I'M
KEITH
HERNANDEZ

I'M
KEITH
HERNANDEZ

A Memoir

—

KEITH
HERNANDEZ

Little, Brown and Company

New York Boston London

Hachette Book Group supports the right to free expression and the value of copyright. The purpose of copyright is to encourage writers and artists to produce the creative works that enrich our culture.

The scanning, uploading, and distribution of this book without permission is a theft of the author's intellectual property. If you would like permission to use material from the book (other than for review purposes), please contact permissions@hbgusa.com. Thank you for your support of the author's rights.

Little, Brown and Company
Hachette Book Group
1290 Avenue of the Americas, New York, NY 10104
littlebrown.com

First Edition: May 2018

Little, Brown and Company is a division of Hachette Book Group, Inc. The Little, Brown name and logo are trademarks of Hachette Book Group, Inc.

The publisher is not responsible for websites (or their content) that are not owned by the publisher.

The Hachette Speakers Bureau provides a wide range of authors for speaking events. To find out more, go to hachettespeakersbureau.com or call (866) 376-6591.

ISBN 978-0-316-39573-1 (hc) / 978-0-316-55243-1 (large print) / 978-0-316-41981-9 (signed edition) / 978-0-316-52686-9 (Barnes & Noble signed edition)
LCCN 2017963935

10 9 8 7 6 5 4 3 2 1

LSC-C

Book design by Marie Mundaca

Printed in the United States of America

This book is dedicated to my mother and father, my three daughters—Jessie, Melissa, and Mary—Kenny Boyer, Lou Brock, Jack Buck, Héctor Cruz, Bob Kennedy Sr., George Kissell, Joe "Ducky" Medwick, Tony Santora, A. Ray Smith, Carl Vallero, Bill Webb, and, most important, my loving brother, Gary

CONTENTS

I'M
KEITH
HERNANDEZ

INTRODUCTION

I LOVE BASEBALL.

But I find most books about baseball players boring. There seems to be a standard template for how you write them. Maybe it's because there are so many of these books out there, but it feels like they've become a paint-by-numbers exercise, dictating *what* you talk about and *how* you talk about it.

Forget that. I'm Keith Hernandez. I want to write this my way.

When I was a kid, my father would come home from his twenty-four-hour fireman shift and bring fresh San Francisco sourdough bread from the local bakery. If we were lucky, he also would have stopped by the Spanish market and picked up chorizo sausage. The bread would still be warm from the baker's oven, and Mom would spread some butter or jelly over it and give it to my brother and me. Soft on the inside with a crust that made your teeth work just the right amount. It was wonderful. I want to make this book something like that. Something that you set your teeth into and say, "Keith, that's pretty good. More, please."

So I'll need to keep things easy and moving along. I want you to feel the spontaneity I feel when I reflect.

And I have specific periods I want to focus on. (In the broadcast booth, I find that when you try to talk about everything, you wind up saying nothing. People just tune you out, and even if they don't, they can't possibly learn very much.) I want to talk about my development as a baseball player and how it got me to the major leagues; I want to talk about how I gained the confidence to thrive in the bigs despite a grueling haul; and, finally, I want to talk about how my development as a young player affects how I see the game today from my seat in the broadcast booth.

Because I've spent most of my life around baseball, I have good stories to tell. And I love sharing them with others.

Like the other night: I was sitting at a table at Harvest on Fort Pond in Montauk, New York, with my good friends Paul and Chantal Weinhold. The place was packed with folks enjoying the cozy environment and excellent food, and I had brought a couple of bottles from my wine cellar for the table. We were happy, and the talk was easy and fun. It's always that way with Paul and Chantal, a married couple I've known since my playing days with the Mets.[*]

Somewhere along the way, we started talking about baseball— specifically, this year's Mets team. Paul, who's a psychologist and finds the mental aspects of the game fascinating, asked about a Mets starting pitcher, a flamethrower who was successful at getting batters out but had a tough time holding them on base during the rare occasions they got on. The opposing team had made five swipes against him a few nights earlier.

"He's been doing it one way for years," Paul said, referring to the pitcher's delivery to home plate. "And now people expect him to change. Can he?"

---

[*] I met Paul, who's nickname is "The Mayor" because he can start a conversation with anybody, at the old Vertical Club, which was located on 60th Street, between First and Second Avenues, right by the 59th Street Bridge.

"Why not?" I said. "Doc [Gooden] did it at the start of his major league career. He had the same issue."

"But how difficult is that sort of adjustment?" Chantal asked. "After all, like the rest of us, aren't baseball players creatures of habit?"

I said it would take time, and, yes, some players get stuck when opponents expose a weakness.

"It's more about mental toughness than the actual adjustment," I said, and I told them how Nolan Ryan would storm around in between pitches, strutting like John Wayne ready for a gunfight in the town square. "You got the feeling that, if he had to, Nolan could throw the ball with his other hand and still find a way to get batters out. For this guy on the Mets, he's got to tap into that sort of mentality: *This is my mound, and I will do anything to protect it.* After that, it just becomes a matter of decreasing his delivery time to home plate while not giving up any of his outstanding stuff. It's that simple."

Then I recalled a story I had been told years earlier. To me, it defines that territorial attitude a pitcher must have to be successful.

"Did I ever tell you what Don Sutton told me? About what he did when Tommy Lasorda tried to mess with his pregame routine?" I asked while topping off the glasses with a 2007 Insignia. Paul and Chantal shook their heads, and I could see they wanted me to go on. I mean, it's Tommy Lasorda and Don Sutton, two Hall of Famers, so it was not a hard sell.

The Dodgers were in Pittsburgh for a series. They lost the first game, and Tommy Lasorda, the Dodgers' then-manager, was bent out of shape because the Pirates had stolen, like, five bases during the game. This was 1979 or

1980—Lasorda's third or fourth year as their manager. So Lasorda, who liked to cuss, came into the visitors' clubhouse after the game and began screaming at his pitchers. All of them. He yelled "You motherf—ers" this and "You c—suckers" that, and he told them that they all were coming out the next day, before the game, to practice holding runners on base.

Don Sutton, a veteran who was having another stellar season, raised his hand and said, "Hey, I'm pitching tomorrow. You still want me to come in at three?"

"You're goddamn right!" yelled Lasorda.

"Okay, I'll come in at three," Don said.

The next day Sutton and the rest of the starting staff showed up. It was the middle of the afternoon and on lousy Astroturf, so it was, like, 100 degrees. Lasorda had them all out there in the heat for about forty minutes, working on holding runners on base.

The game started and Sutton took the mound in the bottom of the first. Omar Moreno, the speedy base-stealing center fielder, led off for the Pirates, and Sutton gave up an immediate single. *On purpose.*

"I just threw a BP fastball down the middle" is what Don told me later. Sutton had great control and command of all five of his exceptional pitches: In the sixty-four times I faced him over my career, he walked me *twice*. That's 1 per 32 at-bats, and I averaged 1 walk per 6 at-bats over my career against the rest of the league. So if Don Sutton wanted to give you something you could slap, he could do it. The question was, why?

Now Sutton had Moreno on first—the exact situation Lasorda had him and the other pitchers working on before the game—and Sutton looked for his sign from the catcher, went into his stretch, and balked! On purpose!

"Lasorda never messed with me again," Sutton said.

Even though they're not ballplayers, Paul and Chantal understood the psychological significance of this story. Sutton was saying, *Okay, Lasorda, this is my day to pitch and my mound. I'm in control! Don't you dare screw with that again.* And a pitcher who's got that sort of cojones—giving a batter a free pass to second base just to make a point to his manager—will also have the guts and the grit to figure out how to keep winning ball games. He will make adjustments.[*]

"Now," I said to Chantal and Paul, "all quality major leaguers—pitchers and hitters—have that sort of moxie. Sutton had it in spades, of course, but everyone's got to have at least a little bit. Because a baseball career is really just a series of adjustments. Those who adjust get to continue, while those who don't need to find another line of work. So if this kid from the Mets is going to be around awhile, and I think he will be, he'll make the necessary adjustments and get over this speed bump, because it's his mound and nobody's going to take it away from him. He'll do what needs to be done, period. And the longer he can do that, the longer he'll be in the league."

Then I couldn't help myself—here we were talking baseball, and it brought me to another place. *Another time.* So I told my captive audience that I had one more story for them:

---

[*] It also shows a certain tenacity and stubbornness that is required in an athlete. But I wouldn't recommend this approach if you're a marginal, struggling, or striving young player. You're talking about a future Hall of Famer and a 300-plus-game winner in the prime of his career!

It was 1978, the year after my first breakout season with the Cardinals. The Reds were in town, and they had Tom Seaver going on the mound. Tom, of course, pitched a brilliant complete game and beat us 2–1 with vintage Seaver stuff. *Hard, off-the-table breaking ball, blazing fastball, painting the corners like a Dutch master.* And I remember coming back to the bench on that hot and humid night in St. Louis, after my second or third futile at-bat, and blurting out, "Goddamn, he's throwing hard!" And sitting next to me was Lou Brock, who simply said in his very soft and understated manner, "You should have seen him in '69."

Eleven days later, we were in Cincinnati and, lo and behold, Seaver was back on the mound, and I went up to the plate and dug in with my back foot *extra* deep to get ready for the heater. But to my surprise, I saw that Tom had nothing on his fastball. He couldn't break a pane of glass, as we say. *Is he playing with me?* So in my second at-bat I was suspicious and got ready for the gas. But it was the same thing—*no fastball!* This wasn't the Tom Seaver from eleven days ago—it was some "cunny thumber," throwing big, sweeping, slow curveballs and sinking changeups over the outside corner, spotting fastballs, and throwing sliders inside just enough to keep me honest. He was *tossing salad up there*! But he made the most of what he had, and he never missed over the plate—if he missed, he missed out of the strike zone. All of this showed the intelligence, *and confidence,* of the man—he must have known in that first inning or warm-up session that he had zero and adapted accordingly.

"And what was the result?" I asked the table.
"A no-hitter," said Paul.

"That's right!" I said. "The only no-hitter of Tom's career. Imagine that! There had to have been a bit of satisfaction knowing that he'd achieved it without anything close to his usual dominant power stuff."[*]

"Had you ever seen an adjustment that stark by a player?" asked Chantal.

"Never," I said. "Before or since. One night he was Dr. Jekyll, the next, Mr. Hyde. It was amazing. But, again, Tom just understood what had to be done and made it happen."

From there, the conversation at the table moved away from baseball, but the theme of performance and mindset hung around, a steady driver for the rest of the evening's talk. And that's the beauty of a good baseball story. It not only slides well into conversation but also feeds conversation. That's why it's the national pastime: it fits in with our own stories, ballplayers or not. Baseball is additive rather than disruptive or merely benign.

So how do I start *my* baseball story? How about this:

> Hi. I'm Keith Hernandez—*former St. Louis Cardinals and New York Mets first baseman turned broadcaster. If you didn't follow the game in the 1980s (or catch today's telecast), you may think we've never crossed paths. But you have seen* Seinfeld, *right?* Oh, that Keith Hernandez. *Yup, that's me.*

I guess that could work, but I'd really just be selling us both short. Because when you're fortunate enough to be around the game and in the public eye as much as I've been, you develop standard responses whenever people want to know something

---

[*] Whenever I see Tom, we laugh about his magnificent start. I tell him he had nothing, and he agrees.

about you. Even if you're good at "being yourself," you still have your go-to's. And that sort of a beginning would send me on a path of a lot of go-to's.

Throw it on the boring pile...

I want to go deeper. I want to strip everything else away to reveal something about myself you can't "discover" in a Google search. *I want to get to the core of my baseball story.*

I should note that my original intention was to slog through my life, dragging you, the reader, along with me in this slow, chronological procession. Like a death march (and standard operating procedure for a sports memoir). Interestingly, I think my brief time on the *Seinfeld* set those many years ago has helped inspire me to do otherwise. Because it was there, seeing Jerry and company at work, that I first caught a glimpse of storytelling's creative process. Going into the week of shooting "The Boyfriend" episodes, I had thought that we would simply stick with the script. But once I was on set, I saw that the script—the original idea—was really just a starting place. There were three writers in addition to the show's creators—Larry David and Jerry—and then, of course, the incredibly talented principal actors. All of them had input into each scene. It was very experimental—*Let's try this; how about this?*—and I was fascinated by just how much the original scene could change once the ensemble's creative juices were flowing. And when you think about it, that inventiveness and spontaneity is actually a lot like playing in a baseball game, where you're forced to improvise almost constantly. Well, then, that's the way I wanted to go about this endeavor: loose and ready for anything.

Then it hit me one day in the grocery store:

That plane ride to Florida... 1972... My first spring training...

That's where I want to start the book! So I thought for a while until I hit on another plane ride:

The year 1979...My manager told me, "You'll be in the line-up every day, even if it costs me my job."...My season turned around...

And those became my goalposts: Every time I tried to move beyond '79, I came back to that span of years—particularly to '74, '75, and '76. Those were the hardest yet most instructive years.

Talk to any player who was able to achieve a sustained career in the major leagues and ask him what the most important years in his career were. He'll say, "The hard ones." Because it's in those struggles, when you're fighting to survive, that you're actually learning how to *thrive* in baseball. (Though you may not realize it at the time, it's happening.) But first, the game will have its pound of flesh. And for some of us, like me, it was more like two pounds. You have to keep fighting. You have to bare your teeth and growl and claw and scratch until one day, still hanging on, you realize, *Hey, I'm a bona fide big leaguer and a damned good one!*

So that's what I want this book to be. A story about a promising talent who became a professional ballplayer with a lot of expectations but not necessarily with the moxie to "own it"—to get in the box against guys like Tom Seaver, Don Sutton, and Nolan Ryan and say, "Okay, I'm gonna go toe-to-toe with you, and I'm gonna win."

That sort of confidence came, but it took a while, and *that* journey—*the making of a player like Keith Hernandez*—feels like something worth sharing.

Something to chew on.

I realize that if you're an '86 Mets fan or you're looking for the story behind Whitey Herzog's '82 world-champ Cardinals, this book is a prequel to the movie. The in-depth stories about those teams are terrific but have also been exhaustively celebrated in magazines, films, and, of course, books (I've written a couple of them). My hope is that after reading this, you will better appreciate my role in and contribution to both of those storied teams and franchises.

I don't want to gloss over my "hard" years. They're too important to me—to my love of baseball. Because after withstanding them, I could withstand anything.

Okay. Let's begin our journey.

Part I

BRICKS AND MORTAR

CHAPTER 1

I'M IN A GROCERY store in South Florida, buying eggs.

But anybody looking at me standing here would say I'm staring at the eggs. There are rows and rows of them—dozens of raw eggs in delicate shells tucked away in soft packaging. One misstep by any of their handlers—human or domesticated fowl—en route to this shelf and *splat,* there goes the chance to become somebody's omelet.

I chuckle at this notion. *Kind of like the perilous route from Little League to the majors.*

And now I'm looking past the eggs—I'm a hundred miles away. I'm thinking. No, wait, I'm dreaming. I'm lost in something that happened years ago.

The phone buzzes in my pocket. It brings me back.

"Hello?"

It's my book agent.

"I was just thinking of a good place to start the book," I say.

The book agent gets excited, but I cut him off.

"I gotta buy some eggs. Can I call you back in twenty?"

He says okay, and I hang up and grab a dozen eggs. I go for the organic because that's what my present company at the condo wants. She's famished.

Publix Super Markets are king in South Florida. Every region of the country has their mega chains, and in the lovely Sunshine State, it's Publix. They got one on every corner. And you never know who you might run into. A bunch of former players live down here. I sometimes hang with Rusty Staub, Jim Kaat, Jim Palmer, and Mike Schmidt, to name a few. It's kind of like Disneyland—all these characters from the sport's yesteryear walking around. And they all shop at Publix. But I don't run into anyone today—it's just me and the eggs.

I drive home and park the 2006 Mercedes-Benz C55 AMG next to the 2015 BMW 650i. The Benz is great—the best car I've ever owned. *Zoom!* But the BMW has a convertible top, and that sure is delightful in the warm Florida winters. Such decadence. But you know what? I've worked hard my entire life to get where I am, and as with my poultry companions in the passenger seat, it wasn't a smooth ride by any stretch. More than once, I ended up with egg on my face.

I get home, and Hadji, my fifteen-year-old Bengal cat, greets me at the door. My Sancho Panza. I put the eggs in the fridge, step outside onto the balcony, and call my book agent back.

I'm standing out on the balcony, looking over the Intracoastal Waterway. It's a beautiful day, and there are a lot of boats on the water. A bunch of teenagers are on one; they're listening to music and the girls are sunbathing. My agent picks up and wants to know more about my idea for the book's opening. So I tell him the story I was thinking about back in the grocery store.

1972. I was getting ready to go to my first spring training. My dad, who was this tough Depression-era guy and hated blue jeans because they reminded him of his adolescent poverty, said he was going to help me pick out my wardrobe for the plane ride east.

"C'mon, Dad," I said. I was a kid of the '60s, so jeans were cool.

But he just shook his head, and we went out shopping. We came back with a long-sleeved solid purple shirt, a pair of black knit slacks with cheesy patterns stitched into them, and white patent-leather shoes.* *Ouch.* When my summer league baseball coach, Tony Santora, stopped by the house to say goodbye and wish me luck, he saw my outfit and said, "Keith, you look like the Cuban flag!"

"Thanks, Tony."

I hugged my parents goodbye at San Francisco International and flew east with this other kid, Marty DeMerritt, a big red-headed pitcher from South San Francisco who the St. Louis Cardinals had drafted twenty rounds before me. Marty wore an outfit that was somehow worse than mine—red on red. He looked like Bozo the Clown.

We'd faced each other in high school and summer leagues, so I knew Marty competitively, which is why we both acted like it was no big deal when the plane flew into a giant thunderstorm over the Gulf of Mexico. But I'm sure, deep down, Marty was terrified and, like me, thought we were going to die. I had never flown before, and there was all this lightning and the plane was bouncing up and down. Having been on a lot of airplane rides since, I can easily say that approach into Tampa is number one on the chart of check-your-lunch flights.

Safely landed in the Sunshine State, I was still scared to death—I was eighteen years old and suddenly on my own.

We collected our bags, and a Cardinals representative escorted us to a waiting van for transport to St. Petersburg, a small city less than thirty miles from central Tampa and home to the Cardinals' spring training complex. As we headed out, I felt like I

---

* Patent-leather shoes, believe it or not, were "in" back then and worn by most of the big leaguers.

was in a foreign country. Gone were the Northern California red-woods and sequoias, the coastal mountain ranges; instead there was a flat landscape dotted with palm trees and prehistoric-looking birds called pelicans.

Strange.

We came up to a series of cheap roadside motels scattered on both sides of the highway. Marty and I had been told our motel assignments in advance, and I was dropped off first. I stepped out of the van into the hot, sticky air, said goodbye to Marty, and headed to the motel's little office to check in. I can't remember the name of the motel, but it certainly wasn't the Ritz—just two twin beds, a shower, a black-and-white television, and one of those electric AC units hanging out a window.

As with the other five hundred players in camp, this would be my home throughout spring training.[*]

I settled in quickly—I didn't have much stuff—and went to my suitcase for my Strat-O-Matic, a board game popular at the time and sort of the precursor to fantasy baseball. There were pitcher and player cards, and you'd roll three dice for the outcomes: hit, strikeout, walk, out, error. I'd invested months in the game over the winter, playing the entire National League 1971 season, managing all the teams, playing both sides. And I'd gotten through 127 games of the 162-game schedule.

That's 762 games.

Multiply that by the half hour it took to play one game, and I'd spent over two weeks of my life dedicated to the 1971 Strat-O-Matic season. I'd stashed the game, along with the fat spooled notebook where I kept extensive statistics game by game, month

---

[*] Also taking up residence were more than a few giant cockroaches. Floridians call them palmetto bugs. I didn't care what they were called; I had never laid eyes on a bug that large and they terrified me. *Where the hell am I?*

by month, at the bottom of my suitcase beneath my clothes. But the Strat-O-Matic wasn't there. It was gone!

Instantly, I knew why.

"Dad, where's my Strat-O-Matic?" I frantically yelled into the receiver of the motel phone. My parents had said I could call home, collect, once a week.

"You gotta concentrate on real baseball, Keith," my dad said. "No Strat-O-Matic."

Oh, the horror. Dad had been one step ahead of me — he'd figured it out and taken the game from my bag before I left. I telephoned my brother, who was on the road somewhere with the University of California Golden Bears baseball team — Gary was their starting first baseman — but he was little help. He just laughed and laughed. But I was crushed. I would never know who won the pennant that 1971 Strat-O-Matic season.[*]

There was no escape now — I was a professional baseball player, and no roll of the dice was going to help me get through.

---

[*] I never did finish that Strat-O-Matic season. When I went home after the season, I never took it back out. I guess that's what a year of professional ball does to a person: he craves the real thing.

CHAPTER 2

I VISIT MY OLDER brother and only sibling, Gary, in San Francisco, and we take the eighteen-mile drive south down the Cabrillo Highway to Pacifica.

There are easier, more direct routes, but we're taking it for old times' sake. Back in the '50s and early '60s, this was the only way to get to Pacifica from the city. We make our descent from the coastal hills of Daly City into the beach communities of Edgemont, Sharp Park, and Vallemar, and continue south over the small mountain crest just past Rockaway Beach, down into Linda Mar Valley.

Gary makes the left turn onto Linda Mar Boulevard, and a half mile inland we turn right onto Hermosa Avenue. "My God," I say to Gary, who's probably thinking the same thing. "It's so small." When we were kids, the street seemed about a mile long. But now I see it's only a bit more than a hundred yards. And I wonder how many times we walked and rode our bikes on this block—to school, to workouts—in rain, fog, wind, and sun.

We pull into the cul-de-sac in front of our old house. There is now a second story, and the small front yard has been replaced by a concrete walkway, but the brick facade and wishing well are still there. As little kids, Gary and I got a few days off from school to help Dad brick the wishing well. He loved using bricks to dress up the house. When Mom wanted a flower bed, he installed one across the front of the house with bricks.

That's still here, too.

But the fence he made—a ranch-style fence with wooden rails and, of course, brick pilings—is gone.

We get out of the car and stand in the cul-de-sac that was our first baseball diamond, and I wonder if there are any kids in the neighborhood still breaking windows with line drives. We must have broken the Barretts' window five times, and Dad would always immediately go over and clean up the glass and get a glazier over to replace the window. The Barretts never complained. It was just kids playing.

Gary and I stand in the street for another minute and take a last look at the house. There were four of us living here, plus a dog, Tex, then after Tex died, a Persian tomcat, Sinbad—1,100 square feet purchased with $12,000 and some help from Dad's GI Bill.

More than half a century ago.

I peek down the side of the house to the backyard. When we were boys it was just a quick scale over the backyard fence to the large artichoke farm, where we'd play hide-and-go-seek and sometimes cut through to get to school. And along the farm's southern edge was San Pedro Creek. The creek begins somewhere up in the surrounding coastal mountains, and as a kid I tried a few times to follow it to its source, but it just kept crawling around, up through the hills. So I never did find it. Mom didn't like us going down to the creek, but we'd sneak off anyway, playing cowboys and Indians with the other neighborhood kids. But between the dirt on our clothes and the painful poison-oak rashes, she'd usually find out. Eventually, she gave up—*boys will be boys*—and sometimes we'd head down to catch rainbow trout in one of the stream's deeper pools, and Mom would cook them on the stove for our lunch.

We're back in the car. Gary takes a right out of the neighborhood, back onto Linda Mar Boulevard, and I catch a glimpse of the old drainage ditch that trickles into the creek. We pass a mini mall with a pizza shop, where Ed and Jim's Union 76 used to be. The gas station sponsored our Little League teams. Ed was the old man and Jim was the son, maybe early forties, and they'd come over to watch our night games after they'd closed up for the evening. I remember Dad sketched out the design of the uniforms on a piece of paper—not only the shirts but also the pants, socks, and hats—and Ed and Jim paid to have them made. Mom cut out the letters and ironed them on the hats for all the kids on our team. *A family affair.*

The baseball fields aren't much farther—close enough that when we were kids we'd ride our bikes or walk—but they're gone, too. A private Christian school now stands where my friends and I played five years of Little League and Pony League ball, where Dad taught us everything, from baserunning and cutoffs to double plays and rundowns.

Gary and I talk about Mr. Otenello, another coach who helped Dad build the fields. He brought an earthmover from San Francisco to level the pasture, and we realize that he couldn't have driven one of those monstrous vehicles on the Pacific Coast Highway—he must have loaded it up on a flatbed and hauled it down.

And after they'd prepared the field, Dad would head out in the early mornings to water the seeds so they would take root and grow strong.

Pacifica, 1959

I am five and I spend hours standing on our front lawn, throwing a tennis ball against the side wall of our garage about fifteen feet away.

The wall isn't smooth. Its facade is brick, with mortar inset between the brick. So if I throw the ball against the wall, it might hit a corner of the brick or an indentation within the brick itself and not come straight back.

It is unpredictable, just like a live batter.

That's what makes it fun. The ball might hit flush and bounce back straight; it might hit on a lower angle and come down hard; it might hit the upper part and speed through the air; and if it hit the side, it could go left or right. Sometimes I have to dive. Sometimes I have to charge. Sometimes it's a blooper and I have to leap. And as I get better, I move in closer and closer, which gives me much less time to react. All good for agility and quickness. Lord knows how many times Mom scrubbed the grass stains out of my jeans.

Pretending I am an All-Star shortstop like Pittsburgh's Dick Groat, I will play games against the wall: a clean fielding with a sharp throw is an out; a ball that gets by me up the middle is a single; down the line is a double. If the bases are loaded with less than two outs, I'll move in closer and play the hot corner over at third.

I love these imaginary games and will play them until Mom calls me in for dinner or the sun goes down. Sometimes Gary will join me—we'll be middle infielders working together. Otherwise, I'll be by myself, off in my own little world.

CHAPTER 3

MY ROOMMATE FOR 1972 spring training finally showed up around 9 p.m. Mets fans remember Mike Vail well because in 1975 he set a modern MLB rookie record with a twenty-three-game hitting streak, which not only began with his first MLB at-bat but also was the longest hitting streak in Mets franchise history.[*]

Imagine that, setting a franchise hit record right out of the gate...

But at that time, Mike was just another Bay Area kid, drafted out of De Anza College in Cupertino. A couple of doors down from us were Jerry Mumphrey and Larry Herndon, two African Americans who would have long careers in the big leagues. Jerry was from Tyler, Texas; Larry hailed from Sunflower, Mississippi.

I remember one hot, humid evening we were sitting around outside our rooms, and Larry and Mumph were eating something out of a big glass jar.

"You want one, Keith?" they asked.

"What the hell is it?"

"Pickled pigs' feet," they told me.

I declined, and they just laughed and said, "What's wrong with you?"

---

[*] Both records have since been eclipsed.

This was part of the beauty of coming into the world of Major League Baseball: it plucked me out of my little Northern California bubble and introduced me to a wide variety of people from across the country. And, of course, there were plenty of players from the Caribbean and Latin America. St. Petersburg of 1972 and every other town I played professional ball in after that was a heck of a place for a young person to meet folks from all over.

But besides baseball, there wasn't much for our eclectic bunch to do: St. Pete's small downtown was a long bus ride away (no one had a car) and seemed to be inhabited exclusively by retirees and octogenarians. The one thing that saved us from complete boredom was the ill-maintained shuffleboard court on the motel property.

Food, unfortunately, was just as scarce as the entertainment. Before workouts, we were given breakfast, which consisted of toast, bagels, and cold cereal along with coffee, milk, and juice. There was also a lunch of soup and crackers. It was hardly enough sustenance for a professional baseball player trying to make the cut. So after practice we would take the city bus down Fourth Street to Morrison's Cafeteria, an all-you-can-eat restaurant chain.

Thank God for Morrison's.

It was six dollars for dinner—a good thing because we weren't paid a salary during spring training, and our weekly allowance was just seventy-five dollars (ten dollars a day for food and five dollars for laundry). There would be around twenty of us scarfing down plate after plate, the grayheads at the rest of the tables watching in shock and awe.

It didn't really matter that there were more things to do on the moon than in St. Pete, because after a long day's practice and stuffing ourselves to the gills at Morrison's, we were exhausted: a few rounds of shuffleboard, then we'd hit the sack. Team busses started rolling to the complex at 8 a.m., and we were expected to be in uniform and ready to go by 10.

The practice regimen consisted of calisthenics, running, drills, fundamentals of all sorts, more running, and then actual live batting practice, shagging, and, for us infielders, lots of ground balls until the lunch break at noon. *Soup anyone?* Then we were back out on the field with more BP and "fundies" until everyone—all 500 of us—had hit. At around 4 p.m., the day was finished off with yet more running, then we'd shower and bus back to the motel, and it was off to Morrison's again.

Of the 500 players, only 175 would find a spot on one of the Cardinals' seven minor league teams. Competition was keen, and the workouts had to be well structured in order for each player to show his abilities to the minor league brass, managers, hitting instructors, and pitching coaches. They all would be scattered around the four fields, in the batting cages, and up in the observational tower located in the middle of the complex. As a player, you felt their eyes upon you at all times, and you tried *very, very* hard to impress them. That was the goal: *to make a good impression.*

So what was their first impression of me?

Well, have you ever seen the movie *The Natural?* It's one of my favorites. Robert Redford is perfect as Roy Hobbs, an immensely talented baseball player with a cryptic past who, after years of suffering, finally gets a second chance to play with a big-league team. In the film, there's this great scene where Hobbs takes his first BP session. It's in the big ballpark, and all the players and coaches are there, halfheartedly watching Hobbs, who's pushing forty, step into the batter's box. He takes his first cut and crushes the ball over the right-field fence, putting it way up into the seats. The next ten swings yield a similar result: Hobbs, the natural, hitting balls so pure and long that even the great Ted Williams would be envious. Only in Hollywood! (But Redford has a nice, athletic swing; and Randy Newman's music score is off the charts.)

Well, the circumstances surrounding *my* first professional BP session on that opening day of camp couldn't have been any more different, or less magnificent.

First, I was still a kid, just old enough to buy cigarettes and girlie magazines from the drugstore (hypothetically). Second, I wasn't a nobody; in fact, I was a "bonus baby," which meant the Cardinals had paid big money to sign me. I knew the Cardinals' brass and coaches as well as some informed players would be watching the $30K buy from the forty-second round of the draft. Third, and I'm not proud of this, I whiffed on my first swing.

I guess I thought everyone was going to be hurling 190-mile-per-hour fastballs, and, in retrospect, I should've taken the first pitch. But I swung before the ball was even halfway home. Of course, there were tons of players and coaches around the batting cage to witness this whiff on 85-mile-per-hour cheese, and I heard a few chuckles coming from behind the cage.

The second pitch came in, and this time I murdered the ball . . .

Just joking. The pitcher jammed the crap out of me, and I sent a dribbler halfway to first base. So it wasn't exactly a Hollywood introduction. But by the fourth pitch or so, I got my bearings, worked back over the middle of the plate, and had a decent BP session. (As it turned out, I wasn't the only one nervous that day: my flight buddy, Marty DeMerritt, threw a curveball over the batting cage his first time out pitching. I'd never seen that before.)

So why was I a big-shot "bonus baby"? Again, I'd been picked in a distant galaxy otherwise known as the forty-second round of the June 1971 amateur draft; usually guys taken that late aren't even signed, let alone given big money. The short answer is that I should have been taken in the early rounds, but my high school coach was a bit of a jerk, so I didn't play baseball during my senior year. It wasn't until *after* the draft and I kicked butt in summer ball that the Cardinals said, "We really gotta sign this kid." Otherwise, I was off to college (I'd been heavily recruited by Stanford and Cal for both baseball and football, and I'd received congressional consent to the Air Force and Naval Academies).

So it all worked out. I had been a good student in high school, but I wasn't interested in anything other than playing professional baseball. If there had been any doubt about that, it went away after I signed with the Cardinals and Dad insisted I enroll in a semester's worth of classes at the junior college while I waited for spring training. *Screw that.* Instead, I'd head out of the house every morning, drive my parents' car to the San Fran airport, and park in the old high school lovers' lane to watch the planes take off until I went to sleep. I got incompletes across the board, and, of course, the report card was sent home.

"Keith, that's on your permanent scholastic record," my brother, who was a senior at Cal Berkeley, told me. "You should've just dropped out if you didn't want to go."

Well, I didn't know all that, and I didn't care. Dad was mad, but not as mad as I thought he'd be. Of course, it wasn't an adult conversation we had—Dad liked to fly off the handle and yell and scream—but he relented, and I sensed that he was impressed by my single-mindedness: *baseball superstar or bust.*

Back to camp.

Initial cuts were made, and those of us remaining were organized into groups corresponding to the respective minor league teams we would most likely be playing for that season. At the lowest level of the Cardinals' minor league food chain was the Gulf Coast League. They would play their season at the spring training facility with no fanfare and all day games. The next step up was A ball, and there the Cardinals placed three teams: Cedar Rapids, Iowa, was the lowest A ball classification in the Midwest League; St. Petersburg in the Florida State League was a tough midlevel A league; and Modesto, California, was the highest A ball classification in the California State League. Then came AA at Little Rock, Arkansas, in the Texas League, and finally AAA Tulsa, Oklahoma, in the American Association.

I was placed at St. Petersburg in the Florida State League under the command of chain-smoking hard-ass Roy Majtyka. I remember one day in early spring training, Roy was hitting me fungoes at first and I was flashing my future Gold Glove leather, making all the plays, catching everything to my right, then left, soft, then hard. After about twenty-five minutes of hitting grounders in the Florida heat, an exhausted Roy said, "Okay, that's enough." When I told him I wanted more, he just laughed. "Come see me in ten years—it'll be enough then." So I guess the manager expected that I'd be sticking around for a while.

Cuts were always made on a Sunday before Monday's new payday for the upcoming week. But I really didn't have to worry about being cut that first spring training because the organization had invested a lot of money in me as a prospect. It meant I had time to develop, which is comforting to a young person who's away from home for the first time and trying to get his bearings in a highly competitive field. Otherwise, it would have been a very stressful period—you could sense the tension building within most of the players as the numbers whittled down. I'm confident I would have made it—bonus baby or not—but baseball is about rhythm for me, and it would have been much harder to find that rhythm with the extra pressure of making the cut.

While I relaxed, Mike Vail, my roommate, was convinced that his head was on the chopping block. Poor Mike spent the whole night before final cuts pacing back and forth in our room.

"I'm toast," he'd woefully announce every five minutes.

"You're not toast. Go to sleep." I'd seen Mike hit. He had a nice swing, and besides, he was a fourth-round pick by the Cardinals.

"That's easy for you to say, Bonus Baby!"

"You're right. You're toast. Now please shut up and go to sleep."

Well, that approach didn't work either, so we both were awake most of the night. But Mike survived the cut, of course, and he and I finished camp with our dreams of one day playing in the major leagues intact.

One night during that final week of camp, some of us took the bus downtown to watch the major leaguers play. Our games usually coincided, but this was an exception. The lights were on at Al Lang Field, and the Cardinals were playing the Mets. The organization had given us tickets and put us in the peanut gallery. But spring training stadiums are really just minor league parks, and I was excited to see a big-league game this close up.

We sat down, and there they were—the mighty Cardinals—taking infield and dressed in their home "whites": Gibson, Brock, Wise, Matty Alou, Ted Simmons, and last year's batting champ and MVP, Joe Torre. It just made me want to be there on that team and in that uniform: the red birds perched on the yellow bat, my last name printed in an arc above my number on my back.

It was all so close, I could feel it.

And yet so far. Within a few days of breaking camp and starting the A ball season, I fractured the ulna in my right forearm. It had been just a routine putout play following a swinging bunt—something I'd done already a million times at camp—but the hard throw from the third baseman sank down toward the churning knees of the runner, who also happened to be about six inches inside the foul line. *Crack!* The doc put a cast on my arm, and I missed the first 48 games of St. Pete's 132-game schedule.

Good grief.

CHAPTER 4

Pacifica, 1960

MOM AND DAD THROW *Gary and me into the Mercury station wagon and, together, we head up the Pacific Coast Highway to San Francisco. We make this trip twice a month to pick up Dad's paycheck and then visit my grandparents. Dad drives and we listen to the radio, Mom dialing in Don Sherwood on KSFO. Gary and I laugh as Sherwood does his crooner impersonation between songs.*

On this particular trip, we pick up Dad's paycheck but don't go to my grandparents'. Instead, Dad steers along Taraval Street near the Fleishhacker Zoo to Flying Goose Sporting Goods. We aren't a rich family—Dad often has to make sure he deposits his fireman's paycheck on the first and fifteenth of each month to be able to cover the mortgage, utilities, and grocery bills—but the Flying Goose will become a regular destination in the future. Dad, a former professional baseball player, will make sure his boys always have the proper equipment.

Dad is a first-generation American. His parents emigrated from Spain via the Pacific, arriving in San Francisco in 1916. He is proud of his Spanish heritage, frequently gathering Gary and me together and asking, "Now, sons, who are you?"

"Spaniards, Father!" we say, trying to match his gusto.

"And where is Spain?" he asks.

We'll find the globe in Gary's room and point to the place Dad has already shown us a million times. "In Europe, Father!"

"Correct! Don't forget this!"

But Dad loves America. "In America," he says, "you can do anything you want so long as you put your mind to it and work hard enough." That "thing" for Dad, like for many San Francisco boys growing up during the teens and twenties of the twentieth century (including one named Joe DiMaggio), had been baseball. A standout at Mission High School, John Hernandez broke all kinds of school records, leading his team to a championship game at Seals Stadium, where he hit five doubles, was named MVP, and was christened by the city as the next big star to come out of the Bay Area.

But Dad's father, Pa, who spoke no English, never knew much about his son's baseball accomplishments. While his son played on the ball fields, Pa worked long hours for the Simmons mattress company as an upholsterer. Being European, he did not understand baseball and always chided his son to stop playing silly games and go to work. The only game he ever went to was his son's championship game at Seals Stadium, and only after seeing that his son was obviously very good and everyone in the crowd was talking about him as the next Joltin' Joe did Pa seem to care.

"He had no problem taking an interest then—after I'd done all the hard work," Dad will sometimes say.

So Dad had never gotten the support that he is now determined to give Gary and me, his two sons, and an hour after parking the station wagon, he leads us out of the sporting goods store carrying two brand-new wooden bats. On the way home, Dad switches off the radio and says, "Hitting lesson number one, boys: Always have a bat in your hands that you can handle. Never too heavy. Never too light. You should swing the bat, not let the bat swing you."

As usual, Dad parks the station wagon on the street in front of our *house. There is a two-car garage, but Dad is always creating something in there. He loves working with his hands—woodworking, masonry, or artistic endeavors—so he needs the space for his saws, tools, and workbench. The washer and dryer are in there, too. It's not a mess, but it's tight. He'll squeeze the car inside once he's finished working for the day.*

Gary and I shuffle out of the car and follow Dad into the garage. The bats are official Little League and much too long and heavy for us. Dad saws the barrel ends down, then secures the bats in a vise and sands them. Finally, he hands each of his two sons a custom-fitted bat.

Then he takes us outside, closes the garage door, and begins throwing batting practice against it. He throws tennis balls because they are soft and don't hurt if they hit us. We are so young—just learning this game—and he wants us to be at ease, without fear. He wants us to love baseball.

We'll take BP off Dad any day he's home from work—twice a day in the summertime. Dad works a twenty-four-hour shift at the fire station and then is home for forty-eight hours. He leaves in the morning and is back the next day for breakfast. After a nap, he's all ours for two days.

CHAPTER 5

THE FLORIDA STATE LEAGUE in 1972 was (and still is) a pitcher's league—the big ballparks and heavy summer air made it more difficult for the hitters to put up high averages or power numbers. Being a Northern California kid, I'd never experienced anything like that tropical swelter, and my uniform would be soaked before the end of the national anthem.

But I was eighteen and strong, and after missing the first 48 games because of my fractured forearm, I played the remaining 84, hitting .256 with 16 doubles, 5 triples, 5 home runs, and 41 RBI. To me, a guy who had hit well over .400 his entire baseball life, that .256 was a hard pill to swallow; but my teammate Mike Potter, who would play with my brother in Modesto, later told Gary that it was the "hardest hit" .256 he'd ever seen.

It's important to note that back then power numbers were not emphasized like in today's player development. If the coaches and brass felt there was power potential in a kid, they would let it come at its own pace. For me—a player who was not interested in hitting anything but line drives and a .300 batting average—this was extremely helpful. It meant that I could concentrate on my game and not worry about "lifting" the ball over the fences.

Part of the reason organizations could be so patient with their prospects was because they mainly drafted kids out of high school, and there wasn't any rush to bring them up. They loved to get a player at the tender age of eighteen and begin teaching him the proper way to play the game. The upside was if the kid progressed naturally, he could be in the bigs in his early twenties. So that gave me time to develop at the plate. As for defense, I was coming along just fine. Some execs, scouts, and coaches claimed that young Keith Hernandez was the best defensive first baseman—at any level—they'd come across in quite some time.

The biggest adjustment was just playing so much baseball. High school players practice two hours a day and play two games in a week. That all changes when you become a professional: 90 percent of your time is spent playing baseball or traveling for away games.

And it's not like the travel is five-star. For the closer Western Division games, we'd bus to the parks in uniform, play the game, and bus back for a shower at our clubhouse. Then we'd sleep in our own beds, report to the clubhouse the next afternoon, and bus back to the same ballpark for game two of the three-game series. For away games to the Eastern Division, we'd stay in "el cheapo" motels. Real fleabag places. One time in Daytona my teammate Mark Gasperino was bitten on the neck by a spider in the middle of the night and had to be rushed to an emergency room. Mark would be okay, but not before his throat swelled to a life-threatening softball size. I didn't sleep a wink the rest of our stay, but such was life in the minor leagues, where even the budget for such crucial items as baseball bats was tight.[*]

---

[*] We were each asked at the beginning of the season what bat model we liked. "Henry Aaron R43 model, thirty-five inch, thirty-three ounce," I told them, and the bats came in. Then our owner, Ralph Miller, who couldn't have made much money on the team, relentlessly gathered all the broken bats over the course of the long season to trade them in to the Louisville Slugger and Adirondack bat companies for discounts on the next season's bats.

But all that was part of the charm of the minor leagues and Florida in the '70s: lots of baseball and sunshine with little pay and few amenities. Towns like West Palm Beach—now a bustling mass of suburbia—were only small seaside communities yet to be consumed by overcrowded roads, shopping malls, and golf courses. So I enjoyed the bouncing around. Unfortunately, due to my fractured forearm, I missed the southern swing, which included a series against the independent team in Key West—that sleepy little village at the tail end of the country and a remnant of old "Hemingway" Florida.*

Speaking of old-school, Early Wynn, a Hall of Fame pitcher from the '40s, '50s, and early '60s, was the manager of the Orlando Twins. I went up to him during BP before a game and introduced myself, a young starstruck kid. But Mr. Wynn very coolly shook my hand and walked away, a look of disdain on his face. Instantly, I understood the message: *Never talk to the opponent.* My father, a former minor league ballplayer, preached the same tough, Depression-era philosophy.

Oh well...at least I got to shake the hand of a three-hundred-game winner.

But I didn't always have such a tough skin that season. That was evident during one twi-night doubleheader when I experienced my first intense razzing. It came from about half a dozen college-aged kids seated a few rows back on the first base side and lasted throughout the first game. *Please, God,* I thought, *don't have them stay for the second game.* But when I walked out of the clubhouse to the field, there they were. Waiting. Stupidly,

---

* I finally did make it to Key West in 2012. But by then it was overrun with tourists shuttling back and forth from countless cruise ships and rum bars all playing the same five or six Jimmy Buffett tunes. I was on my honeymoon with my second wife, and after a couple days, we'd had enough of "Margaritaville" and pulled anchor.

I challenged them to come over the fence: "I'll kick all your asses," I yelled, and of course that was all the encouragement they needed. It got the best of me, and I made two errors in the second game: a towering pop-up that I got in my glove only to drop, and an easy, long pickup at the bag.

Cue the jerk-offs!

After the game, manager Roy Majtyka called me into his office, closed the door, and went through his spiel about how razzing is just a part of the game and a player needs to let it roll off his back. I started to respond but instead broke down in tears. And Roy, cigarette in his mouth, leaned forward, put his hand on his forehead, and blurted, "Oh Jesus." But he calmed me down, and that was the end of it. I guess it's one of the downsides of dealing with kids right out of high school—they can be tenderfoots—and walking back to the motel, I felt like the world's biggest wuss.

I did need a pick-me-up every now and then during the long season, and at some point my high school sweetheart came for a visit. Around four days into her stay, Dad called me and was livid—someone in the organization had tipped him off.

"Get her on a plane, ASAP!" Dad boomed. "Suppose you get her pregnant! You don't need the added responsibility of being married at your age and at this stage of your career! I've seen careers ruined in the sheets! You need to be focused on making it to the big leagues! What the hell's wrong with you?"

But Dad was right—the relationship wasn't practical, and she eventually made it home. She would meet someone else later that summer, and that was the end of us. It hurt, but I got over it, and I suppose it had to happen.

Sometime after that, I hit my first professional batting slump, and I didn't handle it well. Fortunately, I had my brother to lean on. Gary, an all-American first baseman with Cal, had been drafted by the Cardinals in the seventeenth round of the June 1972 draft and sent to Sarasota's Gulf Coast League in the late summer. We talked on the phone weekly. When I hit my drought at the plate, Gary must have sensed I was down in the dumps, and a few hours after hanging up, when I was warming up in front of our dugout before our game in St. Pete, I heard, *"Hey, Keith!"*

"Gary?"

I couldn't believe it! My big brother, along with a couple of his teammates, was in the house. We chatted before the game, Gary pumping me full of confidence, and I broke out of the slump that night with a multi-hit/RBI game. Despite needing to return to his apartment and get a good night's sleep because they only played day games in the Gulf Coast League, he stayed the entire game and came into our clubhouse afterward. Only when he was satisfied that his positive vibes had done the trick did he drive the ninety minutes back to Sarasota.

Over the course of a long season, you inevitably run into two or three slumps. By slumps, I mean an 8 for 60. That's, like, fifteen games—or two weeks—of coming to the park and feeling like a monkey humping a football. It's as if you'd never had a baseball bat in your hands before. I'd call home and say to Dad, "I'm feeling crappy at the plate," and we'd talk through my at-bats. My father knew my swing better than anyone, and he could decipher what I was doing wrong based on just what I told him: "Sounds like you're shortening up"; "Keep your hands back"; "Step up in the box to catch that sinker before it breaks." But sometimes he'd just say, "It sounds like you're solid, son. Just keep swinging the bat."

But it's hard to be patient in a slump. In that first year, I tended to handle them with anger, and a bad temper only makes it worse. I never broke any watercoolers, but I did slam my share of helmets. What galled me most was when I smoked a BB right at someone for an out. That would send me through the roof. *How can I get out of this slump if every time I rip the ball it's right at the other team?* It really does feel like you're jinxed.

I remember one home game when I came up to the plate with the bases loaded. It was in the later innings of a tight game, and I hit a bullet at the third baseman. He caught it for the out, and I took a deep breath, seething inside, but Majtyka had been trying to get me to calm down in situations like this. So I walked back to our third base dugout, trying to keep my composure, and just before I reached the first step down into the sunken dugout, my teammate Pat McCray greeted me with a big "Hang in there, Keith." He meant well, of course, but I snapped—not at him, but at the situation—and I kicked the ground, and dirt splattered into Pat's face. I was mortified and apologized profusely to Pat, who spent the next few minutes getting the grit out of his eyes.

It was also unfortunate that some of the brass had witnessed the outburst. Joe Medwick, the Cards' minor league batting instructor, was in town, along with the general manager of the Los Angeles Dodgers, Al Campanis, who told Medwick how that sort of player would never get to wear a Dodgers uniform.

The next day, Medwick came up to me and related to me what Campanis had said. "I thought he was being a little hard on you, Keith," Medwick said. "I told him so, but you've gotta quit this tantrum business and remember that the good hitters hit more balls hard right at people than they hit bloopers or bleeders. It's just part of the game."

That was Joe Medwick: a hard-nosed guy who was very honest in his criticisms as well as his praises. He was also chock-full of great baseball stories, and when he was on the road with us, the other players and I would usually find him at the motel pool, soaking in the sun—drink in hand—and he'd start rattling them off.

Joe "Ducky" Medwick had been a member of the famous 1934 Cardinals, aka the Gashouse Gang, and the last National Leaguer to win the Triple Crown (1937). The man was a legend. One of my favorite stories was when Medwick was famously taken out of the Cardinals' seventh-game-blowout World Series victory in 1934 in the bottom of the sixth for sliding hard into third base on an RBI triple that increased the Cardinals' lead to 8–0. The game was played at Detroit's Navin Field, and some Tigers fans thought the slide had been dirty, or at least unnecessary due to the Cardinals' big lead.

"They started throwing all sorts of things at me," Joe recalled. "Bottles, fruit, and whatever else they had on hand." It got so bad, he said, that the commissioner, Kenesaw Mountain Landis, removed him from the game for safety reasons. Joe was obviously from a generation that gave little quarter, but he made it out of Detroit in one piece and went on to celebrate the Cards' world championship unscathed.

Unfortunately, my first professional season ended in less fanfare: we finished 66–66, a distant fourteen games behind the Western Division champion, the Daytona Beach Dodgers.

But I was learning a lot about baseball to go along with that humbling .256 average, and even more about myself.

CHAPTER 6

Pacifica, 1961

I AM SEVEN; GARY *is nine. We're standing in the outfield grass along with the other boys trying out for Little League. Technically, I'm not old enough to play—I have to wait another year to join the ranks. But my dad, who organized the draft, lets me fart around in the outfield and shag balls with the older kids.*

I wait my turn in line. When it comes, Mr. Otenello—one of the league coaches—smacks a high popper in my general direction. I get under it, catch it, throw it back, and ready myself for his next swing. This time it's a line drive. I get a bead on the ball, chase it down, and catch it. I throw it back. I shag a few more balls and return to the line with the other kids to wait for the next round.

At some point during this repeated process Mr. Otenello calls my father over.

"Hey, John!" he yells. "You need to see this."

Mr. Otenello hits me a series of hot smashes—line drives and fly balls. Each time, I scamper to my left or my right, behind me or out in front, and make the catch. Mr. Otenello glances at my father. Then he belts a series of soaring fly balls.

"I can't hit them any higher, John," he says to my father.

My dad will recount this story to me years later, saying, "You were camped under everything and catching on the run like you'd been playing the game for a decade. Some of the other kids could catch, too, but none of them made it look so easy."

CHAPTER 7

AFTER THE 1972 SEASON in St. Pete, I was itching to get back home to San Francisco.

I had been paid only $500 per month during the season— barely enough to subsist on, let alone save—so I didn't have many other options. Dad thankfully gave up the notion that I would take another semester at community college, and I planned to just putter around. But I wasn't home two days when the Cardinals' director of player development, Bob Kennedy Sr., called and said he wanted me to join the Tulsa Oilers, the organization's AAA team. Evidently, the team's first baseman, future Red Sox player Mike Fiore, had injured his hand and was out for the remaining twelve games of the AAA season.

I got off the kitchen phone and told Mom and Dad, who started jumping up and down. I said I didn't want to go and that I needed a break. Really, I was just nervous. But Dad lit into me: "I'll arrange a flight first thing tomorrow morning, and you will be on that plane! Start packing!"

So off I went, and as soon as I arrived at the stadium, I was called in to see the Oilers' manager, Jack Krol. "Keith," he said from behind his office desk, "this is a must-win series for us, so be ready, and welcome aboard."

After that, I met the team. There was Jim Bibby, Mick Kelleher, Bake McBride, Ken Reitz, Ray Bare, and Rich Folkers.

These were good players—one step away from the bigs—and much older: the average age of the Oilers' roster was slightly younger than twenty-five.

I was nervous as hell.

The yard was packed with fans. We were playing the Wichita Aeros (Cubs), managed by former original 1962 Met Jim Marshall. Even though it was a dilapidated complex with bad lights—nothing compared to the major league spring training complexes I'd grown accustomed to in the Florida State League—I'd never played in front of a full stadium before, and the dimness of the lights added to the excitement of this first game against the division-leading Aeros.

I pinch-hit late in the game off submarining right-hander and former Chicago Cub Ron Tompkins. When I got up from the on-deck circle and my name was announced over the PA system, I not only heard the buzz from the fans; *I could feel it.* Tulsa is only about 1,300 miles southwest of St. Louis, and Oilers fans loved watching future Cardinals come up through this final rung on the ladder. Now they were getting their first look at one of the organization's top young prospects, and their excitement seemed to match mine. I don't remember the sequence of pitches or if I hit the first pitch, but I ripped a bullet up the middle that almost undressed Tompkins. Krol sent in a pinch runner for me, and the crowd gave me a rousing standing ovation as I glided back to the bench.

Following the series with Wichita, we were off to Colorado to face the Denver Bears. Here I was on a twelve-hour bus journey and the only person underage—not that anyone was carding. Beer on the bus, card games, smoking, laughing, joking, needling. It was a new experience, and I enjoyed every moment of it. Soon after we checked into the Holiday Inn, I wandered into a poker game going on in one of the rooms.

There were fewer than a dozen players around the bed and some other folks just hanging out. One of them was a fairly attractive woman I assumed was with one of the players, though I didn't know which one. But third baseman Ken Reitz did, and during a break in the action, Reitzie got his hands on the player's room key and snuck away to cut about a dozen silver-dollar-sized holes in the player's bedroom curtains. Later, when the card game finished and the player left with his pretty companion, the rest of us waited around fifteen minutes and then quietly gathered outside their window. *Peep show, anyone?* Of course, it's impossible to contain the laughter and catcalls of more than half a baseball team watching their fellow player get lucky, so the performance was cut short, and a scattering chase quickly ensued.

Such juvenile behavior may seem off-putting, but I recommend these sorts of antics for any minor league ballplayers taking themselves a bit too seriously—something magical happens in such silly moments. I know it made me feel less like an intruder and more a part of a team.

I finished the season with the Oilers, playing in 11 games and hitting .241 in 29 at-bats with 1 double, an RBI, and 6 strikeouts. Not bad for an eighteen-year-old making his AAA debut, and I was home again in September, but not for long. The Florida Instructional League in St. Pete began in early October, and we reported a week early for a mini fall training in preparation for the thirty-plus-game season. This was a very prestigious league. There were fourteen teams from various organizations in our division, and only the top prospects from A, AA, and AAA were invited.

The occasional major leaguer, too.

When I reported to camp, to my surprise, Houston Astro Bob Watson was part of our squad. Bob was twenty-five and coming off his best year in what was his fifth full season in the bigs (.312 / 16 HRs / 86 RBI). He was on loan from the Astros to hone his skills behind the plate. Just being around Bob, a bona fide major leaguer, was instructive. He could play ball, of course, but he was also human: he put on his shoes the same way we minor leaguers did and even struck out on occasion. To witness that—to understand that one doesn't have to be perfect to achieve the next level—gives a player confidence.

The other outsider on the team was Phil Garner, a middle infielder on loan from the A's. Phil was a character. He rode a motorcycle to work, and that's sort of how he went about his day—free and easy, but tough, too. Appropriately nicknamed Scrap Iron, Phil was as solid as they come and would have a long career in the big leagues with the Pirates and the Astros—I just wish I could have played with him during one or two of those sixteen years.[*]

Despite the high caliber of players, our team got off to a horrendous start: 0–6 or something like that. It pissed off the Cardinals' brass, and they sent down George Kissell, baseball fundamentals guru, to whip us into shape. Kissell had spent most of his playing days as a so-so minor leaguer from 1940 to 1952,[†] and he had managed teams in the Cardinals chain from 1950 through 1968 before joining the St. Louis coaching staff as bench coach. In the words of former Cardinals catcher and Mets television announcer Tim McCarver, Kissell was "the father of the Cardinal Way." He literally wrote a complex book on fundamentals for every po-

---

[*] Phil was a member of the 1986 Astros and thus a part of that incredible NLCS against the Mets.
[†] Kissell did not play baseball in 1943 through 1945 due to military service in World War II.

sition and every conceivable game scenario. A true baseball "lifer," Kissell was wed to the game of baseball the way a priest is to the church, and he wasted no time exhorting "the word of baseball" to us.

"You guys are our finest minor leaguers, and you're here because we feel you're the best," he began, addressing us in the clubhouse the day he arrived. "And to play like you've been playing not only reflects poorly on yourselves; it's an embarrassment to the organization. Make no mistake, you will turn this thing around, because starting today we are going back to fundamentals, working hard, and doing things right."

That all may sound a bit corny, but if there was any doubt about Kissell's ability to lead and inspire the troops, it disappeared once he was on the field and in uniform. His love for the game was contagious; his knowledge of all things baseball, including its finer points—like baserunning, rundowns, and relays—was unquestionable. These weren't just different "aspects" of the game to Kissell, they were art forms, and his passion to instruct us in each of them was inspiring. I also enjoyed Kissell's militaristic approach to preparation. Everything from how we played to how we looked—socks lined up, shirt tucked in with letters showing—was important, he said. It fostered pride in and dedication to ourselves and the organization.

Things went so well after Kissell showed up that the brass sent down their big-league manager, Red Schoendienst, along with the great Lou Brock to help instruct the promising talent. *Can you imagine?* Being a recently turned nineteen-year-old kid walking into a clubhouse and there's Lou Brock, Cardinals starting left fielder and no-doubt future Hall of Famer, seeking you out to talk about baseball and shoot the breeze.

All that was like a magic potion, and we went on to win twenty-six of our last thirty-two games and capture the league championship. It felt great—not just the championship but winning all those games en route to it. We were putting the competition away, day after day, despite the bad start. And that lesson in perseverance, stemming from Kissell's instruction on "what it takes to be a champion," was crucial in my early development.*

For the cherry on top, I hit .352 that winter league, winning my first professional batting title. I "wore it out," as we say—my achievements were even recognized in the back pages of the December 4, 1972, issue of *Sports Illustrated*.†

After the championship, I was home yet again, this time for a few months. And I remember my first Friday night back: after saying goodnight to my parents, I was on my way out the door to meet some buddies, and my dad said, "Have a nice time, son. Be home by midnight."

"What? Midnight?" I asked. "Dad, I'm nineteen years old, and I've been on my own all summer."

---

* Kissell, known as "the Professor" to later Cardinals generations, enjoyed one of the longest tenures of any coach or player with one team. Sadly, at the age of eighty-eight and still going with the Cardinals youngsters, George was killed in a car crash when a driver ran a red light. His wake, appropriately held at Al Lang Field in St. Pete, was a testament to the man: scores of players from various eras and levels of success attended the service, and we all told stories about Kissell and how instrumental his lessons were, not only in our careers but in our lives. Reverence doesn't begin to describe it.

† The article was titled "The Phenoms That Bloom in the Fall," and it featured half a dozen prospects who excelled in the fall leagues in both Florida and Arizona. And there, right below the headline, was a photo of me in uniform. In the article, I stated, "I believe I can get to the major leagues in two years. The Instructional League has helped me in every aspect of the game. Now the rest is up to me." *Really, Keith?* What chutzpah! The funny thing is I don't remember being that confident, but there it is in black and white.

"If you don't like it, get a job and an apartment. As long as you're living under my roof, you'll do as I say."

Though I might have just won a batting title and been in a popular sports magazine, Dad was still the boss.

But my first year was in the bag, and things were looking up.

CHAPTER 8

Pacifica, 1961

GARY AND I SCARF *our second helpings of breakfast. Dad had bought chorizo and linguica sausage from the Spanish market that morning on his way home from work, and Mom had cooked the sausage and then the eggs in the spicy, salty oils. Delicious.*

Dad folds up the sports section and hands it over to Gary. "The Senators lost again," Dad tells me. "Too bad for Mr. Lavagetto."

Mr. Lavagetto is Cookie Lavagetto, manager of the Washington Senators. I've seen his photograph in Dad's scrapbooks from his playing days. Sometimes we'll take them out and Dad will show us all the pictures and tell us the stories. Mr. Lavagetto and Dad had been teammates on the navy's baseball team during World War II. He had played infield for the Brooklyn Dodgers and had been an All-Star before shipping off to Pearl Harbor. Dad says that he learned more about hitting from Cookie Lavagetto than any other person.

"Like a lot of great players," Dad says, "Cookie had his Major League Baseball career curtailed as a result of his military service."

I've heard this before, but I still listen. I, too, am falling in love with the game. Dad talks and like a sponge, I take it in. And when he mentions the famous men he played with and tells stories of the wartime games they played together, something strange happens: my father becomes almost godlike to me, like I'm living with a character out of Greek mythology, and I love being around this man who used to do all these wonderful things like the other gods I follow through morning-paper box scores.

Like the story about Ted Williams, who played for the Army Air Corps. Williams struck out one time, Dad said, and threw his bat as high as he could into the air. "People say he's temperamental," Dad explained, "but he's really just consistent in his pursuit of perfection. It's why he can hit .400."

Of course, only Dad knows this inside information, because he was on that field, playing first base. So while the other boys in the neighborhood have to rely on magazines for their information, Gary and I have Dad and know all about Williams and other things, like the Gashouse Gang with Dizzy Dean, the Yankees and DiMaggio, and Charlie Gehringer and Hank Greenberg in Detroit. He's told us about the Brooklyn Dodgers' Mickey Owen and his passed ball on a third strike with Tommy Henrich up at the plate in the 1941 World Series, giving a crucial extra out to the Yankees, who would go on to win the game and eventually take the Series, and about Cardinal Enos Slaughter's "mad dash" around the bases to score the deciding run in Game Seven of the 1946 World Series. Dad knows all of that—so his boys do, too.

And it's not just Gary and me who like it when Dad talks baseball. It's Dad's close friends, too. Carl Vallero, a former minor league catcher, and Joe Ortega, a fellow Spaniard who never played but loves the game, will come over with their families or we'll go over to one of their houses for evening barbecues. After the sun goes down, we kids will traipse into the dining room, sweaty from our neighborhood games of baseball, hide-and-go-seek, and tag, and settle down on the rug to listen to the fathers talking baseball over *coffee and dessert.** And it's mostly Dad talking—the other men are as captivated as us kids.*

"The two most important things Mr. Lavagetto ever told me," Dad now says at the breakfast table, "were 'Drive the ball from gap to gap' and 'Know your strike zone.'" And with that, Dad stands up and walks over to Mom. He's tired after a night-watch shift at the firehouse.† He gives her a kiss and heads into their bedroom.

On the breakfast table, Dad's left unopened packs of baseball cards—ten cards and a stick of gum per pack. They're the second treat this morning, after the chorizo. Mom says we can skip our chores, but we clear our dishes and wash our hands to get off the grease. Then we're back at the table, opening up the packs of cards, praying for a Mickey Mantle or Willie Mays, but they're not there—the superstars never are. We count our cards, put our favorites into our pockets along with an extra stick of gum, and Mom tells us to go outside and play so Dad can rest. Gary and I know the drill by now and are thankful that those night watches are only once a month. We head out the front door to see what the rest of the neighborhood is up to.

---

* Looking back, it was very tribal, as in Thomas Berger's classic novel *Little Big Man:* all the young Cheyenne boys sitting around the campfire as the elders and Old Lodge Skins passed down from generation to generation the history of their people.

† Back in those days a lone fireman had to stay up all night as the rest of the guys slept, standing sentinel over the ticker tape, on the alert for any alarms that may sound in the middle of the night.

CHAPTER 9

AFTER SPRING TRAINING IN 1973, I was tapped for AA Little Rock in the Texas League, skipping high-A Modesto in California. This was a fairly big jump, and one that I didn't handle well.

But there were some bright spots. First, I beat out my competition at first base, a player named Ed Kurpiel. The overall eighth pick in the June 1971 amateur draft, Ed was a proverbial brick shit-house at 6'3", 220 pounds and towered over my then 5'11", 175-pound frame.[*] After a full season in Modesto, Ed, like me, was sent to Little Rock but was transitioned to the outfield while I continued to start at first base.

Second—and this is one of my favorite things about all of my minor league years—I loved the fans. Little Rock had some real characters. First, there were "Big Beulah" and "Dirty Judy"—at least that's what we called them. They'd been coming to the games for years, never missing a Sunday doubleheader. In her midforties, Beulah was a head turner: she wore big black sunglasses, and her hair was jet-black and set in

---

[*] The left-hand hitting and throwing first baseman was drafted out of Archbishop Molloy High School in Queens, New York, where in his senior year he set a New York City high school record for home runs. Ed and I would get off to a bad start in 1973 because of the intense competition, but as time moved on, we became good friends and teammates.

beehive fashion; the jewelry was always noticeable above her low-cut neckline, which left nothing to the imagination; and she always had on a tight-fitting black dress with the hemline cut just below the knees. Also well endowed financially, Beulah carried herself with perfect posture and sophistication but wasn't above courting a professional wrestler whenever the circuit came to town. Hilarious.

Beulah's cohort, Dirty Judy, was in her early to midthirties, blond, and a real looker. She'd show up at those hot Sunday games in a bikini. Nothing doctored there, folks—Judy was an all-natural brick house. I should know because she and Beulah sat in the front row, just down the first base line. They would come an hour before the game, and Beulah would talk to the players, including me, in her smooth yet playful Southern drawl. A total flirt. Judy was quieter but equally intimidating to a nineteen-year-old kid—both women just oozed sensuality.[*]

Then there was the state mental institution over the left-field fence. On Sundays, about a hundred of the in-therapy patients would take in the doubleheader, and they'd come marching in together, under supervision, of course. Brad was one of my favorites. He would somehow find his way to the front row behind home plate during BP and shout, "Brad! Brad! The best friend you ever had!" over and over again, continually throughout the game from his seat down the left-field line. Then there was the elderly, silver-haired Willie. He'd dress up in a Cardinals uniform and run up and down the aisles at full speed, ending in a slide, then pop up and yell, "Safe!" both arms signaling the call like an umpire. Back and forth, inning

---

[*] In 1988, when *Bull Durham* hit theaters, the character Annie Savoy, played so beautifully by Susan Sarandon, reminded me of Big Beulah. In fact, the whole film captures life in the minors to a T. Definitely a big thumbs-up.

by inning, game by game—*"Brad, Brad, the best friend you ever had!"* and *"Safe!"* ringing through the ballpark.

Unfortunately, the pitching of the Texas League nearly drove me into a straitjacket: six weeks into the season, I was hitting .190.

I just couldn't get it going. Maybe it was the heat. I know that sounds ridiculous, especially coming from the Florida State League. But that year's spring was one of endless rain for much of the Deep South, and there had been record flooding all up and down the Mississippi, thrusting the entire region into an endless summer of stagnant 100-degree days.

If not the heat, maybe it was the long bus rides. Again ridiculous, but ask anyone who's played in the Texas League about the road trips, and get ready to see that man cry. Because, my God, those were long journeys.

Traveling within our Eastern Division wasn't so bad. The Memphis Mets were only 128 miles to the east, and I liked all the barbecue joints. Next was the three-hour bus ride from Little Rock to Shreveport, a tough sailors' town along the Red River and home to the Brewers outfit. There wasn't much to do there, but just across the river was Bossier City, reportedly loaded with strip joints. *Now we're talkin'!* But our manager wisely thought a bunch of young guys might get into trouble there, so he instituted heavy fines on anyone who dared to venture over. Oh well, I was still too young to get into any bars, so what did I care?

After Shreveport, we'd continue our road trip south another three hours into the very heart of Louisiana and Dixie to the town of Alexandria to take on the Padres. Boy, was I thankful I didn't have to play in that town for a full season. They had the worst ballpark in the minor leagues—old, bad lights, and just over the outfield fence was an endless swamp loaded with cottonmouths and copperheads. *Those are poisonous snakes, folks! No, thanks.* The opposing players told us that sometimes the reptiles would slither onto the field, and the poor grounds crew would go out armed with extra-long rakes and assume battle-line formation to beat them back into the swamp.

It was during one of these Alexandria games that I experienced my first racially tinged razzing from a fan. The man was sitting up close, between home plate and our on-deck circle. "Hey, Hernandez," he went, his tone a relaxed Southern drawl. "What's with your name? You some sort of Mexican? Are you a wetback, Hernandez?" It was like he was trying to engage in conversation—he never raised his voice—but I'd learned my lesson in St. Pete and didn't engage. I never even looked at him, though I did sorta chuckle, and I guess he got bored because he quit after my second at-bat.

I bring this up for another reason: this confusion as to my heritage was something I had to deal with a lot in the minor leagues. Not from the fans, but from the players—the Latin American players in particular. The conversation would go something like this:

"Hey, Keith, what's with the last name, *Hernandez?* Where
    are you from?"
"California."
"Well, what are you?"
"Half Spanish and half Scots-Irish. Spanish on my dad's—"
"You sure you're not a Mexican?"
"Hey, if I was Mexican, I'd say I was Mexican and be
    proud—"
"C'mon, man, you're a Mexican."

I would get that throughout the minor leagues, until finally I got tired of the conversation and just started saying, "Okay. I'm

Mexican." And at some point people started to call me "Mex," which absolutely horrified my father, the proud Spaniard.[*]

Anyway, after the series in Alexandria, we'd hop onto the bus and drive the six hours back up to Little Rock for a home stand, and that was as good as the road trips got, because we'd then head out to the Western Division in the Lone Star State. And as the old saying goes, "Everything's big in Texas."

The first swing was to the Giants' AA squad in Amarillo, then on to the Cubs' outfit in Midland-Odessa.

Ten hours due west of Little Rock, Amarillo was a cattle town right on Route 66 (Interstate 40) in the Texas Panhandle. The ballpark was pretty good, but over the left-field fence, where the wind blew from, was a major rail hub surrounded by enormous cattle stockyards and slaughterhouses. The smell from the stockyards was nauseating, and the giant horseflies, not content to feast upon just the cattle, took a liking to ballplayers. They were everywhere, buzzing around and biting the crap out of us during BP.

After a four-game series and being sucked dry in Amarillo, we'd load up onto the Greyhound and head four hours due south to Midland-Odessa, aka the middle of nowhere. It was just flat country with thousands of oil derricks pumping away 24/7. The ballpark, however, was brand-new with a nice field and clubhouse. Most important, it had terrific lights—mercury vapor lights, an innovation at the time, and they were being instituted in all the major league parks. These lights "grabbed" the field, sharpening even the tricky dusk hour and allowing the hitter to see the ball very well. But we weren't the only ones entranced

---

[*] The nickname stuck throughout my career. All my teammates, they called me Mex. Some I still let—my real, real, real close teammates—but once I retired, I told all my friends, "Don't call me that anymore. I'm Keith."

with these modern marvels; the region's vast tarantula population also found them appealing and would come scampering out onto the field, sometimes fifty at a time. Once again, just like in Alexandria, the grounds crew was prepared for battle: out came the long rakes and tight formations, sending the giant spiders into full, leaping retreat. Fortunately, there was no counterattack during our four-game series in Midland, and we headed back safely to Little Rock, some 700 miles away.

The other swing was to the Angels' AA club in El Paso, 1,000 miles—or sixteen hours—away, then 552 miles (nine hours) southeast to the Indians' affiliate in San Antonio. Then mercilessly back home to Little Rock, about 600 miles (ten hours) away. *No exaggerations!* As my friend former New York ABC Sports news anchor Warner Wolf would say, "You can look it up!" Just remember that we had fewer freeways and a bus that didn't exceed fifty-five miles per hour, the national maximum speed limit at the time. So we weren't breaking any land-speed records.

One road trip I really did almost go crazy.

It started in Memphis, where the owners capped off the weekend series with a big promotional night game on Sunday, usually a getaway day.* It had rained all day and into the evening, so the start time was pushed back even further, and the overworked grounds crew poured gasoline on the infield dirt and lit it on fire to dry it after the owners, hell-bent on getting the game in for the sold-out crowd, had a helicopter hover over the field to blow the water away.

We eventually played the game and sometime after midnight got back on the bus to begin our 1,200-mile trek across two states to El Paso. (That's right: a game out east followed by

---

* Meaning you play a game in the afternoon rather than in the evening so the team(s) have enough time to travel, or "get away," to their next series.

a western swing!) We drove through the night and took turns sleeping on the luggage racks above the seats, like vampires in coffins, lying on our backs, arms folded across our chests, the ceiling of the bus just a few inches from our faces. We pretty much drank ourselves to sleep—we had to; otherwise, there was no escape. At dawn I woke up with the worst hangover and cotton mouth, and happened to look out the window: there, coming up on the right side of the bus, was a road sign: EL PASO 750 MILES. Something like that. And I went, "Oh my Lord," because we'd already been on that bus for an eternity.

In El Paso, we always seemed to have some interesting adventures.

Like one night a handful of us ventured across the Rio Grande into Ciudad Juárez, Mexico. Héctor Cruz, our all-league superstar and native Spanish speaker, served as our interpreter, and no sooner were we south of the border than a cabdriver approached us and asked Héctor if we wanted to see a donkey show. (For those of you unfamiliar with it, a donkey show isn't a carnival ride or circus act but a beastly sex show that's guaranteed to send any viewer straight to hell.) Of course, we all thought it was a great idea, climbed into the taxi—really just an unmarked van—and rode with this nice man about fifteen minutes to the outskirts of Juárez and a dumpy little cantina, where he took us upstairs.

At this point I took a keen interest in knowing where the exits were, and I saw four: one along each wall and covered by a curtain. A man collected our admission fee—I think ten or fifteen dollars a head—and an unattractive older woman dressed in skimpy lingerie came out from behind one of the curtains. She started dancing to some recorded music, and nothing else happened for, like, five minutes until Héctor complained on our behalf. *"¿Dónde está el burro?"* But instead of a donkey, six men armed with clubs stepped out from behind the curtains. They looked like they meant business—no translation required—so I whispered to Héctor, "Maybe tell them we would like to leave now." That seemed to defuse the situation: they kept the money, and we made it back to our stateside hotel safely.

The hotel was a real nice Holiday Inn with a very large pool, which was good because the weather was desert hot. I remember one time a group of television wrestlers was in town performing, and they were all buff poolside with their very large entourage, including several very buxom women lying out in bikinis, but we didn't dare try to jerk their sheets for obvious reasons of self-preservation.* Anyway, it was during either this trip or the one with the donkey show that our carnal interest was piqued. So one of my teammates hired two prostitutes to be in his hotel room after a game and asked if anyone was interested. He'd negotiated a price of ten dollars per head. So we all lined up in the hallway just outside his room, and the girls conducted their business—one on each twin bed—and in quick order. Not our finest hour, and of all the things I was learning in my young adult life, this was one lesson I could have skipped.

Back to baseball.

Remember what I said? Baseball is rhythm. Well, try being in rhythm after strapping into a diesel-fumed tin can and driving fifteen hours through the middle of nowhere. *Impossible.* Except some of my teammates, especially Héctor Cruz, were handling the Texas League just fine. Héctor—who always had a smile on his

---

* If memory serves me right, this pool was also where a bunch of us met twenty-two-year-old actor Kurt Russell. We were told that his father either owned the El Paso minor league team or had a piece of it. At any rate, Kurt had made only two movies at this point and was a part-time middle infielder with the team. We rapped for about thirty minutes, and I remember being very impressed because he could have been an asshole but he was a very nice, normal person.

face and a good joke to tell—never seemed to get down. We were all young and playing baseball, so who cared about long bus trips?

Just enjoy the adventure, Keith.

Héctor was also the funniest person I'd ever met. I remember someone playing a radio on the bus, and when a good dance song came on, Héctor took all his clothes off—he was stark naked—and started dancing down the aisle. "I'm just a good-looking Puerto Rican boy," he boasted with a big smile on his face, and we started catcalling and saying, "Oh no, here he goes again!" because he'd done it before. One time he made a catch crashing into the wall in the outfield. His foot went in between the baseboard and the fence, and he got stuck. He couldn't move. He just lay there, and we had to call a time-out to get his foot out. After that, whenever Héctor did his naked prancing routine or some other antic, someone would always yell, "Why don't you go get your foot stuck in that fence again?"

Héctor could also hit. *Really hit.* That year in Little Rock he batted .328 with 30 homers and 105 runs batted in. And he did all that in only 405 at-bats, because the Cardinals came calling and Héctor went up to the majors—skipping AAA—for the final month of the season.

I envied Héctor. Not for his stats, but for the way he was. I'd look at him, see that big grin on his face, and wonder, *How is he able to stay so loose?* Because I was stuck, still adjusting to the demands of professional baseball. Again, you're not going to hit .400 like you did in high school, and you're not going to have time to regroup and catch your breath. You've got to be okay with both of those things and just weather the ups and downs in a long season against better competition. Guys like Héctor seemed to adapt right away, but it was taking longer for me. I was always on edge, my mood dictated by my most recent performance.

And I didn't have an outlet to just forget about baseball when I went home at night. I still couldn't get into bars, and a lot of the players were older and some were married with kids. I'd also made the big mistake of living on my own, because the previous season my roomie's extracurricular activities with his future wife had kept me on the living room couch watching far too much Johnny Carson and late-night TV. I had wanted my own bed and a good night's sleep, and with the $250 more per month I was making that season, I could afford it. But I just wound up isolating myself from everyone else, and I was lonely as hell.

One day in mid-July, about two-thirds through the season, we played a Sunday doubleheader in 100-plus degrees, and I went 6 for 8, finally kicking my average above .300. It had been a long six-week climb from .190, and I was emotionally exhausted.

Beyond exhausted... I was toast.

So I went back to my place after the game, took a piping-hot bath, and fell asleep in the tub. When I awoke, I had the sensation that my spirit was somehow exiting my body through the top of my head, down to the soles of my feet, moving up toward heaven. I lunged out of the water and frantically pulled what I swear was my soul back in. No joke—had anyone seen this they would have had me committed. I fell back in the tub, trying to catch my breath, convinced that I'd nearly lost everything. It was an indication of how strung out I was, and in three weeks my average plummeted back down to .260.

So, yeah, things weren't good in Little Rock.

CHAPTER 10

Pacifica, 1961

DAD PLACES THE STEPLADDER in the middle of the garage.

He's called Gary and me away from our Saturday morning cartoon routine, which stretches past noon. We stand beneath the opened garage door, watching him climb the ladder, a long, thick rope in his hand. There's no Sheetrock on the ceiling, and he swings one end of the rope up and over the exposed center beam. He ties a knot in the rope and doubles it. Satisfied, he climbs down the ladder and walks over to the bucket of tennis balls sitting next to our custom bats. He reaches down into the bucket and pulls out a tennis ball.

To connect the tennis ball to the rope, Dad uses two thick white athletic socks: he stuffs the ball inside the first sock, pushes it down to the bottom, and doubles this covering with the second sock. Finally, he ties the socks to the rope, and it's finished: a tennis ball swings suspended from the ceiling, hovering a foot above the floor.

"Grab your bats," Dad tells us, and Gary and I argue over who gets to go first. Dad has just built us our own batting cage.

The idea is that you get the ball swinging on the rope, like a pendulum, and the ball will come in and you'll hit it, sending it away and upward until it smacks against the underside of the storage loft and comes swinging back to you, ready to be hit again. The ball hangs at my knees for a low strike. To raise it for a higher pitch in the strike zone, all I have to do is throw the ball up and over the beam—two times around for a letter-high strike.

"Focus on the top half of the ball and drive it," Dad says.

I swing the bat and it connects with the ball. Pop...I look up at my father, who's smiling at me and his wonderful new invention. I let it swing back once, and on the second pass, I'm in my stance and ready to strike. Pop...

I take to this game the same way I took to the throwing of tennis balls against the outside brick wall, and I play every day, constructing nine-inning games by scoring each contact as a single, double, triple, fly ball, etc., depending on where it strikes the underside of the storage loft. In the beginning, Dad will watch and instruct, making sure we move our hands directly back without hitching, our swing is level, our stride is perfect, and our bat is moving directly to the ball. But as time goes on and we know what a proper swing feels like, he'll watch less and let us have our fun.

Pop...pop...pop...

Eventually, I get so good that I can maintain a level swing and "tip" the very underside of the ball—like a golfer's chip shot—off the top of the bat, sending it up and into the storage shed for a "home run." This little trick doesn't exactly meet the Cookie Lavagetto principle of driving the ball, but it does make me more acute, like a marksman, as I'm able to pick out portions of the ball as it approaches.

Pop...pop...pop...All day long. Hundreds if not thousands of swings. Pop...pop...pop.

CHAPTER 11

I CAN SEE THE HEADLINE NOW: NASA LOSES SPACE RACE TO BASEBALL.

If a young player struggles in the minor leagues, like I did in 1973, he's typically sent down to the next-lowest rung or released. In today's baseball world, that process goes something like this: Some computer whiz kid, who either has or hasn't thrown a baseball in his life but has a job in the general manager's office of a Major League Baseball team, gets a notification on his computer that one of the organization's prospects is tanking. Said whiz kid, who is perhaps thousands of miles away from said prospect and has not seen the prospect play, plugs the statistical drop-off into the all-knowing algorithm developed the previous year at MIT and makes a call upstairs to the GM. Said GM uses more whiz kids with more computers utilizing more algorithms to arrive at a decision of what to do with said prospect. The decision is made, and the GM's office calls the minor league team manager. Said team manager, a former professional baseball player who's dedicated his life to understanding the game and may disagree with the analysis, is told the following: drop said prospect from the sixth spot to the eighth spot on tonight's lineup card, keep him there until further instructions, and remember, Big Brother Is Watching. Said prospect understands he is under a microscope, goes into panic mode, and spirals in an 0-for-18 stretch. Said prospect is on the bus to A ball, where he plays sporadically the rest of the season and is placed on waivers thereafter.

Eat your heart out, UPS and FedEx: when it comes to logistics and moving assets around, MLB destroys you. And you guys, Walmart and Target, you thought you were fast pulling product from the shelves. It's no wonder, NASA, your space program is stalled: all the smart kids went into baseball management.[*]

Okay, so I'm being overly simplistic, facetious, and divisive here, but to a large degree, such is baseball now, with its heavy dependence on data and algorithms to forecast player performance and construct rosters. I'm not saying this is the right or wrong way to go about the game. A big part of me dislikes it in the way a master carpenter must dislike IKEA, but whatever—I can roll with change, even if at times it feels like it's eroding our culture and making us all robots. But thank you, God, for holding off on making baseball a computer programmer's joyride until after my time. Otherwise, I'd be going on forty-five years in some business other than baseball.

Fortunately for me, the game in 1973 was still one that took place on the field and was strategized and analyzed by men who knew baseball. For the Cardinals' farm system, that man was the farm system director, Bob Kennedy Sr. He was typical of that era: a baseball executive who had started out as a major league player, became a scout, then a coach, and, in Kennedy's case, a big-league manager for four years. All told, Kennedy was involved in Major League Baseball for thirty-five years before running into the question "What do we do with a struggling

---

[*] Astros GM Jeff Luhnow actually hired a guy from NASA to lord over his analytics division.

Keith Hernandez?" And what all those years in baseball gave him as an answer was "Promote Hernandez to AAA."

Wait. What? Promote?

Why would Kennedy do this? Statistically, I had no business being in AAA. My numbers in AA were atrocious. If anything, I should have been left to shrivel up in that miserable Texas League or sent down to single A. A few years later, after I became a star, I got the chance to ask Kennedy, who was then general manager of the Cubs.

"Bob," I said, "why did you call me up instead of sending me down?"

Kennedy looked at me with a serious gaze—Bob was a man who seldom laughed while in uniform—and said, "Keith, I knew if I left you in Little Rock, you might have hit .230 and been done. If I sent you down, it could have destroyed your confidence and you would have been done. So I took a chance because I knew you had the talent."

Well, I'm grateful to Bob, and I doubt it could happen in today's game. Because Kennedy would be forced to quantify his hunch about me—to flesh it out with complicated statistics—and my numbers lacked the ammunition to make that case. Kennedy thought any problem with me was mental or emotional or both—not physical. He knew that I put too much pressure on myself and had not learned how to play every day. To get me over the hump, he thought that I needed something positive to know the organization believed in me.

I've since discovered that Kennedy's faith in my ability was well known by the St. Louis press. After that first year in St. Pete, he told the *Post-Dispatch* that I was "ready to play defense in the major leagues" and that I was the only young player he'd ever seen who he felt "could make it to the Hall of Fame." And that was after I hit .256!

But I didn't know any of that at the time I was struggling in Little Rock—I didn't read the St. Louis papers. And it's not like we had the Internet. So when my AA manager, Tom Burgess, called me into his office, I thought I was getting sent back to St. Pete or Modesto. But instead he told me I'd been called up.

"Good luck, and show them that you got *a little hair on your bump*," Tom said, employing one of his favorite expressions.

I was flabbergasted, still wondering how it all had come to be as I set out in my little Saab Sonett III the next morning for Oklahoma.

I'd had no idea that northern Arkansas was so hilly and soon realized that I was passing through the country's oldest mountain range, the Ozarks. Scooting around those bald-headed domes, depleted from eons of wind, rain, and snow, in that tiny sports car, which I'd stuffed with all my crap—the stereo system and boxes of LPs taking up most of the space—I had the radio on and the driver's side window open to let in the cool, refreshing air. I was out of that hot and humid Little Rock sweatbox, and any uneasiness I had about the future had been pushed far away. After a day of hard driving and clearing my head, I made it to Tulsa.

I flew out the next morning to join the Oilers for a three-game series in Wichita. Once again, I reported to Jack Krol, the same manager who'd welcomed me to the Oilers the previous season, when I'd been assigned to the team for their final ten days. But this time the Oilers were ten games under .500 and, according to Krol, "out of the hunt."

"You will play every day the rest of the way," Jack said. "There's no pressure, so just relax, play this game you love, and have fun."

Jack must have heard from Bob Kennedy Sr. how tight I'd been in Little Rock. He had an easygoing manner and was a bit of a wiseass, with this infectious, shit-eating grin on his face. I liked him very much. But sitting in that office the first afternoon, I was very uncomfortable and kept shifting in my seat.

"What's wrong?" Krol finally asked.

"I'm sorry," I said, pulling at my pants, "but I think I got the clap."

Jack just stared at me, not saying anything, and I explained that earlier that week a pretty girl had been hanging around my Little Rock apartment building. I'd never seen her before, but she was dressed in nurse's whites, and I don't know if she was stalking ballplayers or what, but five minutes after she came and said hello, we were in the bedroom.

"Oh, Keith," he said, then took a long drag from his cigarette. "Okay, not to worry. I'll get their team doctor over here, but you're playing tonight."

Well, stupid me, and just one more reason I was glad to be out of Little Rock. The doctor injected me with two doses of penicillin—one in each butt cheek—and, boy, did that hurt. But playing for the Oilers turned out to be exactly the medicine I needed, because I tore up the league, hitting .333 in 31 games with 20 runs, 6 doubles, 1 triple, 5 home runs, and 25 RBI. A hefty .525 slugging percentage and .919 OPS (on-base plus slugging) along with a smashing .394 OBP (on-base percentage). As for the Oilers, ten games out of first place when I came aboard, we went 19–10 down the stretch and made a run for the division.

It came down to the last two games of the season, a makeup doubleheader against Oklahoma City. We were a half game behind the Wichita Aeros, and during the early innings of the first game, it came over the PA system that the Aeros had lost their final game. Our home crowd went wild. Now if we took both games, we were divisional champs. And that's exactly what we did, beating Lowell Palmer and Jim Rittwage—two ex–major league pitchers—in the process. Euphoria in the clubhouse. Champagne popping. Hugs and laughter.

But we weren't finished.

Next up were the Eastern Division champs, the Iowa Oaks (White Sox), who were the league powerhouse with a record of 83–53, running away with their division by nine games. We faced off in a seven-game series for the American Association Championship, and for some reason the series opened up in Tulsa. I don't remember much about the series, but I recall that first game.

We were down a run, bottom of the ninth. I was up to bat with two outs and a runner on base. On the hill was Dave Lemonds, a lefty reliever who'd pitched in the big leagues earlier in the season. Full count. He threw a hanging slider, middle of the plate and down. *Crack!* The ball went over the right-center-field wall, and I sprinted around the bases like Bill Mazeroski in the 1960 World Series. I leapt onto home plate as my teammates pounded my helmet, jumping all around me, because we'd just won game one. A walk-off, two-run homer.

It was exactly what I'd dreamed all those years ago in my imaginary games in the garage. *Two outs, bottom of the ninth, down a run, and Hernandez steps up to the plate . . .* Every kid's baseball fantasy, and I got to experience it. Amazing. The next day the pitcher, Lemonds, came up to me during BP before game two and asked me why I'd gone around the bases with all that emotion. He was more curious than angry. I said I had never done that before—won a big game in the ninth, let alone been in a championship series—and I just got caught up in it. He looked at me and said, "Okay." And that was that. I had no intention of showing him up—Dad had taught us never to do that. "Let the bat do the talking," he'd said, "and get your butt around those bases."

We won the series in five games. Oilers owner A. Ray Smith bought up the entire top floor of the Hotel Fort Des Moines for the night, and we partied into the wee hours of the morning. I drank tequila for the first time in my life. Shooters all night. ¡*Borracho con cojones!* I remember the Tulsa Oilers Wildcat Band partied with us. They played at every home game during the season: bunch of old guys playing Dixieland music in barbershop outfits and white panama hats. Late in the night, I got my hands on their big bass drum—its rightful owner probably passed out by then—and I strapped it around my shoulders and beat the heck out of that drum. *Boom, boom, boom,* marching all over the penthouse level of the hotel. I woke up in the morning, hungover as hell, with a blister the size of a silver dollar on one of my palms.

But it didn't matter—we'd won the championship.[*]

Now that the season was over, my monthly salary of $750 was terminated, and I hadn't saved a single dime. So I was headed back to San Francisco to stay with my parents over the winter, and I looked forward to the drive, my first cross-country trip. Having experienced a taste of Denver and the Rocky Mountains, I planned to drive due west, through those mountains, the Sierra Nevada, and beyond.

I called home and announced my plans. Big mistake.

"No, son," Dad began, "you're not driving home alone. You're not old enough yet."

"Give me a break," I said. "This is my second year on my own—I can handle this."

---

[*] A. Ray put together a Junior World Series with the champions of the Eastern League, the Pawtucket Red Sox. A lot of those players would be part of the Red Sox squads that were so good in the mid-1970s, and they kicked our proverbial asses in a four-game sweep. They were better than us by a long shot.

So Dad raised the volume. *"I'm flying out tomorrow morning, and we're driving home together."*

I told him he could fly out, but I wouldn't be there to pick him up. "I'll be six hours on the road by then," I said.

"Son," he said, *"you be at the airport tomorrow or there'll be hell to pay."*

He held all the cards: I didn't have time to get a job, and even if I did, I didn't want to. I'd been playing baseball for eighteen months straight. So I hung up, went to bed, and drove to the airport the next morning. He arrived, and after a lovely dinner at teammate Byron Browne's apartment with Byron, his wife, Chiquita, and their two young children, we went back to my place and I finished packing. Then I went over the route home with Dad.

"No, son," he said. "Not through the mountains. It's late September, and we could get caught in a snowstorm or a blizzard. We're driving Route 66 through New Mexico, Arizona, and Southern California."

Snowstorm my ass—Dad just liked the desert almost as much as he liked giving orders. Again I relented, and side by side—crammed in my little Saab Sonett—we headed out: three long days on the road through endless desert with Dad giving constant orders, telling me how to drive, when to eat, when to piss, where to get gas, when to sleep. *Ughhhhh...*It was like I was fifteen years old all over again.

Finally, we began our climb through the eastern mountains of the Bay Area. It was dark—we'd been driving all day—and San Francisco was just over the next rise when the car blew a water hose. But it was I who exploded: I started shouting at Dad at the top of my lungs, screaming that he had ruined my trip. Up and down, I berated him until the tow truck arrived. I couldn't help it—every ounce of frustration that had been simmering during the previous three days just boiled over. And he didn't say a word, which surprised me. We got home well after midnight, and I didn't talk to Dad for two days. We just ignored each other in that little house.

But it was good to see Mom; and sad, too. Rheumatoid arthritis had struck her when I was in the seventh grade. She just woke up one morning and wham: This thirty-eight-year-old, beautiful, feisty woman, who used to get us up for school chiming, "Rise and shine!" was suddenly robbed of her strength and vitality. And you knew it had to be agony, because Mom, who came from tough Texas stock, was never a complainer.

As kids, Gary and I hadn't known what to do. It had been too heartrending to acknowledge: our dear mother being slowly crushed and twisted bone by bone, joint by joint. And then there were all the medications, each with various side effects: cortisone and prednisone—steroids that blew her up like a balloon—experimental drugs, including injections called gold shots, which had been developed in England and were particularly brutal. So I had slowly become inured to her affliction because, as Gary said, if we didn't insulate ourselves it would kill us.

But once I turned professional, each time I came home, I could see the toll the disease was taking. Bit by bit. I would try to prepare myself before walking in the door, but it would hit me, and I'd have to fight it back.

CHAPTER 12

Pacifica, 1962

MOM JOINS US FOR *today's round of BP. She has a home movie camera in her hands and is positioned near the third base on-deck circle but behind the protective cyclone fence. This is the angle Dad wants—into the body—so we can study our swings once the film is developed.*

More and more, Dad is taking Gary and me to the baseball field for batting practice. He throws hard baseballs now instead of tennis balls because we're comfortable staying "in the box," keeping our front shoulder tucked and striding and driving "toward the pitcher." After each pitch, Dad will tell us where the pitch was: "That's a strike on the outside corner," "That's a couple of inches inside," "That's a bit high," "Right down the pipe."

"Learning the strike zone," he says, "is just as important as learning the proper swing."

Dad throws us round after round of BP, and Gary and I love every moment of it. We bounce back and forth between the batter's box and shagging balls in the outfield while Mom masquerades as the great Alfred Hitchcock with the camera.

"What a team," she and Dad will say after we've finished.

A week later, Gary and I come home from school and see the film projector and retractable screen set up in the living room. Dad must have picked up the BP footage from the developer. Mom says we will watch after dinner, "so get your homework done." Gary and I don't bother to protest—Mom's a stickler when it comes to homework. She makes us a snack and joins us at the kitchen table. (There's no fooling Mom: she loves "pop" quizzes, and if it's math or vocabulary, she'll drill us with flash cards until we're "all square.")

That evening, we watch the footage in the living room, now a darkened classroom. Dad stands behind the projector, dissecting each swing, from the "take back" to the "follow-through." He wants us to be smooth with a "quiet" bat. He doesn't like a lot of extra movement; nor does he like a hitch in the swing (something he says he did when he played).

"It can lead to bad timing," he'll tell us, "and you'll start lunging at the ball."

Gary and I pay attention to Dad—"our professor," as Mom lovingly calls him. After a year and countless repetitions with the tennis ball in the garage and BP with Dad, our swings are developing. So when the professor says things like "Eye on the ball," "Hands back and away from the body," "Front shoulder tucked in," "Stride toward the pitcher," "Butt in," "Don't drop the back shoulder," "Level swing," "Up the middle," "Focus on the top half of the ball," we know exactly what he's talking about.

Dad wants us to be line-drive hitters, and it's becoming second nature.

CHAPTER 13

I'M IN SOUTH FLORIDA, where I spend the off-season, sitting at the dining room table with Hadji, my cat, and we're working on the book. There's a laptop for writing, an iPad for research, and an iPhone for interviews. Yes, I'm starting to feel like a real techie—won't my daughters be proud.

The iPad buzzes, and I see my brother has sent me an email. He's been reading through the book and offers a note regarding Bob Kennedy Sr. Remember, Gary was a minor league player in the Cardinals organization, so he knows the farm system. Here's his note:

> Just saw your bit on Kennedy. Pretty much sums it up—my gosh, they really have turned the game into a giant spreadsheet. No fun. Regarding your promotion to Tulsa, Kennedy did the same thing with eighteen-year-old Garry Templeton [a number one draftee with immense natural talent]. He was doing well on our 1975 FSL Championship team in St. Pete, but as the season wore on, he started to lose focus and his performance began to suffer. (Where your problem was confidence, Tempy's was perhaps boredom.) Our manager sensed it and talked to me and the other veterans about how to best re-engage Templeton. We tried, but it didn't work. So

Kennedy pushed him *up* to AA Little Rock, with the same results you had going to Tulsa: he tore it up. Most guys would
have been sent *down,* but that was Bob Kennedy Sr. again.
The man knew his players.

So there—my older brother agrees that Kennedy was the
man. Anyway, Gary's email is super helpful, and I put it in a special Gmail folder titled "Book."

The only problem is that each of these devices—the iPad,
the iPhone, the computer—is also a source of distraction. Between the texts, emails, Facebook, FaceTime, low batteries,
and all the other things that make for lots of buzzing and
beeping, dinging and ringing, I'm starting to think that a few
legal pads, a rotary telephone, and a library card would save
time.

I find the various mute buttons and get back to business,
when there's a knock on the front door.

Now, who in the hell is that? I wonder.

It's the building manager. She's come to see if I'm satisfied
with some recent repair work. I point out a couple of things that
need to be corrected and tell her that I'll be gone at the end of
the week for the Mets' upcoming baseball season and they can
finish the work after that.

"And will he be staying?" she asks, pointing to the cat. I guess
she's concerned he may go hungry over the next six months.

"Oh no. He comes with me. We're flying up to New York together. I have a carrier for him."

She pets Hadji and talks sweet nothings to him. I guess she's
a cat lover. I glance over at the waiting computer, now in sleep
mode, and she asks if there's anything else she can do.

Then I remember that there actually is something. "I talked to
my AC guy," I say, "and the filters are twenty-one by twenty-one

by one, and I couldn't find them at Home Depot. They had different sizes."

"You have to order them online," she says.

"Ah."

She says goodbye, and I get in touch with the AC guy, who says he'll get me the filters. Then I leave a message with Cookie Knuth, my friend and neighbor who keeps an eye on the apartment when I'm gone, to be on the lookout for the AC guy and the repairmen. Finally, I turn my phone off mute in case Cookie calls me back.

I'm tired now, so I sit on the couch and watch the news. After Cookie calls, I go into the bedroom to take a nap.

I lie in bed and think of my brother's email and how I've always depended on his advice and encouragement. The older, wiser Gary helping the younger, impatient me. And it strikes me that Bob Kennedy Sr., who knew my brother and how our father had brought us up on baseball, would have understood my need for strong mentorship. I mean, who doesn't need a point in the right direction when you're approaching your twentieth birthday? It probably was another reason he sent me up to Tulsa.

Kennedy understood that AAA players are not like A or even AA players; by definition, they are a more select group with more experience and better skills, and nearly all of them had spent time in the major leagues or soon would. Guys like Dick Selma, a right-hander who broke in with the Mets in '65; Dan McGinn, a left-hander by way of the Expos; and Byron Browne, an ex-Phillie and thirty-one years of age. They were all terrific, helpful guys.

Especially Dick Selma. A complete whack job—and I mean that in a good way—Dick was a hard thrower for a little guy and played with the Mets through '68. He was traded in '69, first to San Diego, then to Chicago, where he was a member of that ill-fated Cubs team that was overtaken by the '69 Miracle

Mets. Dick was legendary in Chicago for leading the Cubs fans in cheers from the bullpen down the left-field line during the seventh-inning stretch.

By the time we crossed paths in Tulsa, Dick had lost a few miles per hour on his fastball, so he'd resorted to throwing a "grease ball" and seemed to be covered head to toe with lubricants—Vaseline in his hair, Crisco under his hat, K-Y beneath his jersey. One day I asked Dick to show me how to throw the illegal pitch, and I finally got it while warming up before BP. The problem was controlling it—that was the art—but it sure did sink at the last moment.*

Dick also taught me a lot about the game. I remember one time we were playing in Denver and I was just mashing the ball. I went into the dugout after scoring, and Selma sat down next to me on the bench.

"Keith, what are you thinking when you get up to the plate?" he asked. "Do you have a plan?"

"Dick, I don't know," I said. "I just go up there, look fastball, see the ball, and hit it."

"Okay," he said, "but you do know that the pitchers have a plan, and they are trying to use it to get you out. You are aware of this fact? Right?"

---

* The grip and, of course, the lubricant on the index and middle fingers were key. A player would grip the ball like he was throwing a fastball, but instead of having those two fingers over the seams of the baseball, he placed them over the white leather of the ball. And instead of having his entire two fingers in contact with the ball, he slightly elevated those two fingers by bending at the end joints so the pads of the fingertips were in contact with the ball. Then he would just throw it like a fastball. The force of the throw would allow the ball to slip off the fingertips, thus the ball exited the hand in a rapidly tumbling, vertical orbit. It could be thrown as hard as a fastball or as slow as a changeup. It would approach home plate as if it were a fastball, but at the last moment, the bottom would drop out and the ball would dive about six inches or more. The fact that a hitter could not recognize this pitch (it looked like a fastball) made it doubly tough. Later the split-finger would make its debut, with the same results.

I just shrugged my shoulders like the dumbass nineteen-year-old that I was.

"Well, they are," he said, "and they're always figuring out new ways to get you out. So pay attention to how they're pitching you and your fellow left-handed hitters. See if you can discover a pattern. That way, the next time you face them, you've got an idea of what might be coming down the pike."

As ridiculous as it sounds, Selma was the first guy to tell me that. Previously, I had worried only about my mechanics and never really given the pitcher's strategy the slightest thought. But Selma turned on the light bulb in my brain. It got me thinking before I went up to the plate: *What is this man's plan of attack? Is there a pattern?* It would take me years to get really good at answering these questions, and I never stopped looking fastball 90 percent of the time throughout my career, but I could also play a hunch—sometimes it was correct; sometimes it wasn't. Though my rate of success improved with the more attention I paid.

Selma was the first among many older players who passed along such golden nuggets of advice, and I consider that conversation and the realization of *Oh my God, this game requires that I actually use my brain* as a big moment in my development. Heeding Selma's advice—to pay attention—would make all the difference in the years to come, because if you think about it, the long season was now an advantage. It meant that I would see each pitcher, particularly in our division, maybe 15 to 25 times per season. And with that big sample, I could get a decent read on their arsenal of pitches and how they might deploy them.[*]

---

[*] Remember, there were no computers, printouts, or videos back in those days. You had to really pay attention, catalog and archive each experience, and then store the information in the recesses of your mind.

This wasn't the only advice Dick would give me on how to handle a long season. Somewhere in the Midwest, Selma pulled me aside before BP and asked with a dead-serious look on his face, "Keith, what do you like to drink?"

"Beer," I said. "Michelob or Coors."

"No, I mean hard liquor," he pressed.

"Oh. I don't drink that much booze, but when I do, I like Canadian Club."

"You need to start drinking scotch whiskey," Selma instructed. "At first you won't like it. It's an acquired taste. But the one thing good about scotch is you're having it with either water or club soda. You're hydrating [though I'm positive he didn't use that term], and scotch has no smell of alcohol on your breath, so management will never know if you run into one of them after a game."

Was there truth in this or was it just an old wives' tale? I kind of thought the latter, but I nodded at Dick and he walked away, and from that point on, whenever I had a drink of the hard stuff, it was scotch and water. The rest of my career. So you just had to love Selma—he probably had to see something special in me as a young player and took an interest. He didn't have to do that. After all, he was just trying to get back into the big leagues, so it would have been easy to ignore me. But he and the other guys were just so relaxed within their professionalism that taking time for me was okay, and that in itself—witnessing their easygoing manner while they got things done—helped me understand how to carry and pace myself during the long season.

But I wasn't a veteran. For one thing, I didn't have their balls: they didn't seem to give a shit about the brass or management. I remember when Bing Devine, the Cardinals' GM, got wind of our new team bus and requested we stop in St. Louis on our way to God knows where because he wanted to see it. The detour added a couple of hours to the trip and the veterans were not happy.

It was an amazing bus. It had a small kitchen with a refrigerator, oven, and range, and it could sleep the whole team comfortably: beds came down from the top and the seats would slide into new configurations—like a kid's Transformer—so there would be three levels of bunks and everybody could crash. No more sleeping like vampires up on the luggage racks. The Oilers' owner, A. Ray Smith, who loved his players and took good care of them, had bought and customized the bus at a cost of $100,000 to himself (though I'm sure it was a business write-off). We traveled all over the American Association in A. Ray's wonderful bus, a total luxury. To me, it was a gift from the gods, so when Bing said he wanted to see it, I offered it up.[*]

Not so with the veterans, who were bitching the whole way northeast through the Show Me State. This was pure trespass to them, and when we pulled up in front of Busch Stadium in downtown St. Louis, it was close to midnight, and most of the guys were drinking, playing cards, and pissed. All the lights came on, and Bing climbed aboard, inspecting the bus. Well, they let him have it. "Fuck this bus, Bing!" "We went out of our way just so you can take a look?" "You like this bus so much, you ride in it, Bing!"

Most of the venom came from the players that had never

---

[*] Oklahoma City, just two hours southwest down the interstate, was the shortest trip. Wichita, Kansas, was also pretty close, about three hours (176 miles). The rest of the towns were marathons: Denver, twelve hours west (700 miles). The Eastern Division had longer bus rides. Omaha, Nebraska, was 386 miles away (six hours), followed by Des Moines, Iowa, which was another 135 miles (two hours) farther northeast, and back home to Tulsa, 463 miles away (eight hours). The other eastern swing was to Evansville, Indiana, about 559 miles (eight and a half hours), then to Indianapolis, Indiana, a further 169 miles (two and a half hours) east. Then the long trek back home to Tulsa, a cool 640 miles (ten hours).

made it to the bigs. Minor league lifers like Alan Putz. The players that played in the big leagues and were trying to make it back were less angry. I just sat there, incredulous but grinning from ear to ear. *They're berating the GM—I could never do that!*

But I had it easy: I was on the way up.

I played with a lot of twenty-five-to-thirty-year-olds who had been around for more than a while, some already traded once, twice, maybe three times. Some were on the bubble; others were on the way out. Triple A is scattered throughout with those sorts of Crash Davis players—not willing to give up the dream. They knew their chances were zilch or dwindling fast. They'd been around, so they had to know. But if you're a professional baseball man, you'll take the crappy parts if it means more time doing what you love.

For some of the guys, I imagine, it was a bit unsettling to consider life after baseball. *I've got a family to feed. What will I do for work? Will I survive being home year-round?* All those springs, saying goodbye to their families, and now they were strapping together one last season or two before the inevitable. So Bing was doomed the second he stepped onto that bus. But I'm sure he knew that—he ignored the lambasting and snooped around A. Ray's wonderful hundred-thousand-dollar vehicle. Curiosity sated, he departed and we cast off from Busch Stadium. *How many more hours? Who's counting?* It was late and I was tired, so I pulled down one of those marvelous bunks that snapped free from the ceiling and went to sleep.

What a great time I had those six weeks in Tulsa. I realized it could be fun just trying to get to the big leagues.

Another contributor to my more relaxed mindset? I started smoking marijuana shortly after my call-up to Tulsa. I was living in a motel owned by an ex–minor leaguer. About a week later, a former teammate was called up from Little Rock. I asked him if he wanted to move in with me and split the ten-dollar-a-day rent. So he moved in and unpacked his stuff, including a rectangular package wrapped in newspaper and tied with twine. He cut the twine and carefully began to unwrap the package.

"What's that?" I asked.

"You'll see," he said.

Well, it was marijuana, a big block of it, and I thought, *Oh man, what did I do?* and maybe I should have just paid the ten dollars a night and not had the roomie. I asked him how much was there, and he said it was a pound. *Geez. A pound?* I had never seen more than an ounce before and had smoked the stuff only once, back in high school.

After he lit up, he offered me a toke. After about three or four hits, I was flying. My stereo system was hooked up, and we turned out the lights and I put the needle on side one of *The Dark Side of the Moon,* which had come out the same year. Lying on my back, eyes shut, arms spread out like the Southern Cross, with Pink Floyd aiding and abetting, I began to feel as if I were free-falling in space. That first tumble scared the crap out of me, and I opened my eyes and immediately came back down to earth, but I could not resist going back up there, turning and slowly tumbling, head over heels as if I were a big space station just drifting in the black void.

So I started smoking, and I've got to believe that it helped me relax. Because I wasn't like Héctor Cruz or the other guys who seemed like they could just push the game away and keep it at a distance. It was always on me, like a fever.

But now I had an escape, and I wouldn't take the game home with me. I would just head back to that motel room, roll a joint—all you needed was a few puffs—and go someplace very far from baseball. My roommate wound up meeting a girl he liked (another nurse), and they were always screwing around in the double bed next to me—just like in A ball—but I didn't care now. I was gone, stoned out of my gourd, floating through that pitch-black darkness until I had to get up and turn the LP over. "Excuse me. Sorry." And then I was gone again, because, my God, that pot had to have been laced with some sort of hallucinogenic. I don't know.[*] But I hit the crap out of the ball during those six weeks. It was going great, everything my way, and they couldn't get me out.

I'm still not asleep.

This happens a lot now that I've started the book. I'll just stare at the ceiling remembering things for a bit before drifting off. I start to laugh because I remember the bizarre meeting I wound up having with Roger Waters, the co–lead singer and visionary genius behind Pink Floyd. It was years after my *Dark Side of the Moon* smoking routine and sometime after my divorce from my second wife in 2011. I was just bouncing around New York City when I got a call one night from a gal I'd met about a month earlier, and she said, "Keith, it's Evelyn. I'm over at Roger Waters's town house in Midtown, and why don't you come by?"

Uh, yeah... So I grabbed a cab and went over.

At first, I thought maybe I had the wrong address, because the man who answered the front door (who wasn't Waters) looked like he'd come straight from a country club. Pressed trousers and shirt, V-neck sweater, navy blazer, and perfectly parted hair. I'd expected a houseful of British rockers, not Oxford and Cambridge. In a crisp British accent, he said he

---

[*] Nothing I would smoke after this came remotely close to having that kind of effect on me. Not even Colombian or Panama Red, or hashish, for that matter.

knew who I was, and didn't seem to give a rat's ass one way or the other.

There was a small, eclectic gathering of about fifteen people inside, and Evelyn greeted me and started introducing me around, including to Waters's wife, who was a Long Island girl and a big Mets fan. Everyone else kind of warmed up to me after that, though I felt a bit out of place. I mean, here I come knocking on the door, a perfect stranger in Roger Waters's home, and if I'm Waters, a man of fame, fortune, wealth, and celebrity, I wouldn't want any Tom, Dick, or Harry walking around my home without my permission, and I wasn't sure Evelyn had asked.

But I said hello to Waters, who was shorter than I had expected and not particularly warm to me. *Suspicion confirmed.* He was fairly into his cups, chatting with everyone else and drinking from a wineglass, which never went empty because a young woman, who I guessed was under his employ, kept following him around at a safe distance, and when his glass was close to empty, she refilled it to the brim. All night long, around the room they went: Waters, girl, bottle.

Yap, yap, yap; glug, glug, glug; fill, fill, fill.

Eventually, a group of five or six people led by Waters got into the house elevator because he wanted to show them the music studio. It was on the top (fifth floor), and my friend wanted me to go along. But I wasn't sure Waters wanted me to—Evelyn was very pretty, and now I was there and maybe getting in the way. So I said I wasn't going to get on the elevator, which was tiny, but she said, "Come on. If you don't come, I'm not going up."

So I squeezed in, not realizing I was blocking all of the buttons, and Waters, who didn't share his elitist butler's refined Roger Moore accent (his was more a Michael Caine Cockney), asked me to press five. Well, I didn't know he was talking to me, and I guess he got pissed, because he got right under my chin and looked up at me with a nasty scowl. "Press fucking five! Goddammit!" I said, "Oh, excuse me," pressed five, and up we went.

We were getting a private mix session with the one and only Roger Waters, his genius on full display. If he seemed inebriated before, he was sober now. Totally in control. He was at the massive recording console, working the sliders, and the music went to a video that was being projected on three very large, connected flat-screen TVs set on the wall in front. He was really pushing up the faders, blasting the stuff, and the sound system was amazing. The corresponding video showed Waters in a poverty-stricken village somewhere in Latin America, and he was surrounded by at least two dozen smiling children. They were all following him around the village as if he were the Pied Piper, and he was teaching them how to play a variety of musical instruments.

It was amazing, but after about twenty minutes of it, my ears were ringing, so I decided to explore the rest of the very large rectangular room. I noticed a billiards table and a bookshelf at the far end.

If I'm a guest in someone's home, I don't snoop, but I do check out their library.

Well, I forget what books Waters had, but I do remember his gallery of artwork, which hung down the length of the room. A collection of Andy Warhol original works, all portraits of famous people. Actually, it was more like a rogues' gallery of twentieth-century Communist leaders. Lenin, Trotsky, Che, Mao, Castro—they were all there, these "men of the people" with a penchant for totalitarianism and mass murder, looking out over that man's billiards table and recording studio, perched atop his multimillion-dollar, five-floor town house.

It was getting very late, so we went back down, thanked our

hostess, and departed. The next morning, I watched the news, and there was a report that Waters had been rushed to the hospital. Evidently, he had fallen and cracked his head open sometime after we left and had ended up in the emergency room. I remember thinking, *Well, no surprise there.* But I guessed he was okay, and it had been fun meeting Waters, though I would have liked the chance to tell him how much his music meant to me at a very critical period in my career. Maybe another time.

Only in New York.

CHAPTER 14

I WAS BACK PLAYING for the Tulsa Oilers in 1974, only now for a new manager. Ken Boyer, former Cardinals third baseman and 1964 NL MVP, had taken over the reins, and all us players were crazy about him.

Kenny was young—in his early forties—and just five years out of the big leagues. He knew and had played with or against a lot of the Oiler veterans, and after our games, in the various towns, they would throw parties on A. Ray's hundred-thousand-dollar bus. There would be a few girls and booze, and they'd live it up a little. Not me, of course, as my partying skills were still pretty much nonexistent; I was just smoking grass, listening to music, sneaking into the occasional bar that didn't card me, and playing ball. Still, I loved playing for Kenny. Like those wily veterans, here was another guy to set me at ease over the course of a long season.

I also had a little more money to spend; my salary had kicked up to $1,100 a month. I wasn't rich, but it was the first time I didn't have to watch every dollar I spent. The year before, sometimes the $750 a month had been hard to stretch. Like the time I got thrown out of a game in El Paso in the Texas League. I was fined $100, and one-seventh of my paycheck just went *poof*. Here's what happened:

The umpire called me out on a pitch that was a mile outside. He'd been missing calls all night. I got pissed off and argued with him. He got in my face, and his breath reeked of hard liquor—not beer, hard liquor. He was drunk, this old umpire, and I was stunned. I mean, I'd never encountered a drunk umpire before. Finally, I said, "You're drunk!" right to his face, and he tossed me out of the game. Then he kind of bumped me, and I bumped him back, *hard*. My manager ran out and got between us.

Well, Bobby Bragan was the president of the league. He was the former manager of the Milwaukee Braves back when Aaron and Eddie Mathews were there. Bragan didn't suspend me for bumping the umpire, because he knew the umpire had been drunk. But he fined me one hundred bucks, and I wrote a check to the league and sent it off.

A few days later, the GM of the Little Rock Travelers and former Cardinals major leaguer Carl Sawatski came up to me at my locker and said, "Keith, your check bounced."

And I was like, "Oh my God. I'm terribly sorry. I must've miscalculated."

Someone told me later that Bobby Bragan had had a big laugh about it. He'd just chuckled. It embarrassed me, though—not particularly professional on my part. Anyway, I wrote another check that night and mailed it ASAP.

But in '74, I had more dough, and I splurged on a studio apartment rather than the usual motel efficiency. It was a decent space, and I settled into a nice daily routine in Tulsa.

First, I slept in. I had to, because we played mostly night games. During spring training, we had been on a day schedule: I got up around 7:30 a.m. to be on the field at 10 a.m.;

I would be tired at the end of the day, so I'd have a nice dinner and go to bed. But when the regular season began and we started playing night games, I wound up sleeping later and later and later. So I would wake up in my blacked-out room at noon and have a shower.* Then, at around 2:30, I was off to Denny's, which I considered an upgrade from Burger King and McDonald's. I ate there all year long, a steady diet of patty melts, cheeseburgers, fries, salads, iced tea, and the occasional dessert. If we had a day game, it would be a steak, medium rare, two eggs over easy, hash browns, buttered toast with jelly smeared on top, and a glass of whole milk. Throw in a short stack if it was a doubleheader. I just needed a meal that would stick to my ribs, however many innings were slated that day.

We had to be dressed and ready to go at the ballpark by 5 p.m., but I preferred to get there early. Nobody wants to be in a rush. The routine was no different than it is in the big leagues: home team hits two and a half hours before game time. So for a 7:30 game, we hit at 5; the visiting team hit from 6 to 7.

I always enjoyed that hour when we'd hit. It was also when I'd get my fifteen minutes of ground balls, working on different situations: I'd work on double plays, focusing on the accuracy of my throws to second; I'd play back, as if runners were on first and second or the bases loaded; I'd play up, on the infield grass, as if I was holding a runner on, and I'd throw to the shortstop; then I'd take throws from each individual infielder. We'd all get our ground balls—there was no direct order. We kept things loose,

---

* To this day, I keep my bedroom very dark in the mornings. When I'm on the road with the Mets broadcast and go to a hotel, I'll close the curtains, and if there's a crack anywhere, I'll use pillows, cushions—whatever—to make that room completely dark. I need my cave.

and I needed only fifteen minutes. It's a long season, so you've got to pace yourself, but I always took that time *very* seriously. As my dad always preached: "Don't ever half-ass preparation; you'll form bad habits. Only *proper* practice makes perfect."

While the starting infield took ground balls, the bench players—usually five, six, or seven guys—hit. Then the lineup, including the starting pitcher, had the remaining forty-five minutes to hit. We broke into three groups, according to the batting order: 1-2-3, 4-5-6, 7-8-9. But the pitcher might hit in the first group so he'd have more time to go through his pregame routine. Then we were off the field and into the clubhouse. We changed our shirts because we were soaked, and we had an hour to kill before infield.

Then the home team took infield at 7, after which we had another twenty to twenty-five minutes to kill and get out of yet another soaked tee shirt—it was always hot in Tulsa, and there was no AC in the clubhouse. Ten minutes before the playing of the national anthem, we'd head out of that sweatbox, run a few sprints, and stretch on the outfield grass. Then it was time to go get 'em.

That was the routine—the rhythm of my day.

When the St. Louis Cardinals—the big club—came to Tulsa to play the annual exhibition game on June 13, 1974, I was heating up at the plate and sticking to that routine. *Bring on the patty melts!* Baseball players can be a superstitious lot, and a player might use the same dirty socks for a month if he thinks they're bringing good luck. The problem is that he never quite knows which part of the routine is helping him along. So he sticks to *all* of it, much to the chagrin of clubhouse managers, spouses, and/ or girlfriends.

But it was a big deal for these minor league towns to get

the chance to see the big leaguers play. For Tulsa, that meant Lou Brock, Bob Gibson, and Joe Torre, just to name a few. And some of the players—like Ted Simmons, José Cruz,[*] and Bob Forsch—had played in Tulsa when they were coming up the chain. So the town was pumped.

Remember, the Cardinals' fan nation extended well beyond Missouri's borders. For a long time, St. Louis was the farthest city west and the farthest city south with Major League Baseball. Before there were California or Texas teams, Atlanta, Arizona, Colorado, Seattle, or Kansas City, there was only the Cardinals (and the St. Louis Browns). And there was radio station KMOX in St. Louis—one of the strongest signals in the country— broadcasting the games. You could be up in Wyoming, and Harry Caray—later Jack Buck—would be coming through the ham.

Even with those newer franchises coming on board, Missouri is the only state in the union that borders eight states, and the Cardinals drew from each of them: Arkansas, Oklahoma, Kentucky, Tennessee, Illinois, Iowa, Nebraska, and Kansas. So in Tulsa—and it was much the same in St. Pete and Little Rock—this was not only their minor league team but also their big-league franchise, and when the mighty Cardinals rolled into town, folks would get off work early so they could tailgate with their friends and family. If you were a kid, it meant a chance to stay up late and watch your favorite players—not on television, but in person. It was Major League Baseball comes to Main Street.

Of course, like Little Rock, there were also some great regulars in the Tulsa stands. Like the two women who sat in the fifth row, just behind our on-deck circle. I was attracted to one

---

[*] Héctor's oldest brother.

of them, but our clubhouse man informed me at some point in the season that they were a gay couple. So that never happened, but they were sweet gals, both schoolteachers. They always kept a scorebook and seemed to know the game well. Then there was this super-successful wealthy guy who sat with his family in the front row, behind the visitors' on-deck circle. He had a big, loud, booming voice, and he'd get on the players, even the Tulsa players: "What the hell are you swinging at? Oh, you're in trouble now, fourteen." Stuff like that. It was sometimes more mean-spirited, but he was harmless, and what better training to block out hecklers than to have one behind you every night?

Then there was this dude in his late twenties who had straight, long blond hair halfway down his back and a full beard. He'd always sit to the first base side of home plate in the front row. He wore a cowboy hat and dark sunglasses. And I was like, *Who's this guy?* Because he always had these two great-looking girls with him, and I finally went up to him before a game and introduced myself. His name was Don Preston, the lead guitarist for Leon Russell's *Mad Dogs and Englishmen* concert tour. Russell was an Oklahoma native and had formed Shelter Records in Tulsa in 1969, signing such artists as J. J. Cale, Freddie King, and Tom Petty and the Heartbreakers. A big-time record label.

And there was the great baseball legend Satchel Paige, who lived in Tulsa. He was an old man then, and of course we all knew who he was. They put a rocking chair in the bullpen for him, and he sat, rocking away, talking to the guys and watching the games. He never missed a home game, and it made Tulsa almost a baseball Mecca or a shrine for players and fans to visit. "See that man, kids? That's Satchel Paige, one of the best pitchers who ever lived." All this with the Tulsa Oilers

Wildcat Band, those old guys tooting and blasting and drinking every night.

And when the big-league Cardinals came out in their road gray uniforms for that exhibition game, the packed house went nuts, and I had butterflies in my stomach. Okay, so maybe it wasn't exactly a routine day. I'd been to big-league spring training that year as a non-roster invitee,[*] but I hadn't played in a game, so this was my first competition against major leaguers. I remember them walking onto the field out of the clubhouse: Ted Sizemore, second baseman and National League Rookie of the Year in 1969, and, of course, Gibson, Brock, and Torre. So on the one hand, I was playing against guys I'd met and shared a clubhouse with, but on the other, they were still like Greek gods to me. Future Hall of Famers, former MVPs, and Cy Young winners. And here they were, running out onto the field, dressed in that wonderful uniform I'd worshipped since I was a kid, ready to face off. *Somebody pinch me!*

But for the major leaguers, an exhibition game in Tulsa during the middle of the season was a huge pain in the ass. They were just coming off a ten-day West Coast swing—playing the Giants, the Padres, and the Dodgers—and on their way to Atlanta to play the Braves. But first they had to land in Tulsa, bus to the stadium, and put on a show for the local folks, then head straight back to the airport.

Some off day!

And while we minor leaguers thought the Tulsa complex charming, it wasn't exactly Wrigley. Once you took the fans away, the stadium was really just a dump—straight out of *Bull*

---

[*] The only other non-roster players invited to camp were catchers.

Durham, except we had the Otasco Man sign instead of a bull. The lights were terrible; the visitors' clubhouse was somehow hotter and smaller than ours, which was way down the left-field line and hardly convenient if you needed to take a leak during a game; and just beyond the right-field fence was an auto race-track, and it was loud as hell. *Brrrrrr! Wham! Crash!* It wasn't like pedigree stock car or Indy; it was a low-rent, beefed-up-engine type of thing, and every weekend there'd be that roaring cacophony going on during our games. *

So all the Cardinals regulars would give the sold-out crowd what they paid for with one, maybe two at-bats and get the hell out. Then the bench players would do most of the work. They needed the at-bats anyway. And it's not like they were going to put Bob Gibson on the mound; instead, they threw Mike Thompson, who had been our ace in Tulsa when we won the league the year before. Mike made the big club as their "swing-man," the guy who comes out of the bullpen in long relief or starts the second game of a doubleheader.

Bob Gibson or no, we were facing off against the St. Louis Cardinals—*the second-place team in the National League East*— and though the big leaguers might not have given a rat's ass about the game, we Oilers wanted to win it. At 33–14, and already 11 games out in front in the American Association's Western Division, we were a tough team, and it's not like we didn't have any MLB experience on our side. We had eleven-year MLB veteran Jim Beauchamp (pronounced *bee-chum*), Hal Lanier (who had been the starting shortstop for the Giants when I was in high school), Bobby Heise, Dick Billings, and Jerry

---

  * In 1977, two years after I was gone and a year after A. Ray had moved the
     club to New Orleans, part of the grandstands collapsed and hurt some fans.
     A new stadium replaced it in 1980.

DaVanon. These were all guys with considerable time in the bigs, looking for another chance to go to the show.*

And where there were seasoned veterans, there were usually amphetamines. It was just part of the baseball culture back then. More than a few of my Tulsa teammates had possession of these pills, called "greenies" or "beans." One player had a large jar filled with about five different types of pills in different shapes and colors. There were two pharmaceutical types of amphetamines: one, called an orange heart, had five milligrams of pure Dexedrine; the other was called a green heart, with five milligrams of pure Dexedrine plus a touch of a downer so you wouldn't get the shakes. Sprinkled in was the street stuff called white crosses: tiny, white, round pills with a cross embedded on one side of the tablet. They looked like baby aspirin. The pills weren't very potent, but they were effective. We used to call them the martini olive, a little additive to your boost. It would all be in and out of our system in about six hours, so we'd take them two hours before a game, and they would wear off at around midnight, so we could get a good night's sleep.

This was the first year I ever experimented with amphetamines while playing—never in A or AA ball. I did them very infrequently, though I must confess that I bummed an orange heart for this exhibition game with the Cardinals. I was flying high—on top of the world—totally focused and energized, which was good because according to the St. Louis press, we

---

* Heck, early in the season ex–Baltimore Oriole and twenty-game winner (1963) Steve Barber was a teammate at age thirty-six. Steve was with us for about three weeks until he was picked up by the San Francisco Giants for what would be his last stop in the bigs. He was thirty-six, overweight, and out of shape, smoked cigarettes, and could pound beer. But you bet I knew who he was, and he was great to me.

were going to be hard-pressed to put some runs up on the board and keep the Cardinals from scoring.[*]

But that, ladies and gentlemen, is why they play the games, because, as reported by the *Post-Dispatch* the next day, "the Oilers trumped the parent St. Louis Cardinals with a 12-hit attack for a 6–3 triumph."[†] But wait—there's more! The article goes on to say that "first baseman Keith Hernandez unloaded the big blow of the night with a three-run homer in the fifth inning." *Okay, Keither! Going downtown!* I remember the pitch: fastball, outer half, down in the strike zone. I crushed it over the sixty-foot-high center-field fence. It had to be a four-hundred-foot-plus bomb. At least. And don't forget, this was all in front of the Cardinals' coaches, who were certainly making evaluations along with Cardinals general manager Bing Devine, also in attendance.

Now, a minor league player is delusional if he thinks that one big night in front of the top brass will earn him a call-up to the majors. Because if he's labeled within the organization as just a AAA player—which certainly happens—there's little he can do short of a full body transplant to change the organization's mind. But I was a serious prospect, highly touted, and I knew they were looking at me. How much, I wasn't exactly sure, because, again, I didn't read the St. Louis press (the article I cited previously, along with nearly all the articles I cite, I uncovered during preparation for this book and therefore well after my career).

---

[*] The reporters had a point: So far that season, we'd won our games mostly with good pitching and strong defense. The Cardinals, on the other hand, were loaded at the plate and would finish the season above the league average in thirteen out of seventeen offensive categories. Cardinals stars Bake McBride, Reggie Smith, and Lou Brock would all finish in the top ten batting averages for the National League.

[†] The National League averaged eight hits per game against the Redbirds that year.

But the Tulsa papers had been saying it was really only a matter of time before I went up, and I'd heard from a few of those reporters how Bob Kennedy Sr. and some other executives were comparing me to Stan Musial, saying I was the best all-around player the organization had seen since Stan the Man. So I'd really wanted to have a great game in front of Devine, Red, the coaching staff, and the Cardinals' beat writers, who'd been milling about during BP asking questions of various teammates but mostly focusing their pregame attentions on me.

Remember, we're talking about a young Keith Hernandez here—cocky on the outside, insecure on the inside—and I was hitting only .279 coming into the game. Granted, the sample size was small: only 111 at-bats because I'd missed the first six weeks of the Tulsa season after yet another spring training injury—a slight cartilage tear in my right knee. So there was still room for doubt to do its thing. But with another year of experience under my belt, and learning how to deal with the ups and downs of a season from my ex–major league team-mates, I was waiting for my first red-hot streak, which I knew was just around the corner. I felt solid at the plate, and before the Cardinals showed up in Tulsa, I'd begun to heat up, getting 9 hits in my last 21 at-bats.

But what did all that add up to? With the Cardinals contending and Joe Torre entrenched at first base, I knew I wasn't going to be inserted into the big-league lineup any time soon. And let's face it, I hadn't had a full season in AAA and I wasn't ready.[*] But I was gunning for a September call-up. All I needed was a great second half and to maybe catch a break.

My father always said, "Don't wait for a break; *make* your

---

[*] Prior to the knee injury, reporters from the St. Louis press had speculated that I would be a midsummer call-up.

break." The exhibition game against the Cardinals had been a good start.

Here's a funny sidebar.

When you came into what was then called Oiler Park, the Otasco Man was usually the first thing to catch your eye. An advertisement for auto lubrication, it was a caricature of a man whose shoulders came to the top of the left-center-field fence, and his head protruded high above it—maybe fifteen feet. A giant wooden cutout of a head. Again, he added to the whole minor league charm of the place. But within a month of that exhibition game, the Otasco Man suffered a fatal injury when he was decapitated by a tornado that ripped through the city. I felt sorry for the Otasco Man—I would miss his smiling face. But it was better he die in that wicked storm than I, and I've got to tell ya, it had been a close call.

We were informed early that morning that the evening's game was already canceled, something quite unusual in the minor leagues, where most cash-strapped owners wanted to get every game in—no two-for-the-price-of-one rainout doubleheaders. But Tulsa is smack-dab in the middle of a region called Tornado Alley, and the media outlets warned everyone to batten down the hatches: a big storm was coming. So we got the day off and spent the afternoon preparing for the worst by drinking beer and playing volleyball in the apartment complex's pool. We were just splashing around, escaping the 100-degree swelter with a bunch of other young people living in the complex, most of them in bikinis, and I remember in the late afternoon looking to the southwest and seeing a thick wall of clouds low on the horizon. You couldn't have cut a finer line with a scalpel, and they were the green color of pea soup. Everybody in the pool went, "Oh crap," and ran inside. It was moving so rapidly that within ten minutes the clouds were over us, light turned to dark, and the streetlamps came on.

I sat in my apartment and waited for whatever came next. I had never been in a tornado before, and I left the windows cracked because I'd heard that the drop in barometric pressure could blow the glass out. But then I also remembered reading something about apartment complexes being put together like matchsticks, and I suddenly had visions of me getting sucked up like a hay bale with Dorothy and Toto.

Adorned in only my bathing suit, I ran out of my apartment, through the parking lot, and into a rain gully that was about ten feet deep. I stood in the ditch for about five minutes until a total stillness hovered over me—like the world had stopped. No wind, no sound—just hot, heavy, oppressive air. All at once, a hard, howling, and freezing wind came blowing, along with a deluge of sideways-driven rain. I went from sweating bullets to shivering as the water collected in the ditch almost up to my waist within about five minutes. Then I heard that dreadful sound—the sound of a freight train bearing down upon you. It was earsplitting, and I would've sworn that the funnel was on top of me. I looked to the sky, but it was completely dark, and the water was peppering my eyes. The only thing I could make out were the dark silhouettes of the thrashing trees all around and above me, and I thought one of them could uproot and fall on me.

Brilliant, Keith—now you're gonna drown!

So I clambered out of the gulley and raced across the parking lot to a teammate's apartment. I burst through the door and called for him but got no response, so I went into his bedroom, and there he was, buns up, on top of this girl, and they were going at it. *Okay,* I thought. *Guess this storm doesn't bother them. I'll just go back to my apartment now.*

So that's what I did, and I waited out the worst of the storm alone. Then I got a knock on my door; it was a recently divorced thirty-year-old woman every guy in the complex had been gunning for. She was scared, she said, and asked if she could come stay until the storm moved off. Obviously, my luck was changing. Being a gentleman, I said, "Sure," and we settled on the couch, and soon things went—well, let's just say that survival mode kicks up the hormones a notch.

The next morning the sun was out, but much of the town was a mess—that freight train I'd heard had actually been a mile and a half away, cutting a swath thirty yards wide and taking off all the rooftops along one of Tulsa's most affluent streets. Fortunately, it didn't completely touch down or it would have destroyed everything and probably killed some people.

We got another day off—maybe in memoriam of the guillotined Otasco Man—and bussed the next day to begin a series against the Omaha Royals. Usually, the bus ride to Omaha wasn't bad, just a bit more than two hours. But that's when I started itching all over, and somebody on the bus said, "Keith, you're all red!" *Uh-oh.* I was covered head to toe in a poison-ivy rash. The gully I'd sought refuge in during the storm must have been loaded with it.

We got to Omaha, and my body was on fire. *Smoking.* The Royals' team doctor gave me a massive cortisone injection, which went to work immediately but didn't eradicate the rash for two or three days. Still, I played that whole weekend series in oppressive heat, itching like a dog with mange. *Good for you, Keith.* More important, the poison ivy didn't deter my red-hot bat, and I picked up where I left off.

CHAPTER 15

Pacifica, 1963

CHUCKIE REYNOLDS WATCHES PRACTICE *from the first base dugout. I'd seen him riding up on his bike during the middle of midweek practice. Chuckie is my third-grade classmate and a pal, but in a couple of days we'll be facing off for the Little League minors championship. Like kids playing army soldiers, Chuckie's just here to scout the enemy.*

Dad halts practice and calls the team onto the infield to give us a pep talk for the upcoming game. "I want you to play hard," he says, "and I want you to play fairly." Then Dad turns and points his finger right at Chuckie, still spying from the dugout. "And if Chuckie Reynolds slides into second base with his spikes high again, I will handle it, and Chuckie's father will have his hands full." Dad says this in his controlled yet stern voice, and Chuckie hears every word.

We're 11–0, Chuckie's team is 10–1, their only loss coming when they faced us midseason. During that game Chuckie slid into second base stiff legged and spikes high, and plowed into our fielder. No one was hurt and Dad let it go, but when we got home, he was fuming. "Where does a nine-year-old learn to slide 'spikes high'?" Evidently, Dad felt it was intentional and ordered by Chuckie's father, their team's manager.

So Dad says this to all of us gathered on the infield, and nobody says anything. Our eyes just go from Dad to one another and then to Chuckie, who is already on his bike, pedaling home to tell his father what Mr. Hernandez said.

The game arrives and it's played under the lights. I'm pitching, and I'm nervous. Both bleachers behind the dugouts are full, parents and kids spilling down the first and third base lines. Wow! Standing room only! Mom says I've always got ants in my pants, and sometimes, when I'm really bouncing or just excited, I stutter my words, and she and Dad will gently tell me to slow down. "Your mind is going faster than your lips, son. Just relax and take your time. Slow down." So that's what I tell myself now, walking out to the mound for the first inning. Slow down and throw like Dad taught you:

Front shoulder tucked, not flying open, the arm motion reaching down and back, the delivery coming over the top, almost like a windmill—not sidearm or three-quarters or from the ear like a catcher. And, most important, don't rush the delivery or the arm action. Slow and relaxed.

But I know all this, and my body knows all this, because it's been drilled into me. Before Gary and I were old enough for organized ball, we'd head out to White Field, and Dad would conduct throwing and fielding workouts for us. The two things Dad always stressed with throwing were sound mechanics and a strong arm. The first drill was to warm up properly, then he would separate himself from us, according to our arm strength, increasing the distance little by little as our arms became stronger. We threw with 100 percent effort, in a straight line, without an arc, like an outfielder hitting the cutoff man. This is how I developed the strong arm I carried throughout my baseball career. So as I take the mound in this game, the butterflies in my stomach are there, but I'm also confident because I'm undefeated this season, sporting a dominant 5–0 record. I tell myself to stay within myself and not to rush, just like in practice. And as Dad always says, "Proper practice makes perfect."

I go through my warm-up pitches, and the catcher throws down to second. Here we go. I look beyond the left-field line and notice Dad arriving from work just in time. He's in full San Francisco fireman uniform, looking militarily prim and proper with his badge on his left breast, shirt tucked in. He does not have a belly like some of the other fathers, and his shoulders are square. My teammates sometimes ask Gary and me how strong Dad is, because he's very fit and has enormous forearms that flex whenever he demonstrates things like how to hold a bat properly. He smiles and nods at me. It has a soothing effect—ever since he'd called out Chuckie's dad at practice, the game's prospect had been full of tension for me. But now, with Dad there, I strike out the leadoff hitter and those trepidations wash away.

It's a blowout. We're up 10–0 early, and by the sixth, I'm on my way to double-digit strikeouts. Dad heads back to work because another fireman has been covering for him, and Dad knows the championship is in hand. I strike out the last batter in the sixth to preserve the shutout.

I'm about to start jumping up and down with my teammates when Mr. Reynolds runs out of the opposing dugout to home plate. He's joined by his brother, Dave Reynolds, and both men start screaming at the umpire, Mr. Steiner, accusing him of favoritism toward our team. Mr. Reynolds then grabs Mr. Steiner by the throat and starts choking him. He's got Mr. Steiner up against the backstop, his hands wrapped around his neck, and the other parents from both foul lines are sprinting toward home plate to break it up. I can't see if there are any punches being thrown because more and more parents are crowding around the three men.

Meanwhile, joining me on the mound is Chuckie, and we just

sort of sheepishly smile at each other, shrug, and return our gaze to Chuckie's dad and uncle attacking the umpire, with more than a dozen grown men trying to pry them apart. When they finally succeed, poor Mr. Steiner is left there, just sitting in the dirt, the dust still wafting around him while he's propped against the backstop with his hair matted and sweaty against his pale face and his hands on his throat, trying to catch his breath.

Dad gets home the next morning and is furious. I could sense, after the first game midseason, that he was on a slow burn with Mr. Reynolds. But now Dad is irate at the man, and he'll begin the successful proceedings of having Chuck Sr. and Dave Reynolds expelled from any further Little League activities.

But Chuckie and I will never talk about it. We'll just go on with our lives as before—classmates, friends, and competitors. All this other stuff has nothing to do with us.

CHAPTER 16

THE CHANCE OF BEING killed by a tornado is supposedly one in sixty thousand. According to the Bleacher Report, the chance of making it to the major leagues as a twentieth-round-or-later draft pick is less than 7 percent. So it was something like four thousand times more likely that I would make it to the major leagues than be sucked up by a giant funnel cloud. *Wonderful!*

Those odds were improving, too, because two months after the exhibition game with the Cardinals, I was leading the American Association in hitting, batting .351 with 63 RBI in 353 at-bats, and helping the Oilers to extend their first-place margin. I was so hot at the plate—and, more important, confident—that I even flew my dad out to Denver to meet the team for a weekend series against the Denver Bears.

It was a rare occasion that my father got to see me play since I'd turned pro, and much of that was purposeful. In fact, Bob Kennedy Sr. later told me that he had sent me to single-A ball in Florida rather than the California State League for my rookie year because he had wanted me to establish some distance from Dad and gain a little independence.[*]

---

[*] Probably what had happened was the Bay Area "bird dog" who had scouted me all that summer—a wonderful man named Jim Johnston—became

My dad had brought me into baseball, holding my hand as a little boy and introducing me not only to the game's fundamentals but also to its beauty. He did that for all the kids in the neighborhood. To this day, my brother and I can't go anywhere around Pacifica without running into someone who remembers the countless "World Series" games Dad would host on the neighborhood diamond.

There would be two teams, and Dad would pitch. He showed us how to play the game, including its finer points, like how to turn two, baserunning, relays, rundowns, etc. We were all just seven, eight, nine, or ten years old, but we knew who the cut-off man was on a ball hit to left center with a play at the plate (the shortstop and first baseman), and we knew to hit that cutoff man to his glove side on a line. Dad taught us everything, and there wasn't a single kid or parent involved with those teams who wasn't grateful. He was all about the kids and teaching them the game he loved.

But Dad had a *tough* time letting go, and as I got older, his grip went from holding my hand to a suffocating chokehold. And it wasn't just with baseball: Dad could be heard screaming at me over the cheers in the gymnasium during basketball, or from the stands well behind the sidelines during a football game. And every night I came home from practice or a game, there was the serious threat of a chewing-out session.

It had started when I was in the sixth grade, playing basketball. At first, Dad was great. When he discovered that his boys were interested in the sport, he called up his brother Uncle

---

aware of my father's controlling nature and, despite his high regard for my dad, passed the information along to Kennedy and the powers above. Gary, on the other hand, played for the Modesto outfit, and Dad headed out to watch a lot of his games. But as a college graduate, Gary was older and more mature, so Kennedy was probably less concerned about Dad's influence.

Ralph, who worked in construction, and the two of them built a concrete half-court in the backyard with a top-of-the-line backboard and rim. Dad knew nothing about the game, so he went out and got books and began to instruct us in the proper fundamentals, like how to shoot a jump shot: elbow bent at ninety degrees and tucked into the body, moving up toward the basket, the wrist snaps over for the finish, and the ball rolls off the fingertips.* Dad would rebound the shots and feed us bounce passes as we made our way around the perimeter, baseline to baseline, working farther and farther away from the hoop, but not so far that we were dropping down to shoot from the hip. We'd run drills until the sun went down—Gary and I couldn't get enough.

But when I began playing pickup games with Gary and the older kids in the school yard, Dad began hovering. I'd see his blue Mustang creeping up the street, and he'd go past us, make a U-turn, come back around, and park along the school-yard fence. Same grand entrance every day he wasn't at the firehouse, which meant two days out of three. And he would stay there all day and watch us play. *All damn day.* When the games finished, Dad would finally leave, and I'd walk home with the basketball, dribbling with my non-dominant hand, eyes up—just like it said to do in Dad's copy of Oscar Robertson's book. *Bong...bong...bong...* Down Adobe Road to Linda Mar Boulevard, left on Hermosa Avenue, and the final 150 yards to the bottom of the cul-de-sac. *I could do that walk in my sleep.* Then I'd sneak around the side of the house into the backyard and up to the kitchen window. I'd peer in and see Mom at the kitchen sink, and I'd tap on the glass. Mom knew exactly what I was

---

* His go-to was Bill Sharman's *Sharman on Basketball Shooting*. Dad didn't mess around.

asking—*Is Dad mad?*—and she'd either smile or roll her eyes, like, *Well, you know your father.*

When I got to high school and Dad stepped up his surveillance with football and baseball practice—"Here comes Hernandez's old man in that Mustang again"—I'd get home and wouldn't want to go inside the house. I'd just sit out front for around five minutes, collecting myself, and then I'd open that door and there he'd be. Waiting for me by the foyer steps.

"You're not hustling out there, Keith!" he'd start in. I never understood Dad's definition of "hustle" because I was always busting my ass. To this day, it's one of the great mysteries—I wish he'd lived longer so I could find out what the hell he meant. But the man would be in my face, often *screaming* that I didn't do this and I didn't do that.

The worst part was that it wasn't 100 percent of the time. Otherwise I would have eventually tuned him out the way a soldier might tune out a drill sergeant who had only one volume. But Dad kept me on the line because sometimes I'd come home, take a deep breath, and he'd have a big grin, maybe give me a hug, and tell me how great I played that day. With Dad, you just flipped a coin.

I remember the final basketball game of my high school career. We were playing undefeated Hillsdale, and I needed 24 points to break the school's all-time scoring record, which everyone knew going in. After we blew them out the first half, they came into the second half with a full-court press and tried to slow us down. As the point guard, I destroyed the press—dribbling, passing, running the floor like a field commander in a crack brigade—and we handily won the game. I scored only 14 points and missed the school record, but so what?

We just beat the conference champs!

After celebrating with my teammates at the local pizza place,

I came home and walked into the living room expecting cheers. Instead, Dad started berating me for not shooting the ball more and breaking the record. I was so embarrassed and humiliated because Aunt Florence and Dad's oldest brother, Uncle Henry, were there. I began crying, and all the good feelings that I'd had coming through the door from the game rushed out of my body. I mean here's Dad with all his talk about team play, the stuff he'd drilled into us when we were kids, but now he could give two shits that we'd won the game. All he cared about was his son breaking a meaningless record. Well, by then I was seventeen, and it wasn't the first time I had thought Dad actually wasn't so different from his own father, Pa, who he said could not have cared less about Dad's dedication to something larger than himself. All Pa had cared about was that his son was doing well by the family name because he was a star in some sport that all the others in the crowd seemed to admire. Well, Dad showed the same fault. The same stupid *Spanish pride*. Because it wasn't about the team. It wasn't even about me. It was about Dad and that *he* had raised a son who was a star.

And when he missed the chance to bask in that glory, he was unable to control himself.

At least Gary, God bless him, was there and told Dad off. "You don't know what a great game your son just played," Gary said after I'd gone to my room. "You don't know anything about basketball. Keith played an unbelievable game." But Dad couldn't see it that way.

Yet it was because of Dad and all his instruction and passion for baseball that I was now a professional baseball player and, in large part, doing so well in the minor leagues. I was implementing all the things he had taught me over the years. Ever since those early BP sessions in front of the garage door, whenever Dad pitched the ball, he told Gary and me where the ball was in relationship to the strike zone: *a couple of inches outside, low and inside, just missed down and in, about an inch down.*

As a result, I knew the strike zone like the back of my hand, and later, in my major league career, most umpires would give me the benefit of the doubt on a close pitch. So while I may have been the one stepping up to the plate, it's my father's tutelage that got me there.

And heading to Denver for a weekend series in the middle of an incredible 1974 season in which I felt I'd turned the corner as a professional, I wanted Dad to see it. So I flew him in and had an awesome series, displaying my wares to my mentor, who was pleased and full of praise and pride.

I'd done good.

CHAPTER 17

Candlestick Park, 1963

IT'S SUMMERTIME AND I'M *nine years old. Dad feels like I'm now old enough to go to the ballpark.*

Until this moment, my view into the magical world of Major League Baseball has been limited to NBC's Game of the Week, the nine Giants-Dodgers telecasts from Dodger Stadium each season, and a healthy dose of imagination fostered by radio waves and morning-paper box scores. Like many kids across America at that time, my heroes—Mantle and Mays—lived mostly inside my head.

The Cardinals are in town. Even though I was born and raised in and around San Francisco, the Redbirds are my favorite team. Stan Musial, the team's outfielder and first baseman, is one of the best hitters of all time. He and my dad are former teammates. They played together on the US Navy Ship Repair Unit's baseball team at Pearl Harbor during World War II, where my father had led the league in homers.[*]

Riding up the escalator from the parking lot steps into the stadium, Gary and I are full of anticipation. I can't see the field yet, but I can smell it—green grass—and I feel the hair on the back of my neck stand up. My heart is pounding. It's pumping

---

[*] My dad was at Pearl Harbor for the entirety of the war after it was attacked, but Stan served only in 1945, the last year of the war with Japan.

my little-boy legs in a rush to get my first peek at a major league stadium. Dad has to pull the reins on us like two wild mustangs in need of breaking.

The Giants have a very good team, but the thought of seeing Willie Mays, Willie McCovey, Orlando Cepeda, Juan Marichal, and Felipe Alou isn't what's had me smiling for the past week. Well, maybe a little bit, but they're not the prize waiting in the Cracker Jack box. That would be the Cardinals, who are just a so-so team in the standings. Mr. Musial, whose picture I've seen countless times in Dad's scrapbooks at home, left us the tickets. Each morning, I check the Cardinals' box score listed in the paper. Next to Mickey Mantle, my childhood hero, they're my first priority. Of all things baseball that I love—including Mantle—the Cardinals, aka the Redbirds, are my favorite.

And now we're coming into the park, and the sky is getting bigger and bigger, and I see the grandstands in right-center field, then a bit of the outfield grass, and finally I'm at the top of the steps leading down to our box seats, the entire field sprawled out before me for the first time. I look out to right-center field, the sunlight glistening off that wonderful green grass I'd just smelled, and I see, beyond the outfield fence, San Francisco Bay and the tons of ships, sliding this way and that across the water, the US Navy's Pacific Fleet at anchor in the distance. My father leads us to Mr. Musial's seats behind the Cardinals' dugout, five or six rows back and only a soft toss away from the field.

I sit down, and my eyes come to rest on a player right in front of the dugout. He's playing catch—just tossing the ball.

But he's not wearing his hat.

He's as bald as a cucumber, I say to myself.

I stare. I keep staring. I just can't wrap my nine-year-old brain around it. I lean over to my dad, sitting next to me. "Dad? Who's that?"

I ask this question because I am confused. Something doesn't make sense, and my father is good at making sense of things. How could this athlete, this professional baseball player, be bald? As a kid, I know that isn't possible. Yet there he is, right in front of me.

"That's Dick Groat. He's a great player. You know that," my dad says.

That's *Dick Groat? The Dick Groat?*

Of course I know who Dick Groat is. I've been following the amazing Dick Groat every morning at the breakfast table ever since he hit .325 for Pittsburgh in 1960 and won the batting title and league MVP. As a shortstop! Dick Groat's been turning double plays inside my head for years. I have tons of his baseball cards in the garage chest of drawers back home.

But he was never bald! Then it dawns on me that he always had his cap on in all those baseball card photos.

Many years later—when I'm in my sixties and my brain will do what sixty-year-old brains do, which is forget stuff—I won't re-member much of this game. Nothing that Mays or any of the Giants do this day will carve a lasting impression. But I'll remember com-ing into the stadium and seeing that field and the ships behind it. I'll remember seeing Mr. Musial up at the plate and the peculiar stance he takes—so different from the stance Dad taught me.

And I'll remember Dick Groat's bald head, glistening in the California sun.

There's one more piece that will stay with me. It's such a fateful moment that even if I live to be a hundred and my brain is the consistency of dry toast, I'll remember it. Mr. Musial has instructed Dad to come after the game around the right-field line to the vistors' clubhouse area. Our names are on the list for entry.

Stan greets us at the door and leads us to his locker. The club-house is bustling with activity because it's getaway day: players everywhere, showering, getting dressed, packing their equipment bags; sportswriters huddled around certain players; equipment managers and visiting clubhouse kids gathering up dirty uniforms.

All this excitement, and I'm sitting on a stool next to Mr. Musial when I see Ken Boyer, the Cardinals' star third baseman and my future manager, both in the minor leagues and later with the Cardinals. He, more than any other manager, will help me find my way. Of course, I don't know any of that last bit and neither does he. I'm just a kid whose legs barely reach the floor, sitting on that stool. And he's just a young, famous baseball player, one year away from an MVP season, who probably thinks he will play this game forever.

His locker is two down from Mr. Musial's. He's got a towel wrapped around his waist, and he looks at me and says, "Hi," and I say, "Hi," and he tousles my hair.

Yeah, I'll never forget that.

CHAPTER 18

AFTER DENVER AND MY awesome series in front of Dad, September call-ups were only a few weeks away. But as fate would have it, I would become a major leaguer sooner than that, because on August 28, 1974, the Cardinals' Joe Torre sprained his thumb sliding back into second base.

Well, Torre was the first baseman for the Cardinals, who were only a game and a half out of first place. He was supposed to miss less than a week, but a few games can make all the difference in a tight divisional race, so they called up their red-hot, matinee-idol AAA first baseman, who was busy crushing balls in Tulsa, to fill in.

Me!

We were in Oklahoma City when the news arrived. I was shocked. Sure, I'd been expecting a September call-up, but the organization was now making me an official rookie, and I'd be a Cardinal for the rest of the season, including the postseason if they made it that far. The organization also called up my Tulsa teammate catcher Marc Hill. The best defensive catcher in the organization, Marc was my roommate in St. Pete, sharing an efficiency apartment with me at the luxurious Edgewater Beach Motel, so it was fitting that we were called up together. In fact, I'd like to give a shout-out to *all* my minor league roommates:

without them (and their gals) I might never have discovered psychedelic music, grass, late-night sloth routines, and my distinct ability to ignore sexual intercourse occurring just a few yards away. *Thanks, guys! To be sure, none of this came in handy during my pending life in the major leagues...*

Anyway, Marc Hill and I just stood there in the visiting manager's office in Oklahoma City with these big, stupid grins on our faces as our manager, one Ken Boyer, gave us the news.

"You're on the first flight to San Francisco," Boyer informed us.

Now, in case you missed it, this is nothing short of a "Holy shit, Batman" moment in my life.

First, I was being sent to the big leagues as a St. Louis Cardinal—my childhood dream to wear the same uniform as Stan Musial one day had come true. *Wow!* Second, I was headed to my hometown for my major league debut, where the Cardinals would begin a three-game series against the Giants the following day. *Okay, not optimal, but...cool!* Third, the guy who was giving me this wonderful news—*You're going up, kid!*—was none other than Ken Boyer, the very same Ken Boyer who eleven years earlier, almost to the day, had tousled my hair and said hello to me sitting next to Stan Musial. *Okay, the hair on my arms is starting to stand up now...* And fourth, that had all happened in the very same place where I was now headed: the visitors' locker room in Candlestick Park.

Call it fate, karma, coincidence (I choose the first), but whatever the reason, I was about to come through those clubhouse doors again, only this time as a major leaguer. "Yes, Robin." Or in the immortal words of Group Captain Lionel Mandrake, played superbly by Peter Sellers in *Dr. Strangelove*, "Holy Colonel Bat Guano!"

Unfortunately, my "costume" walking through those doors was going to be as bad as the one I had worn in '72, flying in for my first spring training. Actually, it was worse. Let me explain.

When we got the call, we were on the road in Oklahoma City, and Boyer didn't have any sort of dress code. All Marc and I had in our suitcases were faded jeans and Ban-Lon shirts—not exactly the proper attire to travel with the big club. With only a couple of hours before our flight to San Fran, we said goodbye to Boyer and sprinted to a nearby clothing store.

Remember that great exchange between Dan Aykroyd and the saloon waitress in *The Blues Brothers*?

> ***Aykroyd:*** Uhh, what kind of music do you usually have here?
>
> ***Waitress:*** Oh, we got both kinds! We got country *and* western!

Well that pretty much sums up men's fashion options in Oklahoma City in 1974. Not exactly sport coats and suit pants. This was a cowboy town. I remember we always stayed at the Holiday Inn, and they had a big bar that was straight out of the movie *Urban Cowboy*. It had a mechanical bull, and there were drugstore cowboys in ten-gallon hats and boots, and lots of pretty girls, who were quite friendly, but you had to be careful. I certainly didn't need some hard-ass cowboy with Lord knows how much liquor or crystal meth in his system looking to plant his pointy boot between my legs because his girlfriend was flirting with me.[*]

So Marc and I were forced to shop where those dudes

---

[*] My brother once told me never to get into a fight in a bar over a woman. He said there would be gals who would flirt with me just to get their boyfriends jealous, and the last thing I needed was a drunk and angry BF looking for a fight. "Just say, 'I'm so sorry. I didn't know this was your girlfriend. Please forgive me.' Then *exit stage right.*" Sage advice, and doubly true in a town like Oklahoma City.

shopped, and it was what you'd expect: boots, leather vests, and six-shooters. Even Marc, who was from Elsberry, Missouri—a very small town with maybe 1,500 people in it—was like "What the hell?" The closest things they had to acceptable were polyester cowboy outfits with snaps instead of buttons on the jackets, and more snaps on the shirts' breast pockets. Of course, only two colors were available, so we drew straws: Marc got the navy blue, and I got the other, banana yellow. Another Cuban flag.

We hustled to the airport and flew out to San Francisco wearing our normal clothes, saving our *Bonanza* outfits for the next day, when we'd meet the team at the park. *Won't* this *make a good first impression with the veterans.*

My dad picked me up from the airport, and I was very much on edge. Of all places to make your debut: in front of Mom and Dad and family and about fifty hometown friends. Just arranging all their tickets was stressful. Gary would be my rock, of course, but he didn't arrive until the second game of the series, flying in from Sarasota immediately after his season ended, so I had to withstand all the pressure alone. That's a word I hate: "pressure." Pressure is what people make of an otherwise opportune moment.

Pressure is a challenge.

But in this situation, there is no better word to describe what stirred in my gut. Because everything I'd put into baseball seemed so close to paying off. The hard work, the disappointments, the setbacks. It was all worth it if I could just make this work. It was like making camp on Mt. Everest before the final climb. *I've made it this far, but can I make it to the top?* And to begin that final leg of the ascent in my hometown was beyond nerve-racking.

I stayed in Gary's vacated bedroom with the double bed, and I got a good night's sleep under the same roof where I used to dream of making it to the major leagues. (If only I'd left some clothes in the closet, I could have spared myself the banana suit, but at least when I drove myself to Candlestick Park the next morning I was appropriately dressed for my first gunfight against major league pitching.)

To make room on the roster for Marc Hill and me, the organization waived backup catcher—and fan favorite—Tim McCarver.[*] McCarver, who was on his second run with the club, was a force behind the plate with the Cardinals' championship teams of the '60s. So one special St. Louis career came to an end while two others were hopefully beginning. Such is life in baseball. As my good friend and former teammate Ted Simmons says, "It's a logical progression." How true. But as Teddy—who ironically had taken McCarver's starting job as catcher three seasons prior, in 1971—knows, that doesn't make it any easier for the other veterans, who now have to manage the loss of not only a teammate but a friend. I mean, how many games did Mc-Carver catch Bob Gibson over that glorious decade of the '60s? But now, in that friend's place, is a rookie who by definition doesn't know squat about major league baseball.

So here I was, first day, with a veteran team, feeling out of place, dressed in a ridiculous outfit.

I walked into that clubhouse, and it looked the same as it did in 1963. I immediately peered over at those three lockers and stools where I had sat between Musial and Boyer. *Holy cow.* Then I looked at the lineup card and saw that I was starting at first base and hitting seventh. *Holy crap!* You have to remember, this was not planned. It was not like the team had been grooming me and brought me up on purpose in front of my hometown.

---

[*] The organization also sent reserve infielder Jerry DaVanon down to the minors.

This was all a chain reaction beginning with Joe Torre diving into second base—something he'd done a million times before, just a bit differently on the million and first. And while he was out of commission for hopefully less than a week, the team still needed production at first base, and the Cardinals' brass was hoping I could fill the gap. There was a lot at stake for everybody, and, again, it was all on display for the folks at home.

Left-hander Mike Caldwell was on the hill for the Giants. At 12–3 with an ERA of 2.97, he was having a superb year and retired the first six batters. I drew a walk on five pitches—all sliders—to lead off the third. Taking all the way until I got my first strike, I never swung the bat: the first pitch was a ball; the second pitch was a strike, which I took, and the count was even at 1–1; and then he threw three straight balls that I didn't chase. In my second at-bat, I led off the bottom of the fifth, but Caldwell struck me out.

It's all about getting that first base hit. I knew that once Torre was back I wasn't going to get much playing time. So I needed to get things going. Plus, here I was playing with guys like Reggie Smith, Lou Brock, and Ted Sizemore. The Giants had Gary Matthews, Dave Kingman, Bobby Bonds, and Tito Fuentes, a guy I had grown up watching. I was twenty years old, three years removed from high school. *Are my insecurities on full display?* It was like I was a sapling next to mighty oaks. It was very daunting—it was the major leagues. Then there was my dad in the stands, and I knew how much this meant to him. And sitting next to him was "Constant Mom," wrapped in a blanket to protect her from the wind and chill that were synonymous with Candlestick Park.

Man alive, a base hit sure would be helpful.

It came in the ninth inning: with Bake McBride in scoring position, I singled to right field for my first major league hit and my first major league RBI. Plus, it sent Caldwell to the showers. The Giants won 8–2, so it's hardly like my effort improved the team's lot. But they were my firsts, and the next day, the *Post-Dispatch* read:

> "Sure, I was nervous at bat," said 20-year-old Hernandez. "That Caldwell was throwing some sliders on the corners [of the plate] that I had never seen before. I did get some fastballs that I should have ripped, but I fouled them off. But it was great getting that first hit up there."

Welcome to the major leagues, Mr. Hernandez.

Part II

GET TO WORK

CHAPTER 19

Long Island, New York

THE COUNTDOWN BEGINS WHEN my alarm buzzes at 8 a.m. The Mets have a 1:10 game today, a rarity on a weekday, and I'm working the broadcast. So I get up, feed Hadji and eat breakfast, take a shower, and get dressed. Just before 9 and on schedule, I'm ready to head out the door when a hornet dive-bombs me in the living room.

Uh, Houston, we have a problem.

Whatever the phobia is for bees and such, I have it, so I don't react particularly well when confronted by one. Once, when I was at the plate in Wrigley Field, a yellow jacket landed on my nose. *"Whoa!"* I pulled the ejector button and flew out of the box. Thankfully, the pitcher was still in his windup, and the umpire immediately called time to ask if I was okay. "Damn bee," I explained, and after a few chuckles, we proceeded without further interruption.

Another time, in the early '80s when I was married to my first wife and we were living in Chesterfield, Missouri, I was driving the family van with the driver's side window halfway down, and a wasp flew into my side mirror, got sucked into the van, and landed in my lap. It was either dead or stunned, but of course I freaked—I was, after all, wearing shorts—and we went off the road, and I took out around thirty feet of my neighbor's fence. All my kids were on board, so it could've been a disaster. But thanks to my expert emergency driving skills, the vehicle stayed upright and no one was injured.

So with great trepidation and care, I finally coax this hornet out the now wide-open sliding door.

Recommencing countdown. My house is about seven miles west of Sag Harbor, and the ride from my doorstep to Citi Field is eighty-six miles, usually taking ninety minutes. But all it takes is one accident or stall and you're in deep trouble. It's times like these—when I'm in a rush—that I miss living in the city, where there are no yards or hornet's nests to tend to and everything's just a cab ride away.

So how did a kid from San Francisco who played ball for the Cardinals wind up living most of each year in New York? Well, the impetus was being traded by the Cardinals to the New York Mets in 1983. The next season, I moved into an apartment on the East Side, Midtown, and tried on "city life." As a ballplayer carousing around with his new teammates, it wasn't hard to get used to.

In those early days, our favorite place was Rusty's, owned by my teammate Rusty Staub. But if someone, usually pitcher Ed Lynch, said, "Hey, let's grab some sushi," then we'd head to Tokubei 86, a Japanese restaurant on 86th and Second Avenue (it's not there anymore). It'd be Ed, Rusty, and myself, and sometimes Ron Darling, who lived downtown. (We'd drop Danny Heep and his wife, Jane, off at the Mad Hatter, their favorite post-game establishment on the Upper East Side.) We'd all go and eat and drink. All the restaurateurs loved having us because the Mets, previous doormat of the NL East, were turning things around.

I remember one night we were a little rowdy—there was more sake and Sapporo going around than sushi—and the conversation somehow got on who would be the best lion tamer of the group. *Seems normal, right?* So someone (probably Lynchie) stood up, grabbed a chair in one hand, pointed the four legs at the rest of us, and with an imaginary whip in the other hand, imitated a lion tamer in his best ringmaster voice: "Stand back, everyone. I'll keep you safe from these terrible beasts!" Everybody in the restaurant seemed to enjoy our antics. But the owner came out, pleading with Rusty, the only mature one of us, "Oh, Mr. Rusty, not the chair! Not the chair!"

We were ballplayers—of course we could be obnoxious. Nights after a day game were especially fun: table for ten, dinner at a normal hour, and with Rusty in attendance, fine wine flowing. I remember one night we got loud, and Lynchie left the table to use the restroom. When he returned, he walked by an older couple, and the wife was angrily telling her husband, "I don't care if that is Keith Hernandez. I don't have to listen to that kind of language!"

Oops! (Never got to apologize for that one.)

New York just afforded more opportunities for shenanigans since nothing seemed too far or to ever close down for the night. And as ballplayers on a night schedule, Manhattan was the perfect fix; it was sort of like we were in college, only we used hot new clubs and fine restaurants as our fraternity houses.

I slowed down a bit after I retired from the game in 1991, trading the nightclubs and bars for the next generation, and I enjoyed everything Manhattan had to offer an older, possibly maturing Keith Hernandez. Then, in the spring of 2002, I met my second wife, bought the house out in the Hamptons later that same year, and moved there permanently in 2006 with our dog and three cats. I was doing only around thirty Mets games on the MSG network at the time, and I didn't think my role as television analyst would become anything more than part-time. We settled in, and my summer became those thirty games, barbecuing by the pool, tending my extensive rose garden, and enjoying the bucolic outdoors beneath the embrace of mature oak trees.

Well, that marriage fizzled, too, and now I do about 120 games a season, but I still have the house and its backyard retreat.

So I'm staying.

But there's no way around this commute to the ballpark. I've missed the morning rush-hour traffic, but as I get closer to Manhattan, stragglers are aplenty, and things always begin to back up around exit 39, where drivers can leave the Northern State Parkway and merge onto the Long Island Expressway.

The way home will be *far* worse. The game will finish sometime around 4:30, and it'll be about a ten-minute walk from the booth, through the bowels of Citi Field, past the visitors' clubhouse to the parking lot, saying my goodbyes and see-you-tomorrows to the ushers and vendors along the way. By the time I'm on the highway, it'll be after 5, and I'll be smack-dab in the middle of evening rush hour, everyone going east after a long workday in the city. I'll be anxious to get home, but just like when I stepped up to the plate in the big leagues, I'll have to take a deep breath, count to ten, and tell myself, *No, Keith, the HOV lane is not for you. Just go with the flow and don't weave in and out of traffic just to gain on maybe a car or two.* Finally, after about two and a half hours in the car, I'll be home.

It will go faster if today's game is like last night's broadcast: a nice and tidy two-hour-and-twenty-minute affair. That was awesome. I got home before midnight and had a good sleep despite the quick turnaround for today's day game. I wish all the games could move so quickly, but with so many pitching changes these days and manager challenges, even a low-scoring, well-played nine innings usually takes three hours and change.

Ughhhh . . .

Three hours for an average game is not good for baseball. The only thing it serves is more concession sales and television advertising revenues. The game was meant to be played at a faster clip, and if it is allowed to slow down further, I fear baseball will become a bore: a tedious exercise of managers and general managers trying to micromanage every second of the game. Why do they do it? Because the game, like everything else, has gotten so hyper-analyzed that those in charge—from general managers to managers to the umpires to the commissioner's office—mitigate risk at the expense of the game's pace: e.g., a constant flux in pitchers and "instant" replay.

People—sports television critics mainly—get on me sometimes when I complain during a broadcast about long games; they think my complaining reflects a less-than-enthusiastic tone about baseball. Well, I still love baseball, but if we keep up with these long games, they might be proven correct. Because while baseball was never meant to be played at a frenetic pace, there is, again, a rhythm to it, and with all the stopping and starting—from the batters stepping out of the box for days on end; to pitchers, particularly relievers, who take an eternity between pitches; to 3–2 counts ad nauseam; to an abundance of base on balls; to instant replay every five seconds; to countless pitching changes; to commercial breaks—that rhythm is under siege.

The commissioner's office is trying to crack down, but we've really just seen Band-Aids so far. I mean do they really expect to shorten the time of the game with a silly thirty-second limit for the pitching coach or manager to come out to the mound?

Besides, mound visits have always been part of baseball, as have older managers, who might not be able to make it that far in a sprint.* So the league has tried to heal a broken part of the game by breaking another. To make it worse, while the league enforces such sacrilege, they promote all the replay, which just adds minutes upon minutes of gobbledygook to the running time.

Instant replay was instituted on August 28, 2008. It applied to home-run calls in only three situations: to determine if the ball was fair or foul, if in fact the ball had cleared the fence, and if the ball had been subject to fan interference. Now look where it has taken us: "Manager challenges," which were enacted in 2014, initially gave both managers one challenge at the start of the game and no more than two per game if their first challenge was successful. Then, in addition, a much wider range of calls, beyond the initial scope, were made subject to review. But the commissioner's office wasn't finished. In 2015 and 2016, they made further modifications, allowing a manager to retain his challenge if a play was successfully overturned, and allowing the manager to no longer have to challenge on the field but instead from the dugout. This last bit was done for the sake of saving time.

Saving time? What a joke!

So the league has failed to address the real need: to rein in the beyond-excessive management and umpiring of the game. And it's not like managers or general managers are going to curtail their strategies. They're just trying to win ball games (though I do question the effectiveness of some of these micromanagement strategies—the constant changing of pitchers

---

* Harvey Kuenn, manager of the 1975 and 1982–83 Brewers, was an amputee after suffering a blood clot in his leg in 1980. Will the league start making exceptions for exceptional people like Harvey?

in particular). Those guys have jobs on the line, so it's not like they're going to say, "Hey, this is taking too long. Let's just keep our starter out there," just as the umpires aren't going to say, "Hey, let's skip the replay because I *think* it was a fair ball." It's the league's job to step in here, and so far their measures are inadequate. They have to decide if we're playing a baseball game or conducting a computer simulation. Because people make mistakes—it's part of human nature—and last time I checked, the game was still being played, managed, and umpired by humans.

But if we're going to allow folks to increasingly micromanage every aspect of the game in an attempt to control each and every outcome, then a computer simulation is exactly what we're getting.

I want to add that this isn't an easy issue to solve. Times change; technology increases, as does our understanding of the game; and it would be impossible for baseball to be immune to these forces. When I played, the average game was well under two hours and forty-five minutes, which, according to George Will's *Men at Work,* was still a whopping forty-five minutes longer than games were at the turn of the twentieth century. That's an increase of 38 percent, or, in baseball talk, it's like stretching a normal nine-inning game to twelve and a half innings. I can only imagine a circa 1900 baseball fan watching a modern game. Beyond the strange gloves and testicle-stretching pants, he'd probably think he died and went to eternal hell because the game is taking forever. Interestingly, Will, who published *Men at Work* the same year I retired from baseball, cited that part of the reason for the longer games was batters were becoming more selective with their pitches and willing to go deeper into counts than their predecessors, and "because batters are going deeper into the count, there are more walks and strikeouts, both of which take time."* So I understand the idea that as the game evolves, more time may be required. That said, I would challenge some of our recent game "enhancements" on the grounds that their bad qualities outweigh their good ones, and that they are too disruptive to what is at the very core of baseball: *time* and *rhythm*.

Speaking of time, traffic is moving along nicely. I won't have to call ahead to let my producer know I'm running late. Instead, I want to call my youngest daughter, Mary, to go over the details for a Mets reunion. The franchise is hosting a weekend hubbub at the end of the month at Citi Field. Most of the '86 team will be there, and there will be lots of functions and parties, including a big televised event at the field. My family is coming in—my three daughters with husbands and grandkids, and my brother, Gary, and his wife, Marion. They know all the guys, so it should be a great time. Mary is coordinating everyone in the family, and she really doesn't need my help. I'm just curious, so I give her a buzz.

My girls—Jessie, Melissa, and Mary—are wonderful. They continue to put up with a lot from a father who's had a knack for putting baseball ahead of everything, including them. But we're working on it and have been for a while.

---

* George F. Will, *Men at Work* (New York: HarperCollins, 2010). Pitchers today, versus those from the late '80s, seem reluctant to put a hitter away when they have the decided advantage of an 0–2 count. This careful pitching (to put it nicely) only adds to pitch counts (0–2 quickly becomes 3–2) and elapsed time.

CHAPTER 20

I WAS IN THE big leagues! Even when Joe Torre came back from his thumb injury on September 2, 1974, and I was relegated to the bench, I was like a kid in a candy store.* How could I be otherwise? Every day I got into uniform that September, it was in a new major league city, in a new major league stadium, dugouts filled with players I had grown up following. Remember, I had been familiar with every team's lineup since childhood. As a boy, I had picked up the sports pages and perused the daily box scores, and later I had played Strat-O-Matic baseball, which made me savvier than most fans. My knowledge about the players went much deeper than just the stars; I knew almost *everyone*, their careers, what teams they had played for, and many of their stats and accomplishments. Couple that with the extensive baseball history my dad had taught me, and I understood I was in the presence of not just major leaguers but serious big-league lineage.

For example, after we left San Francisco, my first home stand was in Busch Stadium against the Expos. Playing first base for Montreal? Thirty-five-year-old Ron Fairly. *Who is Ron Fairly?*

---

* In the three games Torre missed, I went 3 for 10 with 3 walks.

Well, of course I recalled that he had started his major league career as a member of the Dodgers teams of the '60s, which I had grown up watching on TV. Pretty much every year those transplanted Flatbush bums had stood in the way of the Giants in their quest for the National League flag, giving the Mays-led Giants the label "The Bridesmaids of the NL." And Fairly was a good, solid player—a .265 hitter averaging 10 home runs and 70 RBI a year with a very, very good glove at first base—but he wasn't a perennial All-Star. In fact, the previous year, 1973, had been his only year as an All-Star.[*]

Yet here I was, a rookie riding pine, thinking, *Holy cow, there's Ron Fairly!* Why? Because I also knew that he had played with Brooklyn shortstop and Hall of Famer Pee Wee Reese.[†] Reese, of course, had been a part of all those great Brooklyn Dodgers teams to face the New York Yankees in *seven* World Series between 1941 and 1956. So he had gone up against Mantle and Berra in '52, '53, '55, and '56, DiMaggio and Berra in '47 and '49, and DiMaggio and Bill Dickey in '41, which had been Reese's first year in the bigs and Bill Dickey's last. Bill Dickey had broken into the league way back in 1921—a late-season call-up—and with *his* keister parked on the bench, he got to watch Lou Gehrig and Babe Ruth lead the Yankees to a World Series title over—you guessed it—the St. Louis Cardinals.

How's *that* for lineage? So, yeah, I was seeing all these big leaguers, and as I said before, most of the time I felt like a sapling in a forest of mighty oaks. But however small, I was now a part of

---

[*] Fairly would also make the All-Star team in 1978, though this time representing Toronto in the American League.
[†] I knew Mr. Reese from my minor league days when he was representing the Louisville Slugger bat company. In fact, he signed me to my first bat contract with Louisville in 1973. I would stay with that company my entire career.

baseball history because I played against a guy who played with a guy who played against a guy who had been a teammate of Babe Ruth, the mightiest oak of them all. And with chronologies like that playing through the back of my mind, riding pine never felt so good.

And then, of course, there were the superstars. Tom Seaver, for one. We faced Seaver and the Mets on September 8 in what looked to be my sixth game in a row of never leaving the dugout. But so what? I was going to watch the reigning NL Cy Young winner, Tom Seaver, go against our ace, Lynn McGlothen. Talk about a show!

I'd faced McGlothen in the minors back in Tulsa when we'd battled Pawtucket in the 1973 Junior World Series. He'd made me look foolish in game one of that series—I'd never seen a hard, snapping curve like that before. Now McGlothen, 16–8, was throwing in his first full big-league season with a chance to be a twenty-game winner for the St. Louis Cardinals. But first he needed to get by Seaver and the defending NL champion Mets, who may have been 64–73 on the season, just beginning what would be another long stretch of disappointing, if not terrible, seasons for Mets fans to endure. But the names were still there: Bud Harrelson, Félix Millán, Ed Kranepool, Wayne Garrett, Rusty Staub, Jerry Koosman, Jon Matlack, and Cleon Jones. So McGlothen had his work cut out for him, while I had plenty of stargazing to keep me entertained. *Yogi Berra is the Mets' manager, for crying out loud!* But, as it turned out, I would be a bystander for only *most* of the afternoon.

We were going for a three-game sweep after Bob Forsch shut out Koosman and the Mets in the opener, 2–0, and Bob Gibson outdueled Jon Matlack 2–1 in the second game. This was the Sunday finale, and we were a game and a half behind the Pirates with twenty-three games left in the season—a real stretch run.

We were losing 5–3 in the ninth when our manager, Red Schoendienst, walked down the dugout toward me and said, "Hernandez, be ready. I may pinch-hit you this inning." I raced to the bat rack, grabbed my bat and helmet, and retreated up the runway a few yards to begin stretching and mentally preparing.

Sure enough, with two outs and nobody on, Red signaled me to hit for Mike Tyson in the eighth hole. Deep breath. The scoreboard in left field had already posted a Pirates victory against the Expos, and I was the last chance for us to keep pace in the NL East.

I strode to the on-deck circle and rubbed some pine tar and resin onto my bat, making sure my hands adhered to it. I then slipped the weighted donut onto the bat and took a few swings to loosen up. During this on-deck circle ritual I heard my name being announced over the stadium PA system, and the crowd of slightly more than 34,000 fans, anxious to see this rookie who'd been in the papers of late, came to their feet in anticipation. I stepped into the box, looked up, and lo and behold, there stood Tom Terrific. A few more deep breaths, and I counted to ten...*I guess I'm ready.*

Not many people in life get a chance to face a Hall of Fame Cy Young winner's fastball, much less one from Tom Seaver. I don't remember the count, but I do know that he threw me a vintage Seaver up-and-in fastball, alive and "rising" with extreme velocity, zinging as if traveling along a telephone wire. And don't ask me how, because I thought the ball was by me, but I just reacted.

Whack! Boom!

I drilled a laser beam to right-center field in old Busch Stadium, where it was 386 to the wall in both gaps. That's a long, *long* way. Had we been dueling in Shea Stadium, that shot would have been a home run. As it was, it smacked above the protective padding off the concrete wall, a foot from a home run, and came bouncing back into the outfield. I dashed around the bases—the roar of the crowd only slightly audible above the pounding inside my chest—and I found myself standing on third base, thinking, *Man, I just got a pinch-hit triple off Tom Seaver.*

Seaver retired the next batter, Richie Scheinblum, on a pop-up, and the game ended. I was bummed, of course, because I wanted to be a part of a big comeback against the one-and-only Tom Seaver. But Tom would have none of it, and we fell two and a half games behind the Pirates with twenty-two to play.

The Phillies came to town the next night, and Red called on me to pinch-hit again—this time against Jim Lonborg, the 1967 AL Cy Young winner for the Boston Red Sox. A freshman in high school during that season, I remember tuning in to the 1967 World Series and watching Lonborg pitch three games against the Cardinals, winning Game Two and Game Five, but losing Game Seven to Bob Gibson on two days' rest. Shortly after that series, Lonborg blew out his knee while snow skiing in Aspen, and the veterans said he was never the same.[*] But I, for the second night in a row, was coming in cold off the bench to face a Cy Young winner whom I'd never faced. *Advantage Hernandez?* I think not! I drew a walk—not exactly a stand-up triple, but I took it. Lonborg got through the inning unscathed, however, on his way to a complete-game shutout and his fifteenth win.

The next night, behind the complete-game pitching of Dick Ruthven, the Phillies beat us badly. I pinch-hit for another walk in the sixth, but it didn't mean much; they'd already put the game away. The much bigger deal was getting to see a huge

---

[*] The handsome Stanford graduate Lonborg was hitting the slopes with actress and super fox Jill St. John when he tore up his knee. From then on, all player contracts would include what is known as the "Lonborg clause," which voids the contract if the player gets hurt while snow skiing.

piece of history being made when my thirty-five-year-old team-mate Lou Brock broke Major League Baseball's single-season stolen-base record. He tied Maury Wills's modern-era mark of 104 when he stole second in the first inning, and he nabbed sole possession of the record with another swipe in the seventh.[*]

And this man was how old? Unbelievable. I remember they stopped play on the field after Lou set the record. Second base umpire John McSherry and Phillies middle infielders Larry Bowa and Dave Cash all shook his hand. I could see that Lou, besides being one of the greats, was well respected and liked by players, teammates, and competitors. We all charged the field and swarmed Lou with congratulations, and then stepped aside to let him soak in the glory. The class act that he is, Brock simply tipped his cap to the 27,000 fans who had sat through the blowout in hopes of seeing the record broken, and I believe it was important to Lou, a St. Louis favorite ever since he'd been acquired by trade from the Cubs in 1964, to break the record in front of the home crowd.[†]

But not everyone was thrilled with Lou when the game ended. Bob Boone, the Gold Glove catcher for the Phillies at the time, was one of the best throwers in the game and *very* difficult to steal on.[‡] Well, he got pissed as hell at Brock in the ninth inning after Lou attempted yet another swipe. I remember I was standing in the dugout, about five feet back from the steps, and

---

[*] Wills had set the record in 1962. Brock would finish the season with 118, a record that still stands today in the National League, although Rickey Henderson stole 130 in 1982 to set the current American League and overall mark. Henderson was twenty-three years old when he set the new mark.

[†] The Cubs traded Brock a third of the way through the 1964 season, and he went on to hit .348 for the Cards for the rest of that season, helping them to a World Series title.

[‡] He was also the son of former Cleveland Indians outfielder Ray Boone, who had been a minor league teammate of my father's at Oklahoma City in 1947. Talk about lineage.

after the out was registered on a perfect throw by Boone, I saw him clench his fist while bending over to grab his mask and curse Lou in no uncertain terms. He was probably already upset that Lou had swiped two off him earlier to tie and break the record—a distinction no catcher would want—and now thought Lou was showing him up.[*]

This little incident, which was probably missed by most, seriously whet my appetite, and I remember saying to myself, *Of all the places in this world, this is where I want to be—amid all this kind of* competitiveness. *I want to stay here and do this on a par and as a peer with these guys.*

So I was seeing and learning quite a bit in a short amount of time. But despite the stargazing, I still very much wanted to play and was happy knowing my plate appearances weren't meaningless. I'd been hitting .350 in AAA, and thought I could really help the Cardinals. But it had been almost two weeks since my last start. *How in hell was I going to get into a rhythm with just pinch hits?* The triple off Seaver probably raised some eyebrows, and the walk from Ruthven was my sixth in seventeen plate appearances. But the team was focused on beating the Pirates for the division, not on developing young talent, and they had a former MVP and batting champ in Joe Torre anchoring first base. I would just have to be patient.

We flew to New York to face the Mets in the first series of a crucial road trip: two in New York, three in Philly, and three in Pittsburgh. We landed at LaGuardia Airport sometime after 2 a.m., and as we were bussing into the city, I got my very first look at the Manhattan skyline. It was a beautiful, clear night,

---

[*] In Bob's defense, he felt Lou was breaking one of the unwritten rules in baseball: neither pour it on late in a game nor, in this case, pad your stats when you're down. After the game, Lou told reporters he was just trying to jump-start a rally.

and I couldn't get over all those buildings, my eyes, of course, scanning for the Empire State Building. Lou Brock, who must have sensed my wonder at the whole thing, reached over to me and said, "Keith, there's a million stories in that city. And guess what? Now you're one of them."

But Lou's inspiring words were quickly tempered when we arrived at the New York Sheraton and George Kissell, Red's bench coach, had me follow him outside the hotel lobby to the street.

"New York City is a dangerous place, Keith," he began. It was past three in the morning, and I couldn't get over the number of taxis still out and about. "It's on the verge of bankruptcy, and there is a major criminal element walking these streets. You can wind up in a bad area and find yourself in trouble."

"Okay," I said.

George then pointed up Sixth Avenue. "That's Central Park," he said. *"Don't go there."*

I nodded.

Then he pointed west. "That's Hell's Kitchen," he continued. *"Don't go there."*

Another nod.

Then he pointed down the avenue. "That's Times Square. *Don't go there."*

And I was thinking, *Where the hell am I? A war zone?*

Finally, George pointed east. "That's the Upper East Side. If you have to go somewhere in this city, *go there."*

George then took me back inside the hotel, escorting me to the elevator, which I took in the only direction left: *up,* and to the safety of my room and bed. Such was my introduction to the city of New York, the place of a million stories and, according to George Kissell, a million ways to die.

Well, I *almost* was the story of the game the next night because I pinch-hit off Harry Parker, a right-hander, in the top of the twelfth and hit a rope to right field.[*] But the right fielder, Dave Schneck—all five feet nine inches of him—leapt up, crashing into the wall at full speed, and robbed me of a home run. So I was back on the bench, and the game stayed tied—until the *twenty-fifth inning! Damn you, Dave Schneck!*

As it turned out, the real "player of the game" was Claude Osteen, who entered in the fourteenth inning and threw 9⅓ innings of shutout relief for us during the marathon, keeping us in the game until we won it on a Hank Webb wild throw attempting to pick off Bake McBride at first. Osteen was another one of those baseball players I knew well because he had played for the Dodgers in my formative years, from 1965 to 1973, winning twenty games twice for manager Walter Alston, in 1969 and 1972. Claude was a super-nice guy and was wonderful to me that September. He was also a dead ringer for Jim Nabors, the actor who played Gomer Pyle on *The Andy Griffith Show;* I started calling him Gomer after a few of the veterans told me it was his nickname. Well, stupid me for falling for that, because Claude pulled me aside in BP one day.

"You know, Keith," he said, "I *hate* being called Gomer."

"Oh, Claude," I said, "I'm so sorry. I'll never say that again." Nor did I take any more of the veterans' advice when it came to nicknames.

Well, that marathon game against the Mets lasted seven hours and four minutes, forcing Red to use nineteen players and seven pitchers over the course of the game. By the time it ended—at approximately 3 a.m.—there was no food and just a smattering of beer left in the clubhouse for the guys who'd played the entire game. Were they pissed...*But, hey! We won, and the Pirates lost!*

---

[*] Near Shea's old bullpen gate.

143

The next night, we were back at Shea for game two. Down 4–3 with two outs and the bases loaded in the sixth, Red pinch-hit me, and I ripped a line drive to right center. This time Schneck muffed it, and the tying run and two go-ahead runs scored. We were now only a game and a half behind the Pirates. Good things happen, including errors, when you hit the ball hard, and some of the veteran players shook my hand in the energetic clubhouse after the game. I can't tell you how awesome it made me feel that I was gaining their respect, my contributions slowly bringing me into the fold.

After showering up, we were off to Philadelphia on a late-night, two-hour bus jaunt down the New Jersey Turnpike. A mixture of veterans and new players, the Phillies were on the verge of NL East dominance. We're talking Dave Cash, Larry Bowa, Greg Luzinski, Willie Montañez, and, of course, future Hall of Famers Mike Schmidt and Steve Carlton. On a five-game winning streak—including a two-game sweep of the division-leading Pirates—the Phillies were now 4.5 back in the standings, and our pending three-game set was crucial for both teams.

So imagine my surprise when I arrived at Veterans Stadium the following afternoon and discovered I was starting the game. *What?!* No one had said to me the night before or that morning, "Hey, Keith, you're gonna be in the lineup." But there it was when I entered the clubhouse, written on the chalkboard: HERNANDEZ, FIRST BASE. Not only that, I was batting fifth—an RBI spot in the lineup—behind Simmons and in front of McBride.

Jim Lonborg was on the hill for the Phillies, and, once again, Jim pitched a brilliant game. He may not have been the power pitcher he was back in '67, but he was smarter than most and could throw a breaking ball for a strike when he was behind in the count.* As a young hitter itching to hit a fastball, that was very, *very* frustrating. I'd be up in the count, say two balls and no strikes, but here would come this big 11-to-5 hard curve. On the black, outside corner, at the knees. *Strike!* Even if I'd been looking for it, which I wasn't at this early stage in my career, I just wasn't used to seeing this kind of quality curveball in triple A.† So Jim, who never seemed to leave anything out over the plate, gave me fits, and I was an insignificant 1 for 4 when he left the game after the eighth.

Fortunately, our starter, Lynn McGlothen, was dealing, and the game went into extra innings, tied 2–2. We eventually won 7–3, putting up 5 runs in the seventeenth inning. This after our twenty-five-inning marathon two days earlier. *Imagine our bullpen!* I went 2 for 3 in the extra innings, taking part in the winning rally: Ted Simmons led off with a single to left; I followed with a single to left; and McBride singled behind me, scoring Simmons and pushing me to third.

Boy, did it feel good to be a part of another big win, especially after not starting for twelve days.

I was back on the chalkboard the next day and went 1 for 5, taking part in a big fifth inning with an RBI triple and a run scored. The 9–2 victory was our fourth in a row and, coupled with a Pirates loss at Montreal earlier that day, propelled us into a half-game lead over the Pirates with sixteen games to play. After the win, my head was spinning, like *Holy cow,*

---

* Jim had the intellect to reinvent himself after the knee injury. But that sort of thing takes time. He hung around, compiling a 27–30 record over 70 starts with the Red Sox, before being traded to the Milwaukee Brewers after the 1971 season. He started turning the corner in 1972, winning fourteen games, then was traded again after that season to the Phillies, where he would play six-plus years, winning 17 games in 1974 and 18 in 1976.

† Even as a veteran, ahead in the count like this, I wouldn't have swung at this "pitcher's pitch"—a quality breaking ball, painted perfectly down and away.

this is amazing. Here I was with the Cardinals, not only in the middle of a neck-and-neck divisional race but in first place! *I could be in postseason play and a World Series, and I'm contributing!*

Back at the hotel and feeling pretty good; I decided to go out on a limb and make my way downstairs to the hotel bar with my buddy Marc Hill.[*] I remember being slightly skittish walking in because Bob Gibson, who didn't seem to have the most patience with rookies, was up at the bar along with Reggie Smith, Joe Torre, and Ted Sizemore. Big dogs. But Ted was always great to me, going out of his way to make me feel at home since I'd walked in the door in San Francisco.

So as casually as we could, Marc and I strode up to the bar to hang near—if not with—these baseball giants, and Reggie Smith, who was a little in his cups, immediately started laying the rookie stuff on me. It was just a typical razzing, nothing mean-spirited, that basically culminated in Reggie saying, "Go someplace else, rook." So I left the bar with my tail between my legs and tried not to take it personally. *What was I thinking, anyway?* I mean, we're talking about Reggie Smith here—a guy who nine days prior to my fourteenth birthday was helping Boston get to Game Seven in the 1967 World Series against the Cardinals with a 2-hit, 2-RBI performance. And now, as a Cardinal, Reggie was on his way to slugging .528 for the season! So big deal if he'd razzed me a little bit. He'd earned the right. As for me, I was just

---

[*] The soon-to-be infamous Bellevue-Stratford, an old and historic hotel on Broad Street, gained worldwide notoriety in July of 1976 when several American Legionnaires on convention were stricken by an unknown disease, later called Legionnaires' disease. Evidently the bacteria thrived in hot, damp places—in this case, the water of the cooling towers for the air-conditioning system—and spread throughout the hotel via the air ducts, killing 29 people and sickening 182 others, none of them major leaguers. The hotel closed later in November of that year.

some young pup, technically not old enough to be in the bar in the first place.

Oh well. Lesson learned.

I didn't play the next day, but we finished the series Sunday afternoon with a 3–1 victory to sweep the Phillies, defeating Steve Carlton, a feat in itself.[*] Rookie Bob Forsch outdueled Carlton, and with another Pirates loss in Montreal, we extended our lead to one and a half games. We boarded our little Ozark Air Lines "Green Goblin" aircraft and took off for Pittsburgh. The first-place, red-hot Cardinals were on a five-game road winning streak with fifteen games remaining and flying high!

It was a huge three-game series against a Pittsburgh lineup that boasted many of the same players as the 1971 World Series bunch: Al Oliver (best left-handed number-three hitter I ever saw), Willie Stargell (team leader, ferocious cleanup hitter), Bob Robertson, Richie Hebner, Manny Sanguillén, Dock Ellis, Bruce Kison, and Dave Giusti. Missing were '71 World Series hero Steve Blass (inexplicable wildness), Dave Cash (traded to Philly), Bob Moose (on the DL), and, of course, the late, great Roberto Clemente. The new offensive additions to this squad were Rennie Stennett, Richie Zisk (.313 / 17 HRs / 100 RBI), and a young Dave Parker (future MVP, two-time batting champ).

All mashers.

Newcomers to their pitching staff were starters, beginning with control master and Cardinal killer Jim Rooker (15–11 / 2.78 ERA), hard-throwing Ken Brett (13–9 / 3.30 ERA), and another hard thrower, Jerry Reuss (16–11 / 3.50 ERA). All lefties.

---

[*] After the Cardinals traded Carlton—over a contract dispute—to Philadelphia eight days before opening day on March 25, 1972, Steve exacted revenge by dominating his former team. There is an old saying in baseball about a player's dominance: "He could've gone out there without a glove and thrown a shutout." Well, not so this day.

The first game matched Bob Gibson against Jerry Reuss. It was Gibby's fourth September start, and he was brilliant, going nine innings, allowing five hits, one run, and one walk, and striking out one.* *Dealing!* I didn't play because of the lefty Reuss, who remarkably went thirteen innings in this extra-inning affair and surrendered only one run in the first twelve frames, when Torre tied the game in the seventh with an RBI double. In the tenth, Red went to the whip with Al Hrabosky, aka the Mad Hungarian, who twirled *four* hitless innings in stellar relief for the win, striking out six, including Richie Hebner, aka the Gravedigger, to end the game with runners on first and second.

Our winning formula in the thirteenth? Something I would get used to in the next two years: a leadoff single by Brock, who then stole second; Sizemore bunted him to third; an intentional walk to Smith; followed by a sac fly by Simmons. That three-four of Smith and Simmons was the best switch-hitting combo I ever saw. And Pirates manager Danny Murtaugh had to pick his poison. Either way spelled death. In this case, he chose to walk Smith over the slow-footed Simmons in hopes of an inning-ending double play. But it didn't happen. Simmons came through, and we Cardinals had a two-and-a-half-game lead with fourteen to play.

After the game, the veterans were pumped up, and I could feel that we had the momentum, like *Hey, we're going to win this division*. I was just a kid, so what did I know? But I loved being a witness to all the energy in that clubhouse. *Could it happen?*

---

* In July, before my call-up, Gibson became the first pitcher since Walter Johnson in 1923 to reach three thousand career strikeouts, although it had been a subpar season for Gibson, who by the end of August had a record of 7–11 with an ERA of 4.19. But Gibson, the old warrior, soon to be thirty-nine years of age, had now turned it on and would continue to dominate down the stretch, posting a 4–1 record with a 2.55 ERA in a whopping fifty-three innings pitched in September.

Not if Jim Rooker had anything to say about it. He bested us the next game, giving the Pirates a critical win to end their six-game losing streak. *Typical.* Jim was a left-hander who would continue to stick it up our asses for the next six years.[*] He threw a complete game, allowing a single run and beating our ace, McGlothen, who now wouldn't get to twenty wins on the season.[†] Talk about a big swing—if we'd won that game, it would have increased our lead to three and a half with thirteen to play.

I started the next game, the rubber match. *Can you believe it?* Red put me in the lineup *in Pittsburgh!* I went 1 for 3 with a single off Bruce Kison, and then Torre pinch-hit for me when Murtaugh brought in Ramón Hernández, a real tough veteran side-arming left-hander. Torre went 1 for 2 with a single, but we lost the game when their closer, Dave Giusti, struck out the side against the meat of our order to end the game, and the Pirates climbed back to within half a game.

A disappointing end to an eight-game road trip. We'd had our chance to further damage the Pirates. But to their credit, they bounced back from an opening series loss and a six-game losing streak to take the series and close to a half game. From our standpoint, we had opened the road trip two and a half games behind and returned home a half game in front. We'd played and won three extra-inning games (twenty-eight total extra innings) and come from behind late in another. Quite an exhilarating road trip, and we had to feel good about returning home for six games—three with the Cubs, then another three-game set against the Pirates.

The next night at Busch Stadium, I got my first taste of the

---

[*] Over his NL career, Rooker started 29 games against the Cardinals. In those starts, he was 18–9 for a .667 winning percentage and an ERA of 2.46.

[†] McGlothen finished the 1974 season at 16–12 with a 2.69 ERA.

famed Cubs-Cardinals rivalry: a sea of red with a smaller sea of blue, and by the sixth inning, brawls had begun in the stands. You just don't see that in the minor leagues.

Speaking of the minor leagues, my buddy from AAA, Pete La-Cock, who had been called up about ten days before me, was starting in right field for the Cubs. Pete had played for the Wichita Aeros, and a bunch of those guys had become friendly with us during the minor league season. Pete was hilarious. The twentieth overall pick of the 1970 draft, he had spent most of his bonus-baby money on a yellow supercharged Porsche, and he'd go 110 miles per hour on Wichita's back roads, which were all S turns, and I'd be going, "Oh man," totally helpless in the passenger seat.

Pete would also get me into bars—he knew everybody. We were in a dry county, so it was bring-your-own-booze in these establishments. We'd walk in with a half-pint of something, and they'd take the bottle and ask, "What's your name?" I'd say, "Keith," and they'd put my name on my bottle and set it up on the bar. All they had was tonic water and club soda and other mixers, so I'd go up to the bar and say, "I'll have a Keith and tonic," and they'd have all the bottles in alphabetical name order and pour my drink.

Anyway, seeing Pete now brought the minors back to me. It had been only a few weeks, but it suddenly felt like ages since I'd left the Oilers.

We won the first game against the Cubs, 5–2, with Bob Forsch throwing another good game for the win. I started the second game, and we got crushed, 19–4. I went 0 for 4 with 2 strikeouts. The next day was a Sunday afternoon game with 43,267 Cardinals and Cubs fans in the seats to watch Bob Gibson match up against future American League Cy Young Award winner Steve Stone. Spotted 4 early runs, Gibby pitched six strong innings until the Cubs tagged him for 4 (3 earned) in the seventh. I went in for defense late, and Ted Simmons won the game with an RBI single in the bottom of the ninth for a 6–5 win. Another thriller, coupled with a Pirates loss, and we pushed our lead back to a game and a half. Bring on the Pirates!

The Pirates took the first game 1–0 in ten innings, behind Rooker's nine shutout innings and a tenth-inning run off Mc-Glothen. Our lead back to half a game, I started the second game, going 1 for 2 with a walk and getting pinch-hit for when the Pirates brought in a left-hander. The Pirates scored 4 in the sixth and 3 in the seventh, and we lost. We won the final game of the series 13–12 in eleven innings, our fifth extra-inning affair going back fourteen games to that marathon in New York. Down 3 runs, we scored 4 to win, not only avoiding a sweep but thrusting us back into first by a half game.

It was just a total slugfest: 25 runs scored between the two teams, and neither team would quit. As for me, I wouldn't play again for the remainder of the season. Red would rightly start Torre the rest of the way. Joe had begun to heat up and drive in runs on the last road trip, and even if he hadn't, you had to go to your seasoned veterans in a race this late and close.

With an off day on Thursday, we traveled to Chicago, taking two out of the three games at Wrigley, but the Pirates won three of four games against the Mets. So it was all tied up with one three-game series to play for both teams. Nail-biting. The Pirates headed home to face the Cubs, and we headed to Montreal to battle the Expos on the frozen tundra of Parc Jarry, perhaps the worst major league ballpark in history, especially in the waning days of the season. Besides the fact that it really was just a minor league park, it was frigid. The wind would blow directly out to right in a gale, and there was nothing in its way to stop it. Put a ball in that jet stream, even a routine fly ball to the right fielder, and it might clear the ridiculously short and low fence.

Well, we won the first game, and so did the Pirates. *Still even.*

Gibson pitched the second game, and we were up 2–1 with two outs in the eighth. Willie Davis, former longtime Dodger, got a single to put the winning run at the plate for Montreal. The batter was left-hand hitter Mike Jorgensen. Red went out to talk to Gibson on the mound. With Hrabosky ready in the bullpen, Red had a decision to make: leave Gibson out there or bring in Hrabosky, who was his dominant left-handed closer. But could he take Bob Gibson out of a 2–1 ball game that might decide the season? *He's Bob Gibson!* So Red left him out there, and Jorgensen, who was 1 for 2 with a walk, hit a humpback line drive, and the lousy Canadian wind kept pushing the ball farther and farther out to right field. Reggie Smith went back to the fence—that stupid, short, five-foot cyclone fence with padding on the top—and he had it in his glove but hit the wall at the same time, and the ball popped out of his glove and over the fence for a two-run home run. We lost 3–2 and were then a game behind the Pirates. The only game Gibson lost down the stretch.[*]

On the final day of the season, we needed to win, and the Pirates to lose. But it was snowing in Montreal—go figure—and our game was postponed until the next day. So we settled into the Queen Elizabeth Hotel, gathering in the hotel bar for some drinks while radio updates on the Pittsburgh-Chicago game trickled in, inning by inning. The Cubs were up 4–0 in the first, and everyone breathed a little bit easier. They were still up 4–2 going into the ninth inning, but then a report came in: the Cubbies had blown it. They had allowed a leadoff walk, followed by

---

[*] From September 1 through the end of the 1974 season, Gibson, who would turn thirty-nine that November, went 4–1 with 3 complete games and 53 innings pitched, posting an ERA of 2.55. *And this man was how old?*

another, and Ed Kirkpatrick had bunted both men over. Dave Parker grounded to second base to score one and move the tying run to third with two outs. Then Bob Robertson, who had hit a home run the day before to give the Pirates the win, swung and missed on strike three, but the would-be winning pitch got by catcher Steve Swisher, and the runner scored to tie the game.

The Pirates went on to win in extra innings and take the division.[*] Our season was over, ending right then and there in that Canadian hotel, the makeup game with Montreal now unnecessary.

Of course, I was bummed for the team—for the veteran guys like Lou and Gibson and Sizemore it had to be tremendously disappointing—but it wasn't really my team. I was just along for the ride, and what a ride it had been.

I was also a bit naive, not fully understanding just how difficult it is to make the playoffs; the Cardinals and I wouldn't sniff the postseason for another eight years.

KH BATTING

Year	Games (G)	At-Bats (AB)	Batting Average (BA)	On-Base Percentage (OBP)	Slugging Percentage (SLG)
1974	14	34	.294	.415	.441

On the plane back to St. Louis, Anheuser-Busch products were aplenty as well as hard liquor. Most of the guys opted for

---

[*] The Pirates would lose to the Dodgers, 3–1, in the NLCS.

the latter. So we were "opening the cups," and most everyone was getting a bit "boxed." Especially Reitzie, who was ranting that Cubs catcher Steve Swisher had let the ball get by him on purpose. He just kept getting madder and madder, saying that he was going to go after Swisher the first time the Cardinals and Cubs met next April. The guys just let Kenny vent. April was six months away, enough time for even a tough kid like Reitzie to cool down.[*] In the meantime, they figured alcohol would do the trick.

Sonny Siebert, a veteran right-handed pitcher and a really good guy, sat next to me on the plane, and he said to me, "You know, Keith, I'm getting sick and tired of those tired-ass jeans you always got on." It was true. I'd pretty much been wearing them every day since my call-up and God knows how long before that. Well, Sonny grabbed hold of one pant leg and just ripped it, from the crotch down to the floor, and then he got the other one and ripped that, too.

We landed in St. Louis at about 11 p.m. Two trucks were waiting on the tarmac to pick up all the equipment, like bats, balls, players' duffel bags, dirty uniforms, etc., but back in those days players' personal luggage came up in baggage claim.[†] So we went through the terminal and toward the baggage claim area, where all the players' wives, kids, and girlfriends, along with a multitude of distraught, commiserating, and well-wishing Cardinals fans, awaited our arrival. As my future friend Howard Cosell would have said, we were "a sight to behold."

---

[*] Reitzie, who was also from the Bay Area, had attended rough-and-tumble Jefferson High School in Daly City. So he knew how to handle himself in a fight.

[†] Today, there would be two luxury busses waiting on the tarmac to take everyone and their luggage to Busch Stadium. No mingling with the general public necessary.

And now, ladies and gentlemen, under the cheers of the consoling crowd, here come those mighty Cardinals, stumbling into the waiting arms of loved ones while their passed-out third baseman, Ken Reitz, is being carted through the terminal like a wounded soldier—feet dragging, head down, body limp. The man seems completely gone. And look, there's Keith Hernandez, the youngster, his jeans shredded beyond recognition, their underside completely ripped away, providing no more coverage than an American Indian's breechcloth, the promising rookie's season now over.

CHAPTER 21

Citi Field, Flushing, New York

I LEAVE THE CAR in my parking space and begin the walk toward the second security checkpoint to enter the "safety" of the stadium confines—here only personnel, players, and press can roam. If that sounds more like a diplomatic compound than a gathering place for America's pastime, you'd be right. Unfortunately, baseball, like every other good thing in America, had to adjust to this "new normal" after 9/11.

"Mr. Hernandez?"

It's some guy decked out in Mets gear. He's caught me before I can get inside, and he has a baseball card he wants me to sign. Some ballplayers may get pissed: *I'm just trying to get to work here, buddy.* But this guy's all right, and there's plenty of time before the 1:10 p.m. start, so I take the pen.*

"You think the weather's gonna hold off?" the fan asks while I'm signing.

Why is it that people feel the need to fill in the three seconds it takes to sign an autograph with idle chitchat? I'm not complaining; it's just an observation, and I think it's hilarious.

---

* Of course, you get the occasional bonehead. What ticks me off is the fan who asks for a quick picture and then winds up shooting video: *Look everyone, I'm here with Keith Hernandez!* That's a no-no.

Maybe they just want to smooth over any annoyance they may have caused. I mean a grown man did just ask if another grown man could sign his baseball card.

"They'll get the game in if they can," I answer, and in fairness to his question, there is a cold front moving in, and it's been drizzling all morning. I hand the man the signed card and the pen.

"Thanks, Keith! Good luck today," the guy says.

Good luck for what? I'm just a spectator in a broadcast booth. It's not like I have to get up there in the bottom of the ninth with the game on the line anymore.

But I say, "Thanks" and "Go Mets!" and make my way through the stadium's "Checkpoint Charlie," then head for the elevators.

The card I just signed was a 1985 Topps Keith Hernandez Record Breaker card. Most cards don't grab my attention, but that one actually does. First of all, it reflects the 1984 season, which was my first full season with the Mets after being traded from the Cardinals in 1983. Second, it's not my favorite card—the picture on it is ridiculous because I'm swinging and my helmet is coming off my head.[*] And while the image captured on the card reveals a nice follow-through—beautifully balanced and staying on the ball—I can tell from the disappointed expression on my face that I've grounded to the right side of the infield for a probable out. All that aside, I have mixed emotions about the "record" I broke that year. It's for "game-winning RBI," a statistic that came into existence just five years prior and was retired in just a few more.

Why was the stat retired? Well, "game-winning RBI" was well-intentioned—it was supposed to indicate a player's

---

[*] I'd just gotten a shorter-than-usual haircut and my helmet wouldn't stay on, which was really annoying. But clubhouse manager Charlie Samuels got me a smaller size by the third game of the season, and all was well again.

performance in the clutch, like a base hit or sacrifice fly in the bottom of the ninth to win the game. *Okay, that's worthwhile.* But the problem was it was too inclusive; *any* game winner—no matter when it occurred—counted. A player could drive in the first run in the first inning in an 8–0 game and get a game-winning RBI. Well, that's not right—that doesn't have the same weight as a deciding RBI when the game is late and close and the batter is feeling the pressure. So the stat was flawed, and baseball was right to throw it out, because it should have included only game-winning RBI from the seventh inning on.[*]

For my own sense of accomplishment, I appreciate the game-winning RBI stat. I know that a lot of my game winners *were* in late and close situations, and that makes me feel good. So I don't totally dismiss it. But another problem with that Record Breaker card has to do with the *other* Record Breaker cards from the 1984 season. There are two in particular. The first is Dwight Gooden's youngest-player-ever-to-win-twenty-games, breaking "Bullet" Bob Feller's record *set in 1939* by one month. That's a record that stood for forty-five years! Gooden was my teammate, and I consider the fact that I got to watch "Doc" throw every pitch of that amazing year one of the highest honors and spectacles of my career. It was nothing short of incredible—godlike stuff. The second was Pete Rose breaking perhaps the most legitimate and one of the longest-standing records in baseball history: Ty Cobb's all-time hits record of 4,189 set in 1928 when Cobb retired. So although my card is a nice feather in my cap, and it proves that I helped the 1984 Mets win some ball games, it's rather absurd for it to have

---

[*] This improved statistic would much later be instituted in the sabermetrics era under the title *Late and Close,* a stat that I love and one I employ on my scorecard before a broadcast.

the same heading, "Record Breaker," as Doc's or Pete's: their records are of *absolute* importance, whereas mine is just of *obsolete* importance.*

Baseball stats are more than just numbers; they're records of performance. They're benchmarks by which players, management, agents, arbitrators, and fans can compare those performances. *But they are also just numbers and don't tell the whole story.* Sometimes, like with game-winning RBI, they also tell a *misleading* story. I say all this because we are in a new era of baseball, one that is increasingly defined by statistics. And with the new sabermetrics evaluations coming into play, I urge caution, because not all of the worthwhile performances we see every day can be accurately quantified with numbers.

How, for example, can you quantify defense? Errors and fielding percentage were historically the two most often cited fielding performance metrics, but few baseball men put stock in them. My father, for example, was always suspicious of players with few errors because it could simply indicate poor range. Well, that makes sense—the player with great range is going to have more chances to make errors, but he'll also save more runs. So rather than using these somewhat blunt stats to determine a player's defensive value, any baseball man worth his salt would make his evaluations by simply *watching* the player play.

But such *subjective* analysis seems to be increasingly dismissed in today's game—"hard data" yielded by more and sharper metrics is what GM offices want to tell the story of performance. Okay, fine. Show me a stat that accurately reflects a player's range, and I'm sold. Show me a stat that measures a player's savviness and grit and intelligence, like Jeter's "flip play"

---

* Still, I'll take it, and I guess the silver lining for me is that since the stat has been retired, it can therefore never be broken.

in the 2002 ALDS against Oakland when he streaked across the infield, picked up the errant throw bouncing in from right field, and backhand-flipped it to the catcher for the crucial tag at home plate. How is that defensive contribution quantified? As "one assist, save one run"? *That single play was worth a thousand assists and a thousand saved runs!*

Again, show me that stat, and I'll say, "Great, let's use it!" Until then, let's temper our enthusiasm on every new stat coming down the pike, and put the scouts and coaches back into the decision-making process.

And think about this: Jeter had no business being involved in that play. But he surveyed what was going on as it unfolded and anticipated the remote possibility that he'd be needed.* Well, that didn't just happen. Derek was in that spot—on that field, with that team—precisely because he was that sort of heads-up player. He'd been pushed through an appraisal system, which at the time was still very much run by scouts and coaches, and rewarded accordingly. And there's no way those decisions could have been made based on stats alone. Why? Because the metric didn't and *still* doesn't exist. Instead, people just kept saying, "This kid's got *it.*" Well, in today's game, that phrase is becoming less and less acceptable to the powers that be.

But I understand why. Human judgment is far from foolproof, and the story of professional baseball is in large part a story of big-time "busts"—supposed "superstars of the future" who just never panned out despite all the coaches and scouts claiming, again, "This kid can't miss." Quantitative analysis can hedge this perspective, particularly in evaluations at the plate, where

---

* As good a fielder and heady player as I was, I don't know if I would've anticipated and made that play. When I saw that play live on television, I about jumped out of my seat with excitement and incredulity.

quantitative metrics are more useful. *On-base percentage. Slugging percentage. Strikeout-to-walk ratio.*

You also have to take into consideration the successes of more than a few, if not all, general managers who rely heavily on these and other metrics. Jeff Luhnow of the Astros, Billy Beane of the A's, the Mets' Sandy Alderson, and, most notably, Theo Epstein, currently with the Cubs. What Theo has accomplished, bringing World Series titles to both the Red Sox and the Cubs, is unprecedented and historic—perhaps no GM will ever surpass those two feats. These examples—along with a willingness to learn new tricks—have gradually swayed my "old-school" opinions about "new stats."

However, I still think even the most practical, quantitative statistics, like on-base percentage, should be put in context with what's happening on the field: i.e., *What's the situation?* Like when a batter comes to the plate with a runner on third and less than two outs. Depending on the score and the inning, getting the runner home from third may be more or less important than getting on base. Or what if a team is down three or four runs late in a game and the batter comes up with runners on? Again, what the batter should be trying to do depends on the context. *Does the batter represent the tying or winning run, or is the tying run in the on-deck circle? Are the runners in scoring position? Is there a force play? Where is the hitter in the lineup, and who is on deck? Is the infield playing in, at double-play depth, or back? What type of hitter is at the plate?* What the hitter should be trying to do will depend in part on the answers to these types of questions.

Again: *What's the situation?*

Even more important, quantitative statistics cannot capture whether the hitter *knows* what he is supposed to be doing on any particular play or at-bat to give his team the best chance to win the game. Or whether the player is fully committed to that course of action, even if it does not reflect as well on him personally in the box score. *Is the player knowledgeable, committed, and talented enough to understand and achieve a successful outcome or at-bat for the team in each situation?* If so, how can you possibly measure that baseball IQ with a quantitative metric?

And this is my biggest concern with baseball's growing obsession with sabermetrics: it discounts those parts of the game that are not easily captured by such quantitative evaluations.

If, for example, a quantitative approach clearly measures home runs, on-base percentage, strikeouts, and walks, but does not clearly measure situational hitting, defensive positioning, or range, then the latter (situational hitting, defensive positioning, and range) will become less valuable in the eyes of decision makers (GMs) adopting a quantitative approach to the game. And as such attributes are discounted, the game begins to change: players with fewer home runs or a lower on-base percentage but with excellent situational hitting skills are passed over in favor of those with more home runs or a higher on-base percentage. And at some point those players with excellent yet unquantifiable skills begin to disappear from the game. If that happens, baseball loses much of its subtlety and beauty.

Bottom line: While sabermetrics will continue to improve, plain old human evaluations will always be an important part of the game. Only they can account for a player's intangibles—from leadership and grit to aspects of defense and situational hitting.

I take the fancy elevator up to the fancy broadcasting booths and press-box area wrapped in the fancy new stadium, Citi Field. I sort of miss the Mets' old stadium, good ol' Shea, which they tore down after the 2008 season, but it's hard to complain about this new one. Like the original "new" ballparks—Camden Yards in Baltimore and The Jake in Cleveland—Citi Field is a true baseball park. The brick-and-steel facade harkens back to an era when baseball, not football or soccer or rock concerts, was the one and only pastime worthy of a complex that could hold thirty thousand fans eighty-plus times per year in such a way that made the crowd feel like they were entering something special, something sacred.

Now, don't get me wrong. When I played for the Mets, I grew to love Shea, once we started winning and the fans came out, bringing with them the most electric energy I've ever felt in a baseball stadium. And I'd rather play in front of great fans than in a great stadium any day. But Shea itself was just an old park, and not in a good way like the really old parks, like Wrigley or Fenway. Its clubhouse was just so-so, and the field lacked the charm and character of its postmodern contemporaries, like Dodger Stadium or Jack Murphy Stadium (before they boxed it in for more Super Bowl seats). One of Shea's saving graces was that it was an open-air stadium, not a coliseum like Three Rivers or Veterans Stadium. And it had a natural grass surface—there is something about the smell of grass, the feel of grass under your feet, as opposed to the sterile, odorless, synthetic crust of Astroturf.

Anyway, there wasn't much about the building itself that made a player say, "Let's play some baseball!," particularly during those down years after the Seaver trade, when the Mets were a perennial last-place team and couldn't fill up 15 to 20 percent of the stadium. But they've got that in spades at this new park.

Sometimes when I'm in the booth, looking down at that perfectly manicured grass, I say to myself, "Gee, wouldn't it be great if..." *Yeah, right, Keith!*

CHAPTER 22

IN 1975, I BEGAN my second year in big-league camp. Only this time the expectations were higher, because during the off-season, the Cardinals had traded Joe Torre to the Mets. And at twenty-one years old, I was clearly the heir apparent to take over at first base.

That first day in the Sunshine State, I waited all afternoon to see who my roommate was going to be. Lo and behold, the one and only Ron Hunt walked in the door. The man who broke in with the fledgling New York Mets as a second baseman in 1963 before being voted a two-time All-Star, representing the Mets in 1964 and 1966, and then played for the San Francisco Giants during my freshman through junior years in high school (1968–70). You can bet your sweet bippy I was tickled to death. I'd sorta figured I would be paired with someone my age—i.e., a non-roster or minor league player—but the organization must have thought me hanging with a twelve-year veteran was a good idea.

Learn from one of the ancient masters, young one. Zen.

Lesson number one? How to stock a spring training fridge. After introductions, Ron immediately got on the hotel phone and requested a small refrigerator for the room. *Good idea,* I thought. *Perfect for beer, soda, water, and such. Ha-ha, silly Keith. Watch and learn.* Ron went out to the store and came back with a shopping bag filled with vodka, Kahlúa, and cream—the ingredients for a White Russian. He would fix one every night before bed the entire spring. *Not too bad,* I thought, tasting my first nightcap. Later in the spring, however, we got smashed together on those White Russians, and I was throwing up in the bathroom, pleading, "Ron!"

"I'm not your daddy! You figure it out," he suggested. So I wised up, never touching a drop of Kahlúa again.

Fortunately, lesson number two was more easily digested. Here's what Ron, a man who led the National League in "hit-by-pitches" for *seven* consecutive years,[*] told me:

> When you sustain a playing injury to a joint, elbow, wrist, or finger either by a pitched ball or a bad hop, or a sprain of any sort, twenty-four hours of icing is the magic potion. Go home that night with an ice bag and an elastic bandage, wrap the ice bag on the injury, and keep it elevated. You'll wake up around three or four in the morning, throbbing. That's because the ice has melted. Get out of bed, reload the ice bag, and continue the process. This is critical. When you wake up in the morning, continue to ice until you leave for the park. I guarantee you that there will be minimal if any swelling, depending on the severity of the injury, and you will be able to play that night.

It may sound trivial, but over the course of a 162-game season, playing six to seven nights a week, this was vital information. I mean, try playing first base the night after catching a

---

[*] From 1968 to 1974, including fifty times in 1971, which is second all-time to Hughie Jennings's fifty-one times in 1896.

fastball on the elbow or wrist. Ron knew all about bumps and bruises. He used to choke up on the bat about four inches, crowd the plate, and wear body padding beneath his uniform top for protection. He was the first guy I'd ever heard of doing that sort of thing. He would lean into a pitch on purpose, infuriating pitchers.

Steve Carlton and Bob Gibson both told the same story about facing Ron. They would be ahead by more than a few runs, and they knew Ron was going to foul off pitch after pitch, so instead of wasting precious bullets, they'd just hit him on the first pitch. *Go ahead! Take first. I can afford a base runner with my stuff and this lead.* Hilarious, so from that spring on, I adopted Ron's mantra whenever I suffered an injury, no doubt sparing me missed games or trips to the disabled list.[*]

Still, you can't be an everyday player if you can't hit left-handers, and the first thing I recall about the start of the 1975 regular season—besides being the new first baseman for the St. Louis Cardinals—was facing *a lot* of left-handers. That was a bitch. *Nice rookie debut, Keith—try these lefties on for size!*

Left-hander Dave McNally started for Montreal in the season-opening series, and I went hitless; the next day, I notched two singles and an intentional walk late in the game off righty Steve Rogers.[†] On the following day, in the fourth, I hit a two-out triple with 2 RBI that tied the game off another lefty, Woodie Fryman. Rogers was a tough pitcher, and Fryman was a thirty-four-year-old flamethrower. I went 3 for 11 in the series, and we took two of three. So far, so good, but we were just getting started with all these lefties...

---

[*] In fact, I was able to avoid the DL until 1988, my *fifteenth* season in the bigs.
[†] That's right, an intentional pass ordered by Montreal skipper Gene Mauch!

Up next were three games in Philadelphia, featuring Steve Carlton and Tom Underwood, both lefties. I went 1 for 3 with 2 walks and an RBI against Carlton, and I eked out an infield hit (1 for 4) off Underwood, who shut us out. But we took another series, and back home we went for a two-game series against the New York Mets, who ran Jon Matlack and Jerry Koosman at us—two more lefties, and nasty. Matlack struck me out looking with a vicious 3–2 slider in the second, and after I returned to the dugout and took a seat, I remember Gibson saying to me with a chuckle, "I bet you didn't see sliders like that in Tulsa." I was inclined to agree and said as much. I went 0 for 6 with 2 walks.

Then it was Pittsburgh with Cardinals killer Jim Rooker and hard-throwing Ken Brett, both lefties. *Where did they find these guys?* Eleven games into the season and *eight* left-handed starters, with more southpaws streaming out of the bullpen, like the Pirates' Ramón Hernández, six-time All-Star Sam McDowell, and Tug McGraw of the Mets. By the end of April, we'd played seventeen games, I'd faced eleven left-handed starters, and I was batting .188. *Ugh.*

Why were lefties a problem?

First, I'm a left-handed hitter—so a lefty's breaking ball starts at my head and moves down and *away* from me. That's a lot of plate to cover *and* still be able to turn on the inside fastball whether straight or sinking.* It's the same thing for a right-handed hitter against a right-handed pitcher, and it's a big reason why managers will often platoon players to get the matchups they want—lefties against righties, and vice versa. Second, something like 90 percent of the world's population is right-

---

* McNally, Hernandez, and Koosman had hard sinkers. Matlack, Rooker, Tug, and Brett were straight, with varying degrees of velocity. Fryman and McDowell were hard throwers with fastballs that ran in on your hands.

handed, so like everyone else, it wasn't until I got to professional ball—with rosters full of lefties—that I started to see them with more regularity. Even for right-handed hitters, that requires an adjustment. Third, as with every step up the baseball ladder, the lefties were that much better: better location, better movement, better command, better stuff, and all with the same "backward" delivery and pitch action.

With only eight of my forty-one plate appearances in '74 coming against lefties, I was having a hard time against them in the opening weeks of '75. And by the end of April, Red had started to bench me against lefties. I just needed to have more at-bats against major league left-handers to be successful, and it looked like I wasn't going to be getting them any time soon.

By May, I was having trouble against the righties, too. They were bringing slider after slider in on my hands, and my confidence—along with my batting average—dropped with every strikeout or fisted ball. I remember standing in the on-deck circle during one game in St. Louis and a fan yelled, "Stan Musial my ass!" It was just one fan in a sea of others, but at the time, it really bothered me. As a young player, you're just trying to get your feet wet, and coupled with all the high expectations, getting booed at home wasn't cool. (Just ask my future teammate George Foster.) So I started to do what a lot of young players do: I started to *press*.

After an 0-for-9 series against the Dodgers at home ending on May 14, my average was an abysmal .203, and I flew with the team to San Francisco to begin a West Coast swing. I crashed at my parents' house, sleeping in Gary's bed, and the next day, Dad insisted he throw me BP before I headed to Candlestick. Dad, the only person who possibly worried more about my swing than I did, would get a sense of urgency—more than usual—whenever I wasn't hitting well. That could create friction between us, but this time I didn't protest. Red was benching me more and more, so I would take all the extra BP I could get.

We headed out to the local high school at about noon, and Dad threw BP. At the age of fifty-two, the man could still throw good BP, and from the pitcher's mound, the full distance, not halfway in front like all the major league coaches do today. He didn't even use a protective screen, while a major leaguer stood sixty feet six inches away, hitting line drives back at him. When I wasn't fighting Dad—when he had my undivided attention—he would be instructive and positive, and though I don't recall what he said during this session, he probably kept the coaching to a minimum, emphasizing the basics.

We'd been working together since I was five, so, like two jazz musicians, a little nod here or a gesture there was all that was required to communicate without breaking rhythm. I went 1 for 3 in that night's game, scoring a run and drawing 2 walks against John Montefusco, the Giants' right-hander, who had a great slider. So Dad's groove session had helped, but it really was just a Band-Aid that didn't address the larger issue: my confidence. For Dad, it was always about mechanics, like Vince Lombardi in front of a chalkboard with all those *x*'s and *o*'s, describing the famed Packers power sweep. But if you don't believe in yourself, then no physical adjustment or tip is going to do the trick. (Dad could never figure out this part of the game. Maybe he was blinded because it was his son. He always felt he could fix things with mechanics, like tinkering with an automobile engine. He had forgotten the mental aspects, the psyche of an athlete.)

So the rhythm didn't last.

I sat game two and faced Jim Barr, a former USC all-American, the next day. I knew Jim from the off-season—we'd played intramural basketball together in San Francisco along with a few other Giants players. An affable guy playing hoops,

Jim was a mean bastard up on the hill, and he "flipped" me on the first pitch, sending a fastball up under my chin. I hit the deck. The fastball may have missed me, but its message was clear: *Sure, we played hoops together, but uh-uh. Not here. That's the big leagues for you — Good to see ya. Try this one on for size* — and I went 0 for 3 against Jim.

We made it back to St. Louis, where things went from bad to worse, because that's when Harry Walker, aka Harry the Hat, started messing with my mechanics. Not good. Harry had an eleven-year career as a player (1940–51), and a seven-year career as a manager for the Pirates and the Colt .45s/Astros (1965–72). He claimed a career .296 BA and a batting title (.363) in 1947. But with only 10 career home runs, he was an inside-out singles hitter, or "ping" hitter.[*] Then, in 1966, when Harry was manager of the Pirates, he helped the recently acquired Matty Alou win a batting title his first year in Pittsburgh (.342) by getting him to "slap" the ball the other way, much like he had done. Alou, all 5'9", 165 pounds of him, was a perfect pupil for Harry: a singles hitter with no power and good speed — the perfect leadoff man. It worked for Alou, who would go on to hit .300 for seven years.

But now Harry, who served as special assistant to General Manager Bing Devine, came down from the front office and started preaching his ping hitting philosophy to me. He meant well, of course, but what he was offering — for me to deal with

---

[*] I do not want to disparage Harry. He won a batting crown and played on those world champion Musial-led Cardinals teams of 1942, 1944, and, most famously, 1946. In the seventh game of that World Series against the Boston Red Sox, Harry most famously drove in the deciding run in the eighth inning. With the score tied at 3–3, his hit-and-run, line-drive double scored the ever-hustling Enos Slaughter. Slaughter's "mad dash" caught cutoff man Johnny Pesky off guard, and the rest is World Series history. Harry also hit .412 with 6 RBI in that Series.

my struggles by swinging inside out and becoming a banjo or Judy opposite-field hitter—wasn't helpful. He was trying to turn a V8 engine into a V6. Now that can be a good strategy when you're behind in the count with two strikes off a tough twirler, and one I could execute when necessary later in my career, when I was able to foul off pitches and stay in the at-bat until the pitcher made a mistake. I called it my "emergency swing."

But I was first and foremost a line-drive hitter. A gap-to-gap hitter. That's what my dad had preached to me since I was kid. Yes, I was having trouble with the inside pitch, but I'd had only 200 at-bats in the big leagues. I just needed time—*not* a change to my swing. In fact, the year before, Harry himself had told the papers, "Hernandez has the type of swing that you just don't touch."

Well, I guess Harry had forgotten about that, because every day during this crucial period he had me come to the stadium early for extra BP, telling me to hit everything to the opposite field. Even the inside pitch. That was the last thing I needed to do! But what are you going to do when you're a twenty-one-year-old kid? Are you going to say "No, thank you" to Harry the Hat when, with every swing, he keeps saying, "Yes, yes, yes—that's the way to do it. Everything to the opposite field," and if you resist or refuse to go along, he might spread it around that you are uncoachable and a malcontent? No way. So these BP sessions set me back. They not only created a bad habit in my swing but also overloaded my brain with too much advice. Paralysis by analysis. My confidence was evaporating with each passing game.

As crazy is it sounds, my manager, Red, had no idea about Harry's meddling. I mentioned it to Red a few years later, and he just shook his head in disgust, saying he would have put a stop to it had he known. It wasn't the first time Red had heard about

Harry's messing with players, because he told me that Harry had tried to get a young Willie Stargell to go the other way. *Can you imagine?* Big old burly Willie "Pops" Stargell, the man who would go on to hit more than 500 home runs, slapping it to the opposite field! Fortunately, Willie sought a second opinion, asking Red for his advice when the Pirates were in St. Louis and they met before batting practice.[*]

"Harry Walker is trying to get me to hit the ball to left field," Stargell told Red. "And I don't think I should do it. What do you think?"

And Red said, "Willie, you're a big guy. If I were you, I would keep doing what you're doing and pull the ball."

There was Willie, thinking for himself and knowing better than to trust what Harry was telling him. But I wasn't Willie. I wasn't that confident. And I can't blame Red for not knowing what was going on. Managers and coaches didn't show up at the park at noon for a night game like they do today. They were less hands-on and didn't talk that much to players, especially the young ones. They weren't big communicators. At least, for the Cardinals and Red they weren't.

That might be hard to understand, looking at today's game, when it seems that most managers and coaches want to be a player's friend, giving him a slap on the backside for something as benign as a check-swing single. But when I came up, Red and most of the Cardinals coaches weren't so gregarious.[†]

---

[*] This is *highly* unusual—Red was the opposing team's manager—but Red was willing to talk.

[†] Barney Schultz, Red's pitching coach, and George Kissell, Red's bench coach, were the only exceptions. In George's case, I think the Cardinals organization was just letting him get his four years in so he could be eligible for a major league pension. That was their way of saying thanks for all his service to the Cardinals. Again, George's passion was teaching in the minors.

Remember that stand-up triple I got off Seaver for my first hit at Busch Stadium? That bullet off the top of the wall? Well, by today's standards, such a laser beam would have earned me some major kudos from a third base coach. But Red's third base coach, Vern Benson, just came up to me and said, very matter-of-fact, "Two outs. You're the tying run. Get a good lead with the pitch, and be ready to score on a passed ball or wild pitch." *Yes, sir, with a salute!* Vern was an old-school Carolinian with a Southern accent, one of Red's cronies, and that's just the way the old-school went about things—players were expected to take care of their game without the coaches blowin' smoke up their wazoo.

On May 21, 1975, the Padres swept us, but not before I went 0 for 4 in the series finale. Another *oh-fer*—I was like a sputtering engine (not even a V6). We went to L.A. and took on the Dodgers, and I started against a lefty. Why, I have no idea at this point. But it was Al Downing—the old Yankee. Here I was, little Keithie Hernandez, hitting off Al Downing! I mean I was seven years old, shagging balls at my brother's Little League tryouts—too young to play myself—when Downing made his MLB debut. I went 1 for 4, getting a single off Downing in the fifth. The next day, Red had me in the lineup again against another lefty, Doug Rau, and I hit my first MLB home run: a two-run bomb off Rau in the seventh to put us up for good, 3–1. It was a fastball up and in—the same thing that Seaver had thrown in 1974—and I don't know how I hit it. I just reacted, which was probably why I hit it, and I cracked the ball to right-center field, way back into the bleachers of Dodger Stadium.

Of course, I called home all excited after the game. Back in those days, we called it "black cord fever," when you had a big game, whether it was a home run or a game-winning RBI, and called the folks back home. Next, I called Randy Moffitt, another good friend from the Giants. He was home in bed and out like a light when I called. "Randy," I said, "I hit my first major league home run!" Then I apologized for waking him up and hung up. The next day I was in the lineup again, and I went 2 for 3 off Don Sutton with a double and a run scored in the seventh. I hit .296 on that road trip with a home run and 4 RBI in 8 games, raising my average to .226 for the year.

But the team was struggling: Don Sutton beat us 7–3 to end a dismal 3–6 road trip, and we headed back to St. Louis. We were 16–22 overall, in fifth place in the East, but only five games behind the pretending first-place Cubs.

I say it on the air all the time now: when you've got a team that's losing and sluggish at the plate, it's tougher on the youngsters than it is on the veterans. Because a bad April for a veteran is "a slow start," and a bad June for a veteran is "a slump." But for a young player, there's no such luxury, because there's no prior body of work to compare it with. Management starts thinking, *He's not ready. Maybe he needs more seasoning.* And remember, like the players, the general manager and manager are paid to win. Their job security is in jeopardy, too, and both Bing and Red probably felt the heat coming down from the owner, August Anheuser "Gussie" Busch Jr.,* that cantankerous, gravel-voiced man who, at age seventy-six, was probably feeling his mortality and wanted another winner before he headed to that great Oktoberfest in the sky, and he made this sentiment known publicly in the newspapers.

We opened up a nine-game home stand against the Padres,

---

* Gussie took over the brewery upon the death of his older brother, Adolphus Busch III, in 1946. By 1957 he had turned Anheuser-Busch Company into the largest brewery in the world. A modern-day robber-baron-type character, he purchased the St. Louis Cardinals in 1953, ironically the year of my birth.

the Reds, and the Braves. For yours truly, it was like Custer's Last Stand, going 2 for 11 against the Pads, then 0 for 10 against the Big Red Machine, which featured hard-throwing right-hander Clay Kirby, super-hard-throwing lefty Don Gullett, and then sinker-balling right-hander Jack Billingham. The part that sticks out in my memory was my second at-bat in the fourth off Gullett, who was pure upstairs, country hardball.[*] He struck me out swinging on three high hard ones, and you just don't forget an ass-kicking like that. He completely overmatched me, and the embarrassing plate appearance took all the starch out of me. The next day, totally defeated, I was 0 for 4 against Billingham.

Management had bet on me, trading away Joe Torre in the off-season, but by the beginning of June, their optimism, along with my confidence, was exhausted, and after that Cincinnati series, it was obvious to everyone in the organization that I was over-matched. I pinch-hit two days later against the Braves and got the call into Red's office after the game. I was demoted to AAA. I don't recall if Bing Devine talked with me or not.

Cry all you want (and, believe me, I went home and cried my eyes out)—you can't blame management. I'd had my oppor-tunity, and I'd failed. I packed my clothes, jammed them along with my stereo equipment and three hundred LPs, safely stowed in cardboard boxes from Tower Records, into my brand-new 1975 burgundy Monte Carlo, which I'd bought in the off-season, and proceeded to drive the 396 miles (five hours and forty-one minutes) southwest down Interstate 44 back to the great city of Tulsa, Oklahoma.

---

[*] Gullett would eventually ruin his shoulder with the Yankees after being the ace of the Big Red Machine, cutting short a Hall of Fame–paced career. What a shame. But, boy, what an arm he had.

CHAPTER 23

Citi Field

IT'S THREE AND A HALF hours before game time, but there's already action in the Mets' broadcast booth. Fox local news is taping a promotional interview for a Mets trivia contest that will air midseason. The cameras and lights are rolling while a reporter tries to stump the formidable team of Gary Cohen and Howie Rose, the Mets' play-by-play announcers for TV and radio, respectively.

"What shampoo did Mike Piazza endorse?" the reporter asks.

Who gives a rat's ass? I want to say. *Ask something about baseball!* But instead I say hello to our stage manager, Cari Loberfeld. Per usual, she greets me with an enthusiastic smile.

"How ya doin', Keithy?" she whispers in her wonderful New York accent, handing me a coffee.

The booth, which is deep enough that you can be off-camera and carry on a quiet conversation, is the stage manager's domain. They're the eyes and ears for the producers out in the production truck and make sure we announcers have what we need for a successful broadcast: stat sheets, advertising copy, water, coffee, soda, popcorn, Cracker Jack, cookies, pretzels, Tootsie Pops, Kleenex, napkins, aspirin, eye drops, and, most important, a tidy work space so nobody trips on a sprint to the john between innings.

"Oh, traffic was a breeze," I say.

"Wait till it warms up and everyone's going back and forth to the beach," says Richie Rahner, our A2 audio engineer. He's our "fixer"—any audio or video issues, and he's got it covered. Every December Richie sends me a Christmas card with pictures of his kids.

"The network promises to get me a helicopter," I joke.

"You and me both," says Cari, chuckling.

So how did I, a former ballplayer, get into this TV business in the first place? Well, I retired as a player after the 1990 season (sooner than I'd hoped), and I divorced myself from the game. I just needed to experience life without baseball for a while. I bounced around the city when I wasn't traveling. I never even considered a new career, because there was nothing I wanted to do: I had no inclination for business, Wall Street was out of the question, and I didn't want to sell real estate. Nothing motivated me. I was put on this earth to hit, catch, and field a baseball. That was my purpose in life, or at least I'd made it that. There was nothing else I wanted to do.

Then one night, about four or five years into my sabbatical from the game, I was sitting at a table at Elaine's, a restaurant in New York City, opened in the 1960s, that attracted a lot of interesting people, especially actors and writers. I was hanging out there—like I always was back then—doing nothing, drinking lots of wine, and Elaine, the owner, who was the real reason anyone worth his salt went there, roamed into the restaurant. She came over and gave me a backhand on the shoulder and said, "What the f— are you doing with yourself? What are you doing with your life?"

I said, "What do you mean?" She sat down—Elaine would always come over and sit with her special customers—and said, "You're too smart to do nothing. You should go be a GM or manager." I said, "Elaine, I don't want to do that. I have no desire. I don't want to get involved in baseball." And she said, "Well, you can't just sit on your ass! Find something! You got too much going for you!" Then she got up and walked away.

It was like a mother talking to her son.

Well, sometime shortly after that I met David Katz, who would become my first media agent. David came up to me at Elaine's, introduced himself, and asked if I'd ever consider doing sports broadcasting. I told him I wasn't interested, so he asked me if we could exchange phone numbers and if he could call every month or two to see if I'd change my mind. He called me once every three months for I don't know how long—it was more than a couple of years—and finally he called one day and I said I'd give it a shot. David took it to the Mets. I started doing thirty games a year, and it moved on from there.

So I owe a debt of gratitude to David, and to Elaine, who died in 2011. She woke me up out of my slumber.

And I do enjoy being back in the game. Working on a broadcast team is, in many ways, like working on a baseball team: you're relying on the person next to you to do their job and do it well. So it's fabulous working with people like Cari and Richie.[*] They keep me out of trouble, because I'm not a trained professional broadcaster, and there are lots of things on the production side that I don't know. It took me five years just to understand what the heck B-roll meant.[†]

---

[*] Dominick Tringali, Cari Loberfeld, and Russ Relkin are our three stage managers for home games. Boots Mehrmann, Dave Ornstein, and Richie Rahner are our three A2s. All are fantastic people. They alternate—there's only one stage manager and A2 at each game—and on this particular day it's Carrie and Richie.

[†] B-roll: "supplemental footage inserted as a cutaway to help tell the story. B-roll includes the shots that are shown to introduce a segment and/or in between the live or taped interviews" (sites.google.com/a/queens buryschool.org/media-production/home/news-package).

If you were following the broadcast back in 2010, there's a good chance you saw Cari. She was the one waking me up when I fell asleep "on the air" during an extra-inning game against the Giants. I was exhausted—I'd been doing a two-day appearance out in New Jersey for Habitat for Humanity, swinging a hammer and carrying sheets of plywood and drywall all over the place from 8 a.m. to 3 p.m. Plus, I was in the middle of my second divorce and an emotional wreck. So we went to commercial break, and I told Cari that I was going to shut my eyes and asked her to please wake me up before we came back from commercial because I might fall asleep. Well, I did fall asleep, and Cari woke me up as planned. But the guys out in the truck thought it was hilarious, so they taped the whole bit with the booth camera and aired it when we came back to the broadcast. Oh boy, did that go crazy over social media, and all the networks had a field day: *Look, everyone, Keith Hernandez falls asleep on the job! Ha-ha-ha!* I caught some flak from some of the local sports media critics and late-night talk-show hosts.[*] I guess they didn't understand that the actual event took place between innings. *It was B-roll, guys! Duh . . .*

When we're on the road, the production team changes: there's a new stage manager and engineer, new cameramen and roadies to help load and unload all the gear. That's also fun, because the personalities from city to city are so different—like in Pittsburgh, they're hard-ass, rust-belt guys with lots of tattoos and Harley-Davidson shirts who look like they can punish a case of beer in an hour. I love working with different types of people from across the country, a real slice

---

[*] David Letterman had a particularly good time with this one. He exclaimed how much fun Yankees games were and showed Yankees radio voice John Sterling doing his routine after every Yankees win, with both arms pumping: "The Yankees win! The-e-e Yankees win!" Then Letterman said, "Unlike the Mets games," and showed the video of me asleep in the booth.

of working-class America. Having grown up in a blue-collar household, living paycheck to paycheck, I feel comfortable around this group, regardless of where they're from or what they look like. That helps me, because it's important for the "talent" to connect with the crew. Not only are they usually wonderful people; if they thought I was just some New York media schmuck thinking he was the cat's pajamas, they could also make my life a living hell. *Screw you and your big city attitude, Hernandez!* So I may not understand all the nuts and bolts of the operation, but I do know it takes an army, and I try to go out of my way to develop a rapport with everyone.

People ask me if I get nervous about being on TV. "No," I tell them. I'm comfortable in front of the camera. But it wasn't always that way. I remember being very nervous when I was interviewed on a St. Louis TV channel soon after my first call-up. I stuttered—something I did as a kid—through the entire interview. But I just told myself the same thing my folks told me as a child: "Slow down. Don't let your mind race ahead." As I got older and more confident in my career and myself, a more casual yet deliberate cadence became second nature to me (though sometimes, even now, I will "get stuck" on a word or two, particularly if I'm excited and talking fast), and after a million interviews on national TV since the late '70s, appearing with Dick Cavett, Robert Klein, Charlie Rose, Roger Ailes, and on numerous morning shows, I'm not the least bit anxious. It's actually kind of fun. Plus, I'm talking about baseball, so it's easy.

That said, America's pastime isn't immune from the larger social and political discussions going on around the country. And that part of the broadcasting job can be stressful. As a member of an older generation with somewhat conservative political and social views that aren't radical but perhaps not mainstream either, I have to watch my step when those sorts of topics make their way into our broadcast. I have, on occasion, gotten myself into a bit of trouble.

For example, I sort of flipped out on the air back in 2006 when the camera showed a woman in uniform in the Padres' dugout. It was during a game, and she was high-fiving Mike Piazza after he'd hit a home run against the Mets. It was the first time I'd ever seen a woman in uniform in the dugout during a major league game.

"Who's the girl in the dugout with the long hair?" I exclaimed. "What's going on here? You have got to be kidding me. Only player personnel in the dugout."

The inning ended and we went to commercial break, realizing we had a problem. The issue was discussed in depth with director Bill Webb, coordinating producer Gregg Picker, and play-by-play partner Gary Cohen. There was disagreement on how to handle the situation. We finally decided to address the issue when we came back on the air. During my mea culpa, I blurted, "I won't say that women belong in the kitchen, but they don't belong in the dugout." I then laughed and said, "You know I am only teasing. I love you gals out there—always have."

How much further could I put my foot in my mouth? In an effort to qualify my comment, I only made it more objectionable. The network formally reprimanded me, I apologized the next day on the air, and we moved on with the rest of the season in hopes that it would soon be forgotten and I would survive the pending firestorm (obviously, I did).

But none of that really answered the fundamental question: Why would Keith Hernandez, a father of three girls, whom he's always told they can achieve anything in life, say such a thing? Right or wrong, I had my reasons, but when you're on live TV, you don't have much time for nuance, especially after a knee-jerk reaction when you need time to collect your thoughts. Now that I have the opportunity, here are my measured thoughts:

I used to get pimples on my ass. Mom thought it was because of the enzymes in the detergent she was using at the time. To this day, I have to shower every morning to make sure I don't break out. But I still have the scars, and anywhere I walk in the buff, there follow two butt cheeks pockmarked in true moon fashion.

It never really bothered me, even as a young player in the Cardinals' clubhouse, where I'd go to and from the showers without ever covering up. But in 1978, after a New York federal judge ruled that the MLB policy banning women reporters from the clubhouse was unconstitutional, I suddenly had to reconsider my level of comfort exposing myself in the locker room.

In his decision, the judge cited that Major League Baseball's policy gave an "unfair advantage" to male reporters and "violated the Equal Protection Clause of the Fourteenth Amendment."[*] As someone who grew up in the 1960s and was proud of baseball's integration as a precursor to the civil rights movement, that sounded like good reasoning to me. Plus, I'd spoken to female sports reporters in the past—not in the clubhouse, but on the field and such—and I thought their questions and angles were great. It sometimes brought a new perspective to the game, and beyond that, it made sense, given the fact that women made up a growing portion of the game's fan base.

But I still had boil scars on my rear end, and I wasn't super comfortable showing them off to strangers of the opposite sex. Well, the Cardinals, old-school themselves, figured out a solution: put curtains in front of the players'

---

[*] Maxwell Strachan, *Huffington Post,* September 25, 2015.

lockers, have the players change in there, and give them towels, secured with Velcro, to go back and forth to the showers. Well, when you put it that way—forgo the expanse of the locker room for a few miserable square feet after I'd just played my seventh game in five days—I guess I'd be okay changing in front of the ladies. So that's what I did. I didn't bother with the curtain, nor did I cover up to and from the shower. I wasn't celebrating anything or trying to make a point, but the judge's decision to open up our locker room to women forced me to make a choice: exposure or freedom of the workplace.* (Out of respect and courtesy to these professional women, I no longer gave postgame interviews in my birthday suit.)

Thirty years later, I witnessed a new frontier: women in the dugout. My instant reaction to that was hostile because once again I saw players having to make a choice: expose your standard behavior—including any bad language, farts, snot rockets, and competitive posturing to the other team—in the presence of a woman or give up that freedom of expression in the workplace. Only now, unlike the clubhouse-interview scenario, players were being asked to do this *during* the game. For me, that went too far, and as a player, I would not have appreciated being put in that position. Because in the heat of battle, I often communicated with my teammates, coaches, and especially the opposing

---

* I did make a bit of a demonstration one night in New York after the federal judge's decision. The visitors' locker room, which wasn't big to begin with, was crammed with reporters after the game, many of whom were women who didn't seem to be there for anything other than the spectacle of the men's locker room. I wasn't pissed, but I decided to add to the circus and proceeded to walk buck naked, on my hands, across the locker room. Silly boy. But I did that only once. Eventually those women who seemed to be showing up in the clubhouses for the novelty stopped coming in, and the ones who remained were the professionals.

team in a way I never would in front of a woman. Again, call me old-fashioned, and if today's players can handle that situation without feeling compromised, all the more power to them.

Obviously, live TV is not the proper venue for such thoughts, and after twenty years in front of the camera, I'm getting better at controlling my knee-jerk reactions. As our SNY executive producer, Curt Gowdy Jr., reminds me on a regular basis, I can always go home, sleep on it, and, if I still have something to say the next day, fire away. But I'm usually glad by the following broadcast that I've kept my mouth shut. *Play ball!*

Anyway, I'm starving. There's a cafeteria next door to the booth, so I'm going to grab an omelet. I can't start my prep work until the news team clears out anyway. Before I go, I catch another trivia question from a reporter.

"There have been only two players in baseball history," he begins, "to record two hundred hits, fifty steals, and twenty triples in a single season. One is a former Met and one is Ty Cobb."

I can see the boys are struggling on this one. "Come on! White Sox," I shout, because the player in question spent eight years in Chicago before signing with the Mets.

"Lance Johnson," Gary Cohen says, picking up on my reference. "Thanks, Keith!"

"Keith Hernandez popping in with a little help," shouts the reporter, and the cameraman turns to me. "He is clutch!"

Buff Stadium, Houston, Texas, 1947: Mom and Dad married at home plate before the last game of the regular season. Dad went on to play two more seasons in the minor leagues before retiring and becoming a San Francisco fireman. (Collection of the author)

Linda Mar, California, 1962: First year in Little League with Pacifica Lumber at eight years old. I pitched a shutout in the championship game. Dad is on the far right. That's me, chewing gum with an oversize first baseman's mitt, next to Mr. Otenello (far left). Look at my "Bucky Beavers"! (Collection of the author)

Linda Mar, California, 1964: Another championship season. Dad is at center with the sunglasses, and the wonderful Mr. Valero is to his right with the baseball cap. I'm the third face from the left. (Collection of the author)

Linda Mar, California, 1965: With Ed and Jim's Union 76. We're looking good in Dad's uniforms, and we're on our way to another undefeated season. (Collection of the author)

Oiler Park, Tulsa, Oklahoma, 1974: On my way to my second batting championship (if you're counting the 1972 Florida Instructional League...I am). Note the box seats in the background. Just to the right was where guitarist Don Preston sat with a couple of beautiful women on most nights. (Collection of the author)

Oiler Park, June 1975: First day back in Tulsa after being sent down from the majors. The humiliation and embarrassment were instantly mollified by my roommate and dear friend, Héctor Cruz. (Collection of the author)

Busch Stadium, 1977: Still figuring things out in the big leagues. Umpire David Davidson gets a close look at my nosedive into the plate for the only inside-the-park home run of my career. (AP Photo)

Busch Stadium, 1978: My beloved brother, Gary, and my second father, Lou Brock. One of my favorite photos. Note Lou's inscription: "Keep on pushing." (Jim Herren)

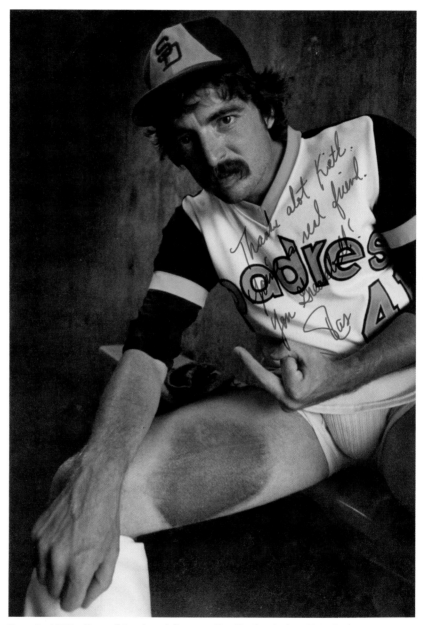

June 9, 1979: Great friend and former Cardinals pitcher Eric Rasmussen sent me this thank-you note after receiving one of my line drives in the leg in a game against the Padres. (Peter Koeleman)

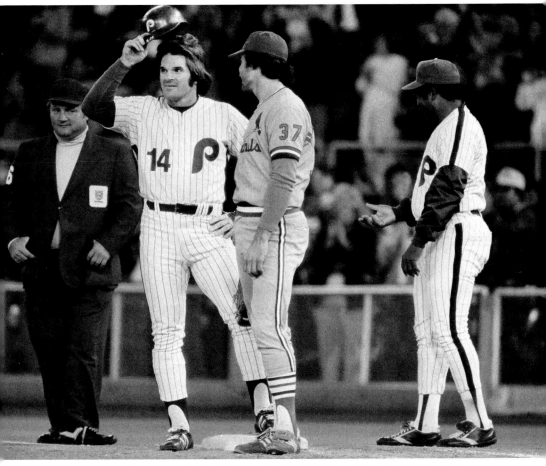

Veterans Stadium, 1979: I look on as the Phillies' Pete Rose tips his hat after striking his two hundredth hit of the season on September 24, 1979, in Philadelphia. Pete was relentless at the plate that September. (AP Photo / Gene Puskar)

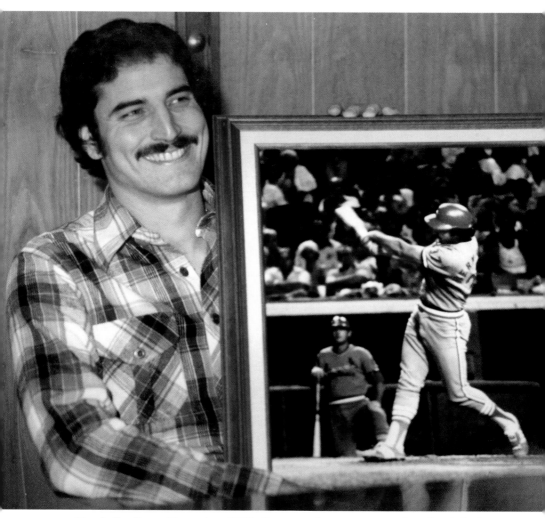

Busch Stadium, November 1979: Press conference announcing that I had won the 1979 NL MVP along with Willie Stargell. Since I hadn't received my award yet, I posed with my 1979 NL Player of the Month Award for August. (Lynn T. Spence / *St. Louis Post-Dispatch* / Polaris)

St. Louis, winter 1980: Making the dinner rounds after the 1979 season. With Stan Musial (left) and St. Louis Cardinals quarterback Jim Hart (right), as well as local television sports anchor and Cardinals television play-by-play announcer Jay Randolph (behind me). (J. B. Forbes / *St. Louis Post-Dispatch* / Polaris)

Cardinals locker room, 1980: Gearing up after the MVP season. I would stay with the Cardinals until 1983, when I was traded midseason to the New York Mets. (AP Photo / David Durochik)

With the Mets at Dodger Stadium, 1984: New colors, same swing. (Icon Sportswire via AP Images)

St. Louis, 1985: Ah…with the kids, Mary, Melissa, and Jessie, at the base of the Gateway Arch posing for an article in *Sports Illustrated*. (Tony Tomsic / Getty Images)

From my condo balcony in Manhattan, 1986: Posing for *Sports Illustrated* prior to the 1986 postseason. Besides helping the Mets win ball games, I was also discovering that "baseball for art" was a good quid pro quo in New York. (Tony Tomsic / Getty Images)

Citi Field: In the booth with former teammate and fellow analyst Ron Darling (left) and play-by-play man Gary Cohen (center). *Play ball!* (SNY Network)

CHAPTER 24

ACCORDING TO THE LABOR laws of baseball in 1975, a player had seventy-two hours to report to his new team. Needing to clear my head after being demoted because of two lackluster months in the bigs, I took all three days to get to Tulsa. When I arrived, manager Ken Boyer called me into his office, sat me down, and asked one simple question: "What happened?" I told him about not getting enough at-bats against the lefties and how the hard slider in on my hands from right-handers was giving me fits. Then I told him about Harry Walker's BP sessions.

"Goddamned Harry!" Boyer said. It seemed Harry's penchant for trying to turn struggling hitters into happy slappers was well known around the organization.* "You're gonna come out every day at three p.m. for extra batting practice," Boyer declared. "I'll throw to you myself, and you're gonna pull *everything*. I don't care if it's on the outside corner, you're pulling it. We're bringing you back."

Two days into those sessions, Boyer made a suggestion. "I've noticed that you stand very close to the plate," he said. "If the slider from righties is giving you trouble, move off a bit."

---

* In fact, I've recently uncovered a letter from roving minor league hitting instructor Joe Medwick to my father expressing his concern about Harry the Hat and his potential for meddling.

"How much?" I asked.

"As far off as you can, but still cover the outside corner confidently," he said.

What Boyer was suggesting—changing only where I *stood* in the box—simplified things. He wasn't messing with my mechanics: telling me to open up my stance, widen my feet, hold my hands higher, or level my bat. He actually wanted me to go back to what I'd been doing all along, only give myself a little more room to do it.

So I tinkered around until I discovered that six or seven inches off the plate was as far as I could move away and still cover the outside corner confidently. But it also meant that I had a new strike zone to perfect—the inside corner in particular.[*] After all, I was battling perceptions and reflexes that had taken years to develop, and recalibrating that decision-making process takes time. But I kept at it, disciplining myself in batting practice with Boyer, and once I made the adjustment, I was somewhat liberated from that pitch in on the hands and could better handle the slider and the hard cutter inside.[†]

My first game back in Tulsa, I was embarrassed because of my demotion. I remember being in the on-deck circle, awaiting my first at-bat and wishing I could dig a deep hole to hide, but I got a very nice standing ovation from the home fans. I then proceeded to hit a little bleeder down the third base line for an infield hit. *So much for pulling everything*... But it got me going.

---

[*] What was on or off the outside corner wasn't an issue, but the inside corner, where you have to be quick with the bat, required an adjustment, because that tough inside pitch on my hands was now six to seven inches inside and I could lay off. But try putting that into effect when you've got less than half a second to pull the trigger...

[†] The key was, I had to learn not to swing at the cutter or slider that was a strike before I had moved off the plate. Now that pitch was a ball. That was hard work in the cage and on the field in BP. Day after hot day K.B. would throw to me until I was back on track.

Now I just needed to continue perfecting my new strike zone, rid myself of that inside-out crap, get hot at the plate, and make my way back to the big leagues. Piece of cake!

To make things easier, I was surrounded by players I knew well and were my own age. The psychological support that gave me—feeling like one of the guys—had been missing in the St. Louis clubhouse, where the average age on the team was pushing thirty. The older players had been great to me—Ted Sizemore, Al Hrabosky, and Lou Brock in particular. Still, they had all seemed like big brothers, even fathers, to me, and it had been hard not to feel like the little kid on the block.

Bob Gibson had been especially intimidating. I remember one incident in the trainer's room. It was early in the 1975 season, and I'd developed a small blister on my finger. I was taping the blister when Gibson walked in and saw me. "What in the f— are you doing in the trainer's room?" he shouted. "Get your ass out of here, and if I catch you in here again, I'm gonna kick your ass, rook!" Evidently, kids with fresh legs weren't allowed to receive medical attention, at least not according to Gibson, whose aged knees had begun to deteriorate at that point. As quickly as possible, I grabbed a roll of tape, a box of Band-Aids, and an aerosol can of Tuf-Skin, and got the hell out of there, never to return to the trainer's room that season.

Even without the reprimanding, Gibby could set a young rookie straight. Around the same time as the trainer's room incident, Reggie Smith and his wife threw a party at their apartment, and the music selection was mostly jazz and R & B. I got into a conversation with a gal who suggested I bring over some of my LPs for a change of pace. *Say no more!* I dashed over to my nearby apartment, grabbed about twenty records, and headed back to the party to crank some rock 'n' roll on Smith's massive speakers.

Let's stick it to the man, everybody!

Well, Gibson noticed me and my stack of LPs as I came through the door, and gave me a look that said, *Looks like you're crowding the plate, young man.* Ask any National League batter who played between 1959 and 1975 and they will tell you that is *not* a good thing. So, very gently, I laid the albums by the front door, vowing never again to attempt to hijack the music at someone else's shindig.

Much later in the evening, I was just sitting on the floor, minding my own business, and Gibson's wife-to-be walked across the room and asked me to dance. *Please, God, no,* I thought. But she said, "C'mon, Keith," and pulled me up off the floor. So there I was, sweating bullets—the most uncomfortable I have ever been in my life—dancing with this beautiful woman while her fiancé, one Bob Gibson, looked on from across the room. *Not good. Can't she just choose someone else?* That song seemed to go on forever, and when it finally ended, I thanked her and quickly resumed my seated position on the floor and as far away from Gibson as possible.

Sit, Booboo, sit. Good dog.

But I can't say that I didn't have any buddies while I was in St. Louis. Ken Reitz, the starting third baseman, was a pal, as was Ted Simmons, who despite being only twenty-five was already a three-time-consecutive All-Star. But neither of those guys was particularly helpful in my adjusting to the major leagues: Kenny was in his third year in the bigs, newly married, and coming off a .271 season the year prior, and it seemed that Simmons, who was very intimidating in his own right and more than a bit moody, was still figuring out his role in the clubhouse as one of the team's top performers. It's rare for someone working through that to walk up to a kid like me and say, "Hey, rook, you stick with me, and I'll help you along."

We were all just sort of thrown into it and left to survive with old veterans and coaches who expected that if we were in the big leagues, we were mentally tough enough to handle it. And it's not like Red was saying to Simmons, "Hey, Ted, why don't you talk to Hernandez and see how he's doing?" Simmons, who'd grown up in Detroit, wasn't naturally inclined to walk up to some California kid and chum it up, because back when he was a rookie, the next-youngest guy on the team was twenty-five-year-old Steve Carlton, who hadn't made connecting with Simmons a priority. It was something cultural about the organization. Again, *old-school*.

Not appreciating this at the time, I put my foot in my mouth when I got sent down, telling a Tulsa reporter that the Cardinals players hadn't been welcoming. It got picked up by the St. Louis press, and a few of my former Cardinals teammates expressed their displeasure, Reitz in particular. *Gee, Keith, you're really making friends fast in the big leagues.* Well, it was a stupid thing for me to have said—I'd been feeling sorry for myself, making excuses. Like the records at Reggie's party, it was just bad form.

But now in Tulsa, I had a whole locker room full of support from guys I'd played with throughout my minor league career: Larry Herndon, Jerry Mumphrey, Leon Lee, Joe Lindsey, Eric (known then as Harry) Rasmussen, John Denny, Marc Hill, and, most notably, Héctor "Heity" (pronounced *high-tee*) Cruz, or "Cruzi Baby." Looking back, I think Héctor was as important to me that year as Bob Kennedy Sr. had been in '73: where Kennedy instilled confidence at a crucial time, Héctor now reminded me how to relax and have fun, taking the sting out of my demotion.

With all those guys in my corner and Boyer giving me my swing back, it didn't take long before I turned 1975 around. In the 85 games I played in Tulsa, I hit .330 with 29 doubles, 48 RBI, and 70 runs scored. All this while my good friend Héctor was named Minor League Player of the Year, batting .306

with 30 doubles, 29 home runs, and 116 RBI. Add "loosening up Keith Hernandez" to that list of accomplishments, and, for me, Héctor Cruz was Player of the Decade.

I was also getting out more socially. Now twenty-one, I could get into bars and clubs after games, but I found the whole experience to be difficult. First, I just didn't know how to strike up a conversation with girls, so I would stand against the wall, listening to the music, hoping a girl would come up to me or give me the eye. Second, it was the drug era, and some of these people were just gone. I remember Don Preston was playing at a club called The Magician's Theater in downtown Tulsa, and I showed up—either it was an off day or I had hustled down after a game. I was high, having smoked a joint during the twenty-minute drive, and I spotted this girl at the bar. She was breathtakingly gorgeous, and after a few pops, I mustered enough courage to slowly shuffle up to her and strike up a nervous conversation. She just looked at me with these beautiful, glassy eyes, smiled, and tried to say something, but her words were garbled. She was totally boxed, and not just on alcohol. After a few more tries to communicate, I gave up and walked away. I never went back to the club again. It was alluring, for sure—A-list bands and beautiful girls—but I was also afraid of it. My whole life, growing up, my dad had warned Gary and me about the evils of hard drugs.

I also went to more than a handful of cockfights in the Tulsa area in '75. Talk about bizarre. It'd be in some old barn out in the sticks with about three dozen farmers in their OshKosh B'gosh overalls with big wads of cash in their hands, making high-stakes wagers. I never bet; I just watched. One of my good Tulsa buddies and wingman, Bob Ferris, who was older and a bit of a hell-raiser, had a rooster that never lost, until, of course, he did. And when they lose, they're dead. But it was an interesting experience—like I'd somehow walked into a Faulkner or Twain novel.

After one particular cockfight, Bob took me to a party packed with pretty girls. They were dressed in the hippie fashion of the times—bell-bottom pants, tie-dye, beads, etc.—and at some point Bob called me aside and said he wanted to show me something. He led me to one of the back bedrooms, and a girl was in there, sitting in a chair. She was stunning. She had her blouse sleeve rolled up, and one of the other folks in the room wrapped a band tightly around her biceps. The guy standing in front of her had a syringe loaded with a clear liquid, and I asked Bob what it was. "Crystal meth," he said. Then the guy stuck in the needle, pushed the plunger, and within a split second, the girl shot out of her chair like a bat out of hell. It scared the crap out of me, which I guess was Bob's intention. He may have been a hell-raiser, but he was looking out for me. He told me after, "That girl's in deep shit. Never mainline, Keith. There's no more rapid sensation and reaction than to the needle. Once you try it, the odds are you'll never go back. Bad news."

So I just stuck with marijuana and the very occasional greenie, which would stay in my system for a while after a game, and I'd hit the bars and dance the night away, *going boldly where Keith rarely went before* because the amphetamine would help me shed my shyness and inhibitions. But again, all that was rare; even if I'd known where to get my hands on amphetamines, I certainly couldn't have afforded them. How the other guys managed to get them, I didn't know, and they certainly weren't going to let me mooch too often and deplete their stash.

As for the harder stuff, I was terrified of it. I'd grown up hearing horror stories of kids lost to drugs, and now in Tulsa I had witnessed it. Like the girl at the nightclub and then the girl at the party, a lot of kids my age back then were checked out. Well, that stuff wasn't for me. I was invested, and I wasn't about to go jeopardizing my career by becoming a druggie.

In September, the organization called me back up to the big leagues—aka "the show." I'd figured they might leave me off the guest list because of my earlier comments in the paper about the Cardinals players not being too supportive. But I got the nod and headed back to St. Louis.

I remember, my first day back, walking through the tunnel that led to the field, when Jack Herman of the *St. Louis Globe-Democrat* stopped me for a few questions in our dugout. It was just past 5 p.m. and the gates weren't open yet, so I said sure, though technically I was a wee bit late since the pitchers were just beginning to hit. Within seconds of Jack's first question, I heard Gibson yelling from behind the batting cage: "There you are, Hernandez, always talking! Talk, talk, talk! Why don't you just shut up and get your rookie ass out here to shag some balls!" So Jack and I just looked at each other and I said, "Sorry, Jack, but I gotta go." Jack, of course, understood. He was an old beat writer who had been covering this Gibson-and-Brock-led team for years.

Gibson wasn't laying off, that was for sure. But if you read his 1968 memoir, *From Ghetto to Glory* (a terrific book), it makes sense why he was tough on younger players. He was raised in Omaha in the 1950s, when the odds of being black and successful were against him. Gibson's older brother recognized his sibling's potential and kept him on a tight leash, not allowing young Bob to get sidetracked or into trouble. Because of that tough love, Gibson says he was able to go on and succeed.

So Gibson was rough with rookies like me and some of the others because that's what his brother had done with him. And the more potential a young player had, the tougher he would be. It was a nurturing thing; at least, looking back, that's the way I take it. Years later, after we'd both retired, I saw Gibson at an All-Star Game, and I went up to him and said, "Bob, you know I just wish that...when I came up, that..." I was nervous, stumbling for words, and Bob, patient as ever, said, "Well, you just played like a damn twenty-year-old, that's all!" So, again, I think in his own way he was just helping a kid grow up.

While my Tulsa buddies were off winning the American Association Championship without me, I mostly rode pine those first two weeks back up with the Cardinals, getting only three pinch-hit plate appearances (1 for 2 with a walk). Because of the somewhat cool attitude toward me in the clubhouse, I had too much time to be alone with my thoughts, and I certainly did not want to stay at the airport motel again, so I accepted an invitation from the two visiting clubhouse managers, Jerry Risch and Buddy Bates, to move in for the remainder of the season. We'd become friends during spring trainings, Jerry turning me on to a lot of music that wasn't mainstream. Stuff like Seatrain, Jeff Beck, and Leo Kottke.[*]

Before I was sent down, the three of us had gone to see Jeff Beck, who was showcasing his new album, *Blow by Blow,* at the old Ambassador Theatre in downtown St. Louis. It was

---

[*] The album that Jerry had was Leo Kottke's second album, *6- and 12-String Guitar,* which was released in 1969. I remember the album because I went out immediately and bought it. I also loved the cover artwork, with an armadillo in the middle on a black background, like a charcoal painting. A few years ago, Leo was playing in Amagansett, New York, at the Stephen Talkhouse, a great little club that has live music all during the summer season in the Hamptons. I love the Talkhouse; the owner, Peter Honerkamp, and the bartenders know me well. So after the show, Peter brought me upstairs to meet Leo, and I was able to tell him how important his music, particularly that album, was for me at a very precarious time in my career. It put a big smile on both of our faces.

my second concert ever, Dad never letting Gary and me go in high school. With songs like "Freeway Jam," "Scatterbrain," "She's a Woman," and "Cause We've Ended as Lovers," Mr. Beck put a spell over the crowd, each guitar lick and phrase softening and bending our senses. Of course, the rolled marijuana joints being passed throughout the theater helped, and I remember one of those joints had a much different, distinct flavor and texture—like velvet slipping down my throat, caressing my lungs. I asked the guy who'd shared it, "What's the deal with this one?" and he said that he'd sprinkled a little bit of opium in it. *Wow.* I took a few more hits—the only time I would ever encounter the drug—passed it back, and let the sounds from Beck's guitar wash over me. Anyway, it was great of Jerry and Buddy to let me crash on the couch in their living room, where Jerry's record collection and stereo system helped me settle back into an otherwise turbulent life in the bigs.

But the biggest boost I got those first two weeks was a phone call from my brother. I was in Chicago, playing the Cubs, and Gary had just wrapped a season in St. Pete.

"I'm driving up for tomorrow's game," he said.

Wait, from Florida?

"Just leave two tickets for me at will-call."

Amazing. Gary and teammate Claude Crockett, born and raised in the Windy City, planned to drive through the night, and I told Gary, my good-luck charm, that he must have already been sending me positive vibes, because earlier in the day I'd hit a three-run shot off Steve Stone in the top of the fourth. Another pinch hit. Gary was pumped, enough to step on the gas a little harder, he said.

I was on the chalkboard the next day, *batting third*. Again, probably Gary's doing: my big brother's selflessness unfolding good things in the universe for me. I dressed and went out to the field, looking for Gary, but he wasn't there. *I hope he makes it,* I thought.

The first thing most players do when they walk out onto the field at Wrigley is look at the direction of the wind, gauging its ferocity. And this was a typical September afternoon in Chicago: a bit chilly with the wind blowing in from left field. So I focused on hitting line drives in BP. *No fly balls—all line drives.* Rick Reuschel was the Cubs' starter that afternoon. A hard sinker baller with a funky delivery, Reuschel released the ball almost underhanded, which gave the pitch a good sink but flattened out his slider. The sinker would jam the crap out of right-handers but could find the barrel of a lefty's bat. (Rick was always double trouble for right-handers.) Still, with that bread-and-butter hard sinker down and away, Reuschel was a tough mark. He got me to ground out to second in the first inning, but I got the best of him in the fourth: our team trailing 6–1, I hit a two-iron bullet line drive to left-center field. Too low for the wind to knock down, the ball cleared the ivy wall, and after days of limited pinch-hit duty, I had two home runs in back-to-back games.

We took the field after the inning, and halfway through the frame, I noticed my brother, maybe eight rows up by our dugout, standing and fist-pumping with that big grin. *Did he see the home run?* Only after the game could Gary tell me that they'd driven through the night and early morning and stopped off at Crockett's house, unloaded luggage, and said hello to his mother before rushing to Wrigley. An hour late, they dashed into the stadium just as my name was announced over the loudspeaker—"Now batting, Keith Hernandez"—and Gary raced through the closest entryway to a view of the field just as the pitch was delivered. *Crack!* He saw the whole thing! Like Glenn Close standing among the seated crowd to rouse Roy Hobbs's sleeping bat in *The Natural,* there was Gary, my talisman, summoning my bat for not just the home run but two more hits that day, and a fantastic rest of the season, as I played in 22 games with 14 starts, hitting .350 (21 for 60). I was back on track.

Thanks, Gary!

KH BATTING PROGRESS (BY SEASON)

Year	Games (G)	At-Bats (AB)	Batting Average (BA)	On-Base Percentage (OBP)	Slugging Percentage (SLG)
1974	14	34	.294	.415	.441
1975	64	188	.250	.309	.362

CHAPTER 25

Citi Field

THE TV NEWS GUYS have cleared out of the booth, and I've had breakfast.

Now I'm preparing. There are stat sheets—pages and pages of stat sheets—to assist me. I flip through and circle the handful of categories, like clutch stats, I may reference during the game. The rest is mostly gobbledygook. I mean, do I really need a listing of who's currently got the lowest ERA in MLB for *night* games? *Can we just play the baseball game already?* As a former player who studied the intricacies of the game from the inside—while it was happening to and around me—I have little patience for the grossly abstract.

Play the game, and I'll react as it unfolds.

And that's precisely what I'm paid to do: lend my expertise as a former major leaguer who took enough pride in the game to know what the heck was going on and share that baseball IQ with an interested audience. It may have said exactly that in the job description.

A big reason I can be so loose with all these stat sheets and preparation is because Gary Cohen is one of the best play-by-play announcers in the business. Gary knows the game and stays current with the latest news across both leagues. So as I'm ripping through pages and tossing most of them into the trash can,

Gary sits at the broadcast desk next to me, quietly absorbing the materials along with whatever extra research he brings. There's no shuffling papers, wildly circling things, or exasperated sighing in Gary's preparation—it's a much tidier, quieter exercise, like a monk studying scripture: elbows in tight, chin resting on hand.

It's really incredible, because whenever I have a question, I can just ask the encyclopedic brain next to me. *Screw the stat sheets!* Like now, I'm wondering what the win-loss record is of the pitcher starting for the Braves. I should probably know that. I flip back through the pages, but that's the problem with too much information: it's nearly impossible to find what you want. More sighs. *Oh, wait! I'll just ask Gary!*

Poor Gary. He's like the studious kid who got partnered with the dumb jock in some everlasting school project and has to carry most of the weight. But it's great working alongside him. Because if there ever was a human being built to announce Mets games, it's Gary. As a kid growing up in Queens, he went to nearly every home game throughout his childhood, and that was during some lean Mets years. So you know he's committed, and Mets lore is embedded in his DNA. Hopefully, I won't have to tax his innate knowledge too much today; it's the final game of the series, so we're all familiar with how both teams have been playing.[*]

The temperature is really dropping—so much for spring. But I'll be just fine if it's a well-played ball game, and, fortunately,

---

[*] I do have to pay more attention to the sheets when it's the first game of a series. That's always the most work. Of course, I know about the Mets and their players because I see them perform on a daily basis, but the visiting team is a whole different ball of wax. I need to research them thoroughly. Fortunately, we also have Dave Fried, statistician extraordinaire, to help us all out. And Dave knows the stats I really like to see and is always right there with an assist when we're preparing and executing the broadcast.

we're seeing more and more of those in the league these days. After the dilution of talent that came with two rapid league expansions back in the 1990s, it's been a slow climb. You have to remember that when they expanded by four teams, that meant forty-eight minor league pitchers were suddenly thrust into the majors. And three of the four teams—Arizona, Colorado, and Florida—were in the National League, so the NL hitters got to feast on thirty-six pitchers that didn't belong. That rate of expansion—three teams over six years—was too much. While it was maybe fun for the hitters, it dropped the level of play, from the major league level on down. Because baseball, like all sports, feeds on competition, and the better the competition, the better the level of play. Conversely, the softer the competition, the softer the level of play.[*]

Big deal, Keith! That was, like, twenty years ago.

Well, I'll say it again: *baseball feeds on competition.* And like any other meritocracy, if you suddenly ration its food supply, that leads to poor results. All you have to do is look at the interleague records of the NL versus the AL. Between 1997—the start of interleague play—and 2003, the NL held its own, winning more than 50 percent of the games in three of those first five years. That even match makes sense because the stock in the league was overwhelmingly composed of players who had come up before the expansion. Their skills could go toe-to-toe with the AL. But as that stock depleted and was replaced by post-expansion players—players who had been raised on a diet

---

[*] I remember a conversation we had with the very humble Hall of Famer Mike Piazza in the booth shortly after his retirement. He commented that he was very fortunate to have played during the '90s expansion—not only was the pitching diluted but in both Denver and Phoenix the ball really traveled. Well, Mike would have made it to the Hall in any generation, but his point is noted: those were really advantageous years for hitters.

of substandard competition—the NL teams started to get their asses handed to them.[*]

Finally those matchups are starting to even out again. I say this in hopes that the rumors about more expansion are untrue—the league has said so, but we'll see.[†] Otherwise, I may have to trade in my baseball affection for something like bullfighting, where the customs, traditions, and quality of the fight are more sacred than any resulting commerce (and I am, after all, 50 percent Castilian). Or maybe a card game like bridge—that pastime may be dying, but the old folks who play it sure know what the hell they're doing.

I glance out the open booth window, onto the field. A light fog has settled in and around the stadium. It reminds me of growing up and playing ball in Northern California on chilly, damp afternoons. But the memory is interrupted when suddenly techno music starts blaring throughout the stadium—*boom, boom, boom*—and an MC on a microphone starts shouting through the PA. He's on the edge of the field, calling out to the thousands of schoolkids bussed in from all over the city to enjoy a day off from school and a game on the house.

"Who's ready for some baseball?" he shouts, like he's working a WWF match rather than America's pastime, and the kids go berserk. They shout back in a roar, feeding the MC, who gets

---

[*] According to the Bleacher Report, between 2003 and 2016, AL teams compiled a 1,765–1,465 record against their NL counterparts—good for a .546 winning percentage—and won interleague play by a grand total of 1,688 runs (from Neil Paine at FiveThirtyEight: https://fivethirtyeight .com/features/the-nl-is-finally-winning-interleague-play-for-now/).That's not winning, that's *dominating.*

[†] Baseball's new commissioner, Rob Manfred, has made known his distaste for interleague play and would like to scale it down. But to achieve this scheduling-wise, there would have to be two more teams added. *Good Golly, Miss Molly!* More diluted and minor league talent in the big leagues? I love the idea of getting rid of interleague play, but at the expense of fifty mediocre-to-marginal players and two El Stinkowski teams?

louder and louder with every turn while the incessant music pumps the frenzy.

Gary looks up, the nonsense outside breaking his concentration. "Why do we treat these kids like they're morons?" he asks.

Out on the field, some of the Mets players run and stretch, and I wonder if the kids even notice that their big-league heroes are out on the field. Whatever attention they can give is being crushed to death by the thumping of some electronic bass drum set to go off precisely every half second for minutes on end, until it is replaced by another electronic bass drum set at some slightly altered but still incessant tempo.*

"That's right, kids," I shout out the window, into this beautiful ballpark that reminds me of a great big Ferris wheel—a throwback to yesteryear. "Let's get pumped up for some baseball! Let's all plug in and get juiced up!"

Gary chuckles—he appreciates the sarcasm—and we both head to the cafeteria for some more coffee and an escape from the noise.

---

* I just want to say that Vito Vitiello, who runs the command center that controls the scoreboard, music, advertisements, in-game recorded cheers—basically the whole shebang—is a fantastic fellow who is just doing his job when it comes to all these bells and whistles that sometimes get on my nerves. It's not his fault; he gets paid to respect today's tastes and play what ownership desires. And he still takes care of us oldies but goodies. Like during every Sunday day game, Vito always plays Bobby Darin's recording of "Sunday in New York," which just happens to be my favorite of all the songs written about Manhattan.

CHAPTER 26

AFTER THE 1975 SEASON—once again without a dime to spend[*]—I headed home to San Francisco, but this time without Dad and his damn desert. Instead, I'd asked my friend Jerry, the visiting clubhouse man, to take the trip. So off we went, westward toward the Rocky Mountains.

We stopped in Denver for a night and headed over to The Loft, an Oilers' favorite bar and a total meat market. Still shy around women, I was more comfortable in social scenes when I had a wingman and a few drinks in me, and after an hour or so at the bar, I started chatting up this very hippieish brunette from Boston. We were a perfect match—I'd let my hair grow fairly long that season and hadn't shaved in a couple of weeks. We went back to her place, a studio apartment that was an absolute mess, I mean a pigsty. We rolled around in her already unmade bed for most of the night while her dog—this huge wolfhound or something—slept on some of the clothes strewn about the bedroom. We said our goodbyes the next morning, and Jerry and I hit the road again, heading west on I-70 with the radio blasting.

---

[*] I had made only $18K in 1975.

In the late afternoon, somewhere in western Colorado, I be-gan to itch. All over. I got home, and Mom was horrified. "You look like something the cat *drug* in," she said. Dad thought I was turning into a hippie and reacted in his usual way. I told them about the itch, which sent them further into a tizzy, so I headed up to Kaiser Hospital in South San Francisco, where the doctor, this old guy, examined me. He looked at me and asked, "Where have you been living? A commune?"

"No," I said.

"Well, you've contracted scabies," he said, explaining that par-asitic mites had taken up residence in my skin, a condition that people get from unsanitary environs.

A light bulb went off in my head: *that gal in Denver . . . her filthy apartment . . . the damn hound!*

The doc gave me a prescription for Kwell shampoo and hus-tled me out the door.

I'd asked my folks if Jerry could stay for a few days, and they said absolutely not. They were pissed off about the whole sca-bies thing. *It's not like it was Jerry's fault . . .* So I called Randy Moffitt, the closer for the Giants, to see if he could help. Randy's wife was a flight attendant, and she had a bunch of coworkers who were always in and out of town. Randy, who knew Jerry from the Cardinals' visiting clubhouse, was happy to help and found Jerry a place to crash with a bunch of the in-flight ladies. Lucky him.

As for me, I headed into my folks' bathroom, filled the tub, poured in the prescribed amount of Kwell, held my breath, and submerged myself. In an instant, little red bumps appeared all over my body. Those little microscopic bastards were fleeing their host in an attempt to save themselves. After soaking for about twenty minutes, they were vanquished. Mom was still pissed, of course. She had already washed my clothes with added bleach.

"You're no son of mine!" she kept saying.

I suppose I was going through my liberal and sympathetic stage of life. The longish hair, the mustache (which had made its first appearance that season), pot smoking, and rock 'n' roll. I was swept up in the way things were back in that period. So I felt a little cramped at my parents' house that off-season—Dad was just too much of a watchdog, and besides, having turned twenty-two that October, I was getting too old to still be crashing with my parents.

Come mid-February, I was back in the Monte Carlo, headed for Florida. Riding shotgun for the first leg of the journey was John D'Acquisto, the fireballing right-hander for the Giants, who was going to Phoenix for his spring training. We stopped in Las Vegas because John had a relative who was in a high position at Caesars Palace on the old strip.* His relation got us a beautiful suite, chips to gamble with, tickets to all the shows, and free meals. He also sent up two high-class call girls, both extraordinarily beautiful, but it wasn't much more fulfilling than the ten bucks a pop back in El Paso. Impersonal at best, it was my second and final dalliance with a woman of the night.

But my parents, along with any future inoculating doctors, had nothing to worry about. Despite my rebellious behavior, my MO was still very much "Baseball star or bust."

In fact, I was taking a gamble driving out east, because there was a good chance that all MLB players were going to be out of work for the foreseeable future. Trouble had been brewing on the labor front ever since the Seitz arbitration ruling had come down against MLB in December 1975. A landmark decision that would forever change the face of baseball, the ruling elim-

---

* I still prefer the old strip to the overcommercialized new one.

inated the "reserve clause" in players' contracts, finally giving them a place at the negotiating table. The owners, who'd enjoyed nearly a century of cheap labor, were, predictably, flipping out and planned to lock out players until an appeals process had run its course. I was young and still trying to prove my worth, so I didn't bother to understand any of this union stuff—I just wanted to play ball.

But I was nearly broke, without enough dough to survive the protracted labor negotiations. For some reason, this hit me after that wild night in Las Vegas (who knows, maybe I was hoping to score at the tables). So from my Vegas hotel room, I called A. Ray Smith, my friend and the owner of the Tulsa Oilers, and explained my predicament. If the owners were bluffing—which was unlikely—I had to be in Florida when camp opened. If, however, they planned to lock us out, it was unknown for how long, and I didn't have the money to survive two weeks, let alone a month. So I asked A. Ray for a loan. Thankfully, he said yes.

I said so long to D'Acquisto, who headed off to Phoenix and the Giants, and resumed the drive east along Route 66. Radio up, smoking doobies, riding high. I stopped in Tulsa and went to the bank with A. Ray, who cosigned on a $2,000 loan. Driving through Tennessee the next day, I wondered if the money would hold out. It did, though I'm not exactly sure how. The lockout pushed all the way to March 17—nearly a month after we were supposed to report—when a federal judge upheld the Seitz ruling and we went back to work.

Three weeks later, the regular season started, and I was, once again, the Cardinals' starting first baseman.

I had two roommates in St. Louis that season: Pete Falcone, a newly arrived pitcher from the Giants, and Héctor Cruz, who was replacing Kenny Reitz at third base.[*] I was sorry to see Reitzie go, but with Lou Brock, Bake McBride, and Reggie Smith in the outfield, third base was the only place left to put Héctor, 1975's Minor League Player of the Year.

With Héctor and Pete in my corner, and my strong finish the season before, I went into the 1976 season a bit more confident. But I hit .147 without a run scored or an RBI through the first 9 games. Games eight and nine were particularly demoralizing. We were playing the Mets at home, and I went 0 for 7 in the first game, an extra-inning affair in which Tom Seaver struck me out *three times*. I followed with an 0 for 4 against Jon Matlack. That game turned into a knockdown match after the Mets hit *two* two-run bombs off our Lynn McGlothen in the first, and Lynn, who didn't care for that sort of treatment, responded in kind with a couple of knockdown pitches.

Do pitchers have a right to intentionally hit a batter? Yes and no. Officially—and this is at the umpire's and the league's discretion—a pitcher who purposely hits a batter should be ejected from the game and/or fined by the league. That's for good reason, as a ninety-mile-per-hour fastball can inflict serious damage. But I can tell you that a good pitcher won't take abuse lying down. He'll come after a guy if he feels intimidated or disrespected. Remember, baseball is a battle between a pitcher and a hitter—neither wants to give ground. So McGlothen drilled the Mets' Del Unser on the elbow in the third inning in retaliation for Unser's two-run blast in the first. Typically a line-drive doubles hitter, Unser *feasted* on McGlothen, taking him deep 4 times in 28 at-bats between '75 and '76.

---

[*] Falcone came over in the same deal that shipped Reitz off to San Francisco.

"[McGlothen] was wild all night," Red told reporters after the game. "I'm surprised he hit anybody if he was trying."[*]

Of course, Red knew it had been on purpose, and as Unser made his way to first base, both teams started eyeing one another. What ensued was somewhat predictable. The Mets' starter, Matlack, retaliated by brushing back McGlothen during his at-bat in the bottom half of the inning; McGlothen then retaliated by drilling Matlack in the hip in the fourth, and a melee ensued.

Dave Kingman immediately charged McGlothen from the Mets' dugout but was, as reported the next day, "tackled" by yours truly before reaching the pitcher.

At six foot six, Dave "King Kong" Kingman was one of the strongest men in the league. When he'd shake your hand, if you didn't get a good grip first, he'd ring it like a rag. Before the offending pitch, I'd noticed him crouched on the top step of the third-base dugout, his eyes ablaze and fixed on McGlothen. He was like a raging bull, pawing the dirt, ready to rush the matador. McGlothen had to have seen him but drilled Matlack on the next pitch anyway.

Both benches immediately emptied, and Kingman led the charge. Ted Simmons, coming up the third base line from his position behind home plate, tried to intercept, leaving his feet and launching at Kingman in full cross-check style. But Kingman, who was as agile as he was strong, ducked Teddy and continued his pursuit. I looked to my right for reinforcements. *Maybe Reitzie from third base?* McGlothen had scurried to my rear, making me the last line of defense. It was like a freshman defensive back in high school taking on an all-state fullback.

---

[*] *St. Louis Post-Dispatch,* April 21, 1976.

Boom!

I barely had time to brace myself. I remember being lifted off the ground from the initial shock of the attack, crashing onto the turf on my backside, and desperately trying to hang on to the V-neck of Kong's jersey as he literally crab-walked over me to get to Lynn. But by then the cavalry arrived and held Kingman down, landing a few punches along the way.*

The next day, I showed up in the clubhouse with a serious red welt on my neck, and Lynn came up to me and patted me on the back with a huge smile. "Thanks, my man!" he said, or something like that, and then strode out the clubhouse door for BP. The rest of the gang was slightly less appreciative, laughing and shaking their heads—even the radio broadcasters were making light of it. Being young and a tad bit sensitive, I may have muttered something like "Well, I didn't see you guys doing anything to protect your pitcher." But whatever. I'm sure that deep down they were all just happy that fate hadn't placed *them* between Kingman and McGlothen. And to be fair, I'd been positively *steamrolled*.

Chivalry or not, I'd stunk it up at the plate, and Red sat me down in three of the next four games. Ron Fairly started in my place.† *Uh-oh, here we go again...*

A week later, we were in San Francisco for a three-game series versus the Giants. *Perfect timing.* I stayed with my parents, and Dad, predictably, was on edge and spouting advice every three seconds. Even during the game, there was no escaping the man.

The final day, Mom, Dad, and Gary were in their usual fifth-

---

* McGlothen was ejected, along with Red and Mets shortstop Bud Harrelson. Following the game, McGlothen was fined $300 and suspended for five days. As for Del Unser, he continued to get the best of McGlothen, going deep on him once again that September.

† Ron had come over from the Phillies the year before and hit .301 for us—which was part of the reason I'd been sent down in 1975.

row box seats behind our third base on-deck circle. I started the game and could see my family from my position at first base—I was facing them whether I wanted to or not. There was Dad, standing up, waving his arms at me, trying to get my attention. He was like a man on an aircraft carrier signaling the planes as they were lining up for takeoff. *Please, God, make him stop,* I thought, and I tried to wave him off.[*] But each time I did, he started demonstrating how I should hold my bat.

This happened for multiple innings—I was waving him off, but he just wouldn't stop. I went 0 for 3.

"What were you doing?" I shouted at Dad after the game. He, Gary, and Mom had been waiting for me just outside the clubhouse door. "For crying out loud, get a grip!"

"Ah, never mind that," he said, dismissing my frustration like I was some fifteen-year-old kid. "I know what you're doing wrong."

"Never mind?" I screamed. "Don't you ever do that to me again!" I kissed Mom, said goodbye to Gary, and stormed off to the team bus without saying anything else to Dad.

The team flew to L.A. that night, and the next day I went 0 for 3 against Don Sutton. I didn't start the rest of the four-game series—just two pinch-hitting appearances, both strike-outs. Ron Fairly started against the right-hander Rick Rhoden, and Red surprisingly put backup outfielder Mike Anderson at first against the left-hander.[†] I could read the tea leaves—Bing and Red were obviously looking into other alternatives.

After losing the afternoon finale, we flew all the way back east to Atlanta, where we played three games against the Braves. We arrived very early in the morning and thankfully had a day off. I

---

[*] Pete Falcone later told me he thought I was going crazy out in the field. He couldn't see Dad's antics from his dugout seat.

[†] Mike had come over from the Phillies in the off-season and was off to a good start, though in limited play.

was in my room, probably just waking up, when the phone in my hotel room rang. *Who the heck is calling me in Atlanta?*

"Hello?"

"Keith, it's Murph."

That was the nickname of my teammate Willie Crawford, whom we had acquired in the off-season from the Dodgers. The left-hand-hitting outfielder was a hard-nosed African American from the L.A. area. A no-nonsense guy who had played with the Dodgers from '64 to '75 until he was traded to us for Ted Sizemore in early March 1976.

"Yeah, Murph?"

"I want you down in the lobby by two p.m. We're going out to the park for extra BP."

"Ah, c'mon Murph," I whined. "It's an off day."

"Get your butt down here by two or I'm coming up!" *Click.*

So I met Murph, as instructed. We got to the park, and I noticed most of the other bench players were there for the same purpose. It finally dawned on me: never a full-time starter in his career, Murph was used to being in a platoon role and knew what it took to stay in shape and be ready. In the past I'd taken extra BP only when I was in a slump. But now, playing sporadically, I needed the extra BP regardless.

Unfortunately, the extra swings had little effect on my immediate performance, and on May 14, the team announced a major change at first base: Ron Fairly would play against right-handers; outfielder Reggie Smith would play third base against right-handers and first base against left-handers; and Mike Anderson would take over in right field. I was officially benched. The move also meant that the team was platooning Héctor at third base, playing him only against left-handers. At the time Héctor was hitting only 3 points higher than me at .181.

The two stars from Tulsa were duds in St. Louis.

CHAPTER 27

Citi Field

"LAST NIGHT WAS A good broadcast," says Gregg Picker, the co-ordinating producer for SNY. We're seated at a table in the press cafeteria, drinking coffee and killing time with Gary Cohen and a few other radio and TV guys.

"I felt flat last night," I say. "I just didn't have any energy."

"Well, the whole game was flat," Gary says. "It wasn't you."

"The game was lousy, but you guys sounded great," Gregg says. He wasn't working last night—a rare day off—but tuned in to the broadcast anyway. I don't know how Gregg does it. Every game is three hours plus. And regardless of how the team is doing, he has to figure out a way to keep things moving along and the viewers engaged. On top of that, he has to worry about every word in the broadcast. So if I stumble on a phrase or a word—let's say the word is "boisterous"—there's Gregg, sensing my stumble and coming in loud and clear in my earpiece, "boisterous," without skipping a beat, and I continue on with my analysis.

Anyone who thinks TV producing is easy should hang out with Gregg Picker for an hour. They'll have a heart attack. Gregg worked years on the USTA circuit with USA Network and ESPN, and if I'm any good at my job as a color commentator, it's in large part because of him. From the very beginning of our collaboration at SNY in 2006, he's always encouraged me to be myself on the air.

"It's a great listen," he says. "It's almost like you guys aren't on TV but in my living room, sitting on the sofa, having a conversation about the game."

Gary laughs. "Well, Keith didn't think we were on TV either," he says, and explains to Gregg that the last thing SNY viewers heard from last night's broadcast wasn't Gary saying his usual "Goodnight," but me saying "Oh, are we still on?"

Everyone at the table laughs, me included. As with ballplayers, a coffee break among broadcasters usually includes a healthy dose of busting chops.

"Nice one, Keith," says Gregg, rolling his eyes before sipping his coffee.

I enjoy this pregame ritual with the guys. When I was a kid and would go with my dad to pick up his paycheck at the firehouse, the other firemen would always be at the table, drinking coffee, talking, or playing cards. Even as a young boy, I sensed that the firemen liked hanging out at the station together—they weren't just spinning their wheels, waiting for the alarm to ring. When I started playing professional baseball, I got something very similar to that. Because I spent *a lot* of time with teammates before and after games, and like the firemen, I enjoyed the hanging around. But when I retired, that part of my routine just went away.

Poof.

So when I came to broadcasting ten years later and was very unsure if a return to "baseball life" was what I wanted to do—the night games, late travel, hotels, road trips—one of the things that eased me back in was a work culture that provided plenty of time to talk shop or just shoot the breeze.

Anyway, it's nice to hear from Gregg that even when we're not on our A game, the broadcast is still conversational. That's something that we all want it to be.

"It's apparent you're never forcing things," Gregg now says. "And you know, the whole entertainment business is in an era where people feel like *I'm on the air so therefore I gotta be this type of personality all the time*. It's very forced and relentless."

Boy, do I agree with Gregg on this last point. At times when I watch sports on TV—anything from baseball to football, even golf—the volume is usually muted. Otherwise, the noise keeps me from why I turned on the tube in the first place: *the game*. It's just talk, talk, talk, while the network puts up all these crazy graphics and sound effects. Nothing ever shuts up. It's like that MC with the kids in the stands this morning—he thinks he needs to yell and scream all the time. And you just want to grab the guy and say, "Hey, buddy, how about a little peace and quiet while they take it all in?"

As usual, Yogi Berra said it best: "It was impossible to get a conversation going, everybody was talking too much." *There you go, Yogi!* I wonder what he and some of the other old-timers would say if they heard some of the broadcasters in the game today. Too many of them emphasize all these crazy stats, like "exit velocity," "trajectory angles," or, and this is my favorite, "percentage rate of someone making a catch." "His probability rate of making that play was sixty-seven percent!" Give me a break. Who cares how many miles per hour the ball traveled once it left the bat, or how high the ball traveled in degrees, or how many seconds it took to leave the ballpark.

When did baseball become NASCAR?

Why can't they just say "Wow, he hit that ball hard!" or "Geez, what a rope"? Did Harry Caray ever talk about exit velocity? Vin Scully? I doubt it. Is that even part of the game's vernacular? When a kid today is playing baseball out in the street with his buddies, does he exclaim "Did you see that monstrous *exit veloc-ity*?" as the ball bounces down to the end of the block? Gosh, I hope not. Hopefully he just says, "I hit the dog outta that ball."

Am I dating myself? Am I a dinosaur? I guess to a degree I am, and I have been called such by a few newspaper critics. But for some reason a lot of commentators and networks think fans need all that extra stuff, *all* the time. Yes, it's the job of every broadcast to keep the viewers from turning the dial, but enough already. *Play ball!* Let the game provide the bulk of the entertainment.

Of course, times change and maybe more noise and chaos is what people want these days. I'm not sure. But that great adage "Less is more" is absolutely true in TV sports, where overindul-gence in production prevents viewers from *seeing* the action. It's like we've combined the techniques of radio days—when producers had to sonically create the action and emotional land-scape with constant narration and literal bells and whistles—with a now ultra-high-def visual experience. Well, that sensory *overload* makes zero sense, and I'm happy that the Mets owner-ship likes our broadcast as is.

Conversational.

"And I think we stay away from the clichéd boilerplate stuff that can kill a broadcast," says Gary as he gets up to head back to the booth. "I mean there's some—it's unavoidable—but we do a good job staying away."

Well, that's true, too. You don't need filler when you know what you're talking about, and, again, none of us is afraid of a bit of silence between talking points. No doubt, that ease starts with Gary's play-by-play. Like the conductor of an orchestra, he's the one who sets the tempo of the broadcast. Ron Darling and I just follow his lead. And if the maestro isn't feeling the need to fill the space with cacophony or race to the next section of mu-sic, neither are we.

That's why I say Gary is one of the best in the business. Not only is his knowledge base substantial; he also has a feel for what's appropriate and when. His sense of timing is terrific. He may never have played the game beyond Little League, but Gary *feels* baseball better than a lot of veterans I played with. And that makes Ronnie's and my job as color commentators infinitely easier. We're just the brass and string sections taking our cues from the man with the baton.

And while I may have the most television experience covering the Mets of anyone in the booth, I am not, as further evidenced by last night's faux pas, a professional broadcaster. I'm just a former ballplayer who happens to know a good bit about the game and can concisely comment about what's going on in the field without getting too much in the way. And for that opportunity, I owe a lot to my predecessors, former players turned broadcasters who blazed a trail for the rest of us. Guys like Dizzy Dean, Tony Kubek, Joe Garagiola, Jim Palmer, and Tom Seaver, to name a few.

But the one I think deserves the most credit is Tim McCarver. He showed, better than anyone, how having a former player with a microphone in his hands can be an asset to a broadcast. Some say he talked too much—overanalyzed. I disagree. Considering the time when Tim came onto the broadcast scene—just when networks were starting to really revamp their broadcasts with more slow-motion instant replay and analytical statistics— McCarver met the demands of those changes with acute, confident observations while maintaining the easygoing manner that, to me, is most complementary to the game. That isn't a simple balancing act, and no one did it better than Tim.[*]

I check my phone for the time. "Oh my God," I say. "We still

---

[*] Tim was inducted into the broadcasters' wing of the Baseball Hall of Fame in 2012.

got fifty-five minutes to kill," and I head back to the cafeteria line to get another cup of coffee.

When I return to the table, I see Ron Darling has joined the fray. It's a pleasure to work with Ronnie—we've known each other a long time, since our playing days with the Mets, where we shared the field together for seven years. That's a good amount of time in baseball. Guys get traded, sent back down, or retire. They come and go. Most go. I remember when Ronnie was called up from the Tidewater Tides in September 1983, soon after I'd been traded to New York from St. Louis, and two things immediately jumped out about him in the five starts he made that final month of the season: one, he was well on his way to having one of the best pickoff moves I would ever see (he'd sometimes even catch me "leaning"); and, two, he had guts and wasn't afraid to go after batters inside. That's what I always looked for in pitchers, and I could see that Ronnie was a mentally tough kid to go along with that Yale intellect, a dangerous combination for a pitcher in the bigs and one that Ronnie would exploit over his career.

So it's great to still be working with him, and I think we're beneficial for the color side of the broadcast. There's no ego or authoritativeness—we're both confident the other guy knows his stuff, and we have a great time together in the booth.

I sit down. Ron and Gregg are talking about last night's starter, Matt Harvey, whose suddenly anemic fastball has cost him a few tough outings.

"Well," says Ronnie, "DeGrom [another Mets starting pitcher] isn't throwing his hardest either. But he's getting by. He's just figuring out a different way to do it until he gets his fastball back. But Harvey's whole persona is to blow you away, and when he's not doing it—when guys are catching up to his fastball—it throws him off. He looks stung out there."

Ron has hit the nail on the head. I said last night between innings that Harvey looked a bit lost out there. But "stung" is better.

"And I've been there before," says Ronnie. "It's tough to deal with that. You just stand on the mound, thinking, *You gotta be kidding me!*"

"That makes sense," says Gregg, who's seen enough professional athletes to know when one of them is mentally struggling. "A lot of today's pitchers want to be *the* strikeout guy. But as soon as the other team chips away and puts up a run or two, it erases the hope of pitching that great, ten-strikeout shutout."

"Well, that happens to everyone," says Ronnie. "You got five days between starts and you wanna kick ass, so you get deflated when things go badly early on."

"But that's the name of the game," I say. "It's all about being able to battle through adversity."

"It sucks, but it's true," Ron agrees.

"It's like that time you told me about," I say to Ronnie, recalling one of my favorite anecdotes about pitchers *learning* to be mentally tough. "You were getting blown out in Tidewater [AAA] and Davey [Johnson] paid you a visit on the mound and said, 'Hey, my bullpen is dead. You better figure out a way to get out of this.' And he left you out there to clean up your own mess."

Ronnie sits there across the cafeteria table, nodding his head the way we former ballplayers do after recalling some crucial moment in our careers. "A good lesson," he finally says. "And you know what? I got out of the mess!"

"Well, that's what Harvey needed last night," I say. "To stay out there and get out of his own mess. But that's not gonna happen with teams pulling these guys in the middle of innings because of pitch counts."

"When they should keep him out there and let him get his ass kicked," says Ronnie. "It's the only way to figure it out."

Unfortunately for the development of talented guys like Harvey, baseball has become, like anything else in which lots of money is involved, too conservative. One reason teams pull their pitchers early is because they're being fed all this data that suggests a high pitch count can ruin an arm, and they need to protect their investment. Well, it's true. You can ruin an arm. Some of the old-school teams and managers used to not give a shit. Why? Because the owners used to pay their players like indentured servants, so what was one arm to them? They could just toss it in the trash heap and find another. Well, I'm certainly not advocating that—everyone should have a chance to play a long, healthy career.

But high pitch counts also provide something useful: an opportunity to work on a pitcher's mental toughness when things aren't going his way. And it's being forgotten. Okay, you want to save the arms because you're paying these guys a lottery check every two weeks? Fine. But realize that your protectionism at every turn is costing them the vital lessons necessary to become a *resilient* pitcher. One that can adapt to adversity. Like Ron Darling in Game Seven of the 1986 World Series—that's the type of pitcher who wins big games. And in my opinion, a good arm isn't worth much if it's attached to a head that goes to Jell-O any time the opposing team lands a punch.[*]

Ronnie probably realizes that we're starting to sound like a bunch of old men, complaining that today's game isn't up to snuff, because he changes the subject. "You ready for your vacation, Keith?"

---

[*] There's nothing worse than a pitcher, particularly a starter, looking down toward the bullpen when things start to unravel. Those are the pitchers you don't want. But there were guys like that when I played, too, and I do feel that the great majority of today's pitchers, like Harvey, are pissed when they get yanked and would love to go nine or pitch their way out of a jam in the seventh instead of handing it over to a reliever and hitting the showers. As competitors, they relish the opportunity to battle back and get stronger.

"You bet," I say. After the game this afternoon, the team will head out on a West Coast swing, but I'm staying home for a little R & R and to work on the book.

Eleven days off! Yes!

"You know," says Gregg, "we're gonna have to get you on the phone during one of the games." I think he's worried Mets fans might forget about me or something.

"Sure," I say.

"Yeah, he loves free publicity," jokes Ronnie, who I can tell is just winding up. "Maybe get a camera on him at the bar at the American Hotel, sipping scotch and watching the game along with everyone else."

"Actually, that's not a bad idea," says Gregg, who is serious.

"Oh yeah, that'd be hilarious," says Ronnie. "Or at the barbecue making a steak. Feeding the cat."

Well, folks, I learned a long time ago that if you can't beat 'em, join 'em, so I suggest, "How about getting a shot of me and Hadji in the living room. Maybe have the TV in the background with some soft porn going? Just a little bit fuzzy and out of focus."

The whole table laughs, especially Ronnie. "Yeah, picture in picture with the game and the porn!" he says, somewhat above the cafeteria din. "It's perfect!"

Uh-oh. Looks like some of those old Mets players are getting loud and obnoxious again…

CHAPTER 28

I SAT IN FRONT of my locker in full uniform, staring off into space.

It was 1976, and I'd just been officially benched. It was hard not to feel sorry for myself. *Keith Hernandez, now twenty-two years old, is a major league* bust...Thankfully, I didn't have much time to sulk because our third base coach, Preston Gomez, came calling. "Come with me," he said, and with a fungo bat in his hand, he led me onto the field.*

Preston was the greatest fungo hitter I'd ever witnessed: any angle, any location, Preston knew the speed and spin it required. He would start nice and easy to warm me up, but as our session progressed, he would pick up the pace until it reached a crescendo, and I'd be drenched in a full sweat, breathing heavy.

---

* Preston was an outstanding third base coach. He had different signs for each of our fifteen position players. That's fifteen individual signs for bunts, hit-and-runs, steals, squeezes, and takes. So if there were two men on base and the bunt was on, Preston would have to give three separate signs. And he did this in extremely fast motion, like someone fluent in sign language. *Amazing!* I remember in late spring training, when all the cuts had been made and the team was set, he took all fifteen of us aside separately and gave us our codes for opening day. I don't know if everybody had the same "indicator" or "wipe off," but it didn't matter; I was focused on my signs. And it made us more alert. "Don't tell your teammates your signs," he instructed. "Players get traded."

That afternoon he worked me doubly hard, and for a moment I forgot my troubles. When the session was over, he told me to come out early every day for ground balls until further notice. Like Murph's insistence on extra BP, Preston was looking out for me. Who knew how long the benching would last, but until things changed, Preston wasn't going to let me slack. *Far from it.*

Those extra sessions did more to increase my range than anything else in my professional career, and I think Preston enjoyed conducting them as much as I benefited from them. He would laugh and shake his head when I made a great play—even after seven weeks, I could still make him marvel a bit.[*] He went out of his way to praise me, probably because he could sense my need for it. Players, whether "screwbeanies" or superstars, desire praise, and at this point I required more than most. Unlike a lot of other coaches of his generation, Preston understood that.[†]

My teammates, too, helped me through. One day in Chicago, Pete Falcone encouraged me to run with him after our day game at Wrigley.

"Run? Run where?" I asked.

"Back to the hotel."

Why not? I've got energy to burn these days... We ran all the way to the Westin Hotel in downtown Chicago—a beautiful late afternoon through Lincoln Park, with more than a few ladies to look at as we jogged. It was a great way for me to clear my head and, most important, stay in shape, so I stuck with Pete's routine

---

[*] I would go the rest of my career searching in vain for a coach to challenge me with grounders like Preston could. He really made you work.

[†] I lost track of Preston after 1976. Years into my retirement, I read in the paper that the almost-ninety-year-old Preston had been struck by an automobile and had survived. I got in touch and thanked Preston for his care in 1976. "Keith," he said, "you were like a young stallion penned up in a stable. You just needed space to gallop." I'm forever grateful that he felt that way. He helped change the course of my career.

the rest of the benching. Even Ron Fairly, the man replacing me against lefties, was helpful. Ron had the disposition of an army officer, so he wasn't overly friendly, but he took the time to show me how to better break in a first baseman's mitt and how to "cheat a little bit" on a close putout at first. "You're moving forward to get the ball with the glove," he explained, "extending your body, and your foot comes off the bag just before the ball arrives." Ron showed me how to do all of that smoothly. "Don't rush it," he said, "or the ump will catch you pulling your foot." I worked on it every day during infield until I had it, and took Ron's sly little move with me for the rest of my career.

Despite all this help, I could still sulk with the best of them. Besides the occasional pinch hit, I was all but forgotten by Red. I remember one night when I was down at the end of the bench, moping after a pinch-hit strikeout. *Wait. Really? We're in a close game, the Phillies jumping out in front of the division, and the twenty-two-year-old punk is off by himself sulking? Not gonna cut it.* So here came Lou Brock, taking a seat next to me, basically telling me to stop being such a prima donna. But it was Lou Brock, so he didn't put it that way. Instead, he very gently said:

What the hell are you poutin' about? No one's gonna feel sorry for you. You getting mad and feeling sorry for yourself? Who's making you mad? You see that guy on the mound? He's making you mad. Get him. Take it out on him. He's the one who's gonna put you into a day job. You wanna go to work nine to five and have two weeks off a year? Then go ahead and do what you're doing. Or get mad at him. He's the one who's gonna take the job away from you.

Without another word, he got up and walked to the other end of the dugout. That was Lou's version of tough love. He wasn't

"My way or the highway" like my dad, or intimidating like Bob Gibson, or all about the silent treatment like Red and most of the coaching staff. Lou engaged with a calm gentleness that was more stirring and powerful. He made you *want* to do better, like your favorite teacher in high school, only this was the great Lou Brock, who would hit .301 that season at the age of thirty-seven.

No more self-pity for this guy.

One thing I'll never forget was watching Lou calm down a seriously pissed-off Wayne Twitchell, a big, hard-throwing starting pitcher for the Phillies. We were in the clubhouse after a game in which we'd pretty much beaten the tar out of "Twitch," sending him to the showers early. He burst through the door—all six feet six inches of him—still in uniform, soaked in sweat. He hadn't even changed his shoes!

"Where's Hrabosky?" Twitchell demanded, referring to our animated closer, Al Hrabosky. Evidently, Al's antics on the mound, which had earned him the nickname the Mad Hungarian, had steamed Twitch.

While most of us just stared, thinking, *This man is gonna kill somebody,* there was Lou Brock, walking forward, quietly saying, "Now, Wayne, calm down." And he put his arm around the 220-pound Twitchell, whose eyes still glowed beneath his cap, and kept talking to him—like a parent soothing an upset child—while he slowly turned him around and walked him out the door. Such was the quiet yet persuasive power of the mighty Lou Brock.

Sometime around the beginning of June, Red called a meeting before a game. We were more than a dozen games back in the standings. He was angry and chewed us out, and ended the meeting by naming Ted Simmons and Reggie Smith co-captains. *Really?* Even I, the twenty-two-year-old, underachieving, emotionally soft, benched first baseman, knew this was a harebrained idea. Sure, Reggie was a premier player—one of the best switch-hitters with power in the game, and a Gold Glove outfielder with a very accurate cannon for an arm—but he'd spent the last month, since being moved to the infield, sulking and brooding in the clubhouse. Everywhere he went, a dark cloud followed. That was not captain material. Besides, there was no doubt in anyone's mind—young players and veterans alike—that the real "captain" was Brock, the longest-tenured veteran of our team.*

After the meeting, I went back to my locker, four stalls away from Lou's. He was pissed and muttering under his breath—one of the few times I saw Lou "angry." I didn't blame him— management was taking him for granted just to appease the disgruntled Smith. But Lou, further proving his class and professionalism, never created a stir. Instead, he came to the park every day with the same work ethic and remained as helpful as ever.

As for Reggie Smith, the olive branch offered had zero effect on his gloom. So at the June 15 deadline, Bing traded Reggie to the Dodgers in exchange for catcher Joe Ferguson.† With Reggie gone, the team moved to yet another "plan B" at first base: they'd stick with forty-year-old Fairly against right-handers and, against lefties, move Ted Simmons to first, with Ferguson behind the plate. Where did that leave me? Same old place—bench city.

What does management do when they have a promising young player who just hasn't gotten over the hump? How long do they continue to ride out his struggles? For me, it wasn't very

---

* Gibson had retired after the 1975 season at the age of thirty-nine.
† The Cardinals also got two minor leaguers: Bob Detherage and Freddie Tisdale. Neither was considered a big-time prospect. Detherage would make it to the majors in 1980 but only for a cup of coffee. Tisdale remained in the minor leagues and Mexican leagues his entire career.

long—the Cardinals just didn't have a lot of patience. In the previous season, that had made sense, because the team was only five games out of first place by the end of May 1975. They weren't in a position to give me more starts, especially when Ron Fairly had gone about his business at first base, hitting above .300. But 1976 was a different story: the team was *fifteen* games behind the surging Phillies and out of contention at the June 15 trade deadline. It was apparent to all that we were going nowhere.

Is the team giving up on me?

Again, the annals of baseball are littered with "can't miss" talent that never panned out. Well, I was determined not to be in that classification. But the chances now were few and far between, because it seemed that everyone *but* me was getting a shot at first base. After the Ferguson trade, it became clear that I wasn't part of the organization's plans for the remainder of 1976. But this was my dream, or as Steve Martin would say, "my special purpose"!

I started the next day because Ferguson hadn't reported yet, and I had a big day: 3 for 4 with 2 RBI. But I sat the next five games. Finally, I snapped and stormed into Red's office. I didn't bother to close the door, and my teammates probably heard every word.

"What's going on here? Why aren't you playing me?" I shouted. Red, sitting behind his desk, responded that they had to give the Ferguson-for-Smith trade a chance to work. What were Red and Bing to do? Not play Ferguson, when they'd just traded away a superstar, Smith, for him?

But I would have none of that. *"You gotta be kidding me!"* I said. "You're just worried about your job!"

Well, Red got all flushed in the face and stood up from his chair. He walked around his desk toward me, and I thought,

225

Oh God, this old man's gonna take a swing at me! Instead, he closed the door, reached into his office cooler, and grabbed a Budweiser. After a long sip, he came back to his desk and sat down.

"Keith, I understand. But we have to make this trade look good."

Now with tears streaming down my face, I said, "Red, we're out of the hunt, and you play a forty-year-old first baseman and a backup catcher?"

And Red goes, "Okay. Now, Keith, I want you to go home and calm down. We're not changing anything right away. But I'll call Bing, and I think he's gonna want to see you tomorrow."

Dad was in town, visiting for the home stand, and we drove home together. This time I was the semi-hysterical one; Dad stayed calm and helped me pull myself back together. He just said, "You did good, son. At times in life you have to stand up for yourself. I'm proud of you. Let's wait and see what Bing Devine has to say tomorrow."

The next day Red called me back into his office and said, "Bing's coming down to talk to you."

Bing basically repeated what Red had said the night before about making the Reggie Smith trade look good. "But I'll tell you what," he offered, "if we're still fifteen games behind at the All-Star break, then you'll play every day the second half of the season. If we get back in the hunt, then I'll do my best to try to trade you to a team you'd prefer—if not this year, then in the off-season."

I felt like saying, *Are you blind? We're already out of it!* But I agreed to the proposal and rode the pine without complaint, coming out early every day, taking extra BP, and fielding ground balls with Preston.

Having stood up for myself, there was nothing else I could do.

CHAPTER 29

Citi Field

THE METS ARE UP 6–0 in the bottom of the fifth.

As per usual, they've done it with home runs, sending three balls over the fence in their first fourteen plate appearances. The first Met to "go yard" was catcher René Rivera. *Good for him.* Drafted in 2002, Rivera has spent the majority of his professional seasons grinding it out in the minor leagues. That's a lot of bus trips, a lot of patty melts.

Leading off the inning for the Mets is Michael Conforto. The young left-handed hitter has one of the nicest swings I've seen in a while, but he's cooled off at the plate lately, going just 1 for his last 14.

"They have really been working him inside this whole series," says Gary, referring to the Braves' pitchers.

Correct. After the young slugger's terrific start, where he continued to demonstrate patience by not chasing pitches out of the strike zone, the pitchers have been probing for weak spots, and the Atlanta hurlers think they've found one. They're pitching him more aggressively—fastballs and hard breaking stuff inside—early in the count, then getting the young slugger to chase the softer, low-and-away stuff if they're behind in the count or once they're ahead. With the rest of the league looking on, it's a safe bet that Conforto will continue to see a steady diet of these pitches until he makes the necessary adjustment and stops swinging at the soft stuff out of the strike zone.

Such is a batter's career in the major leagues, which really can be seen as just a series of adjustments. Those who adjust get to continue; those who don't have to pack it up. Pitchers are always hunting for vulnerabilities, and when they find one, they exploit it. (And let's not forget all those advance scouts in the stands, watching and looking for a weakness.) Then it's the batter's turn to try new things—it could be something as simple as a plate adjustment. Moving closer to the plate or farther away. Maybe up in the box or back in the box.

And around and around we go. It's a game of constant adjustment and relentless tinkering. That's a rude awakening for young players, who are just trying to get used to the quality of the pitching, let alone its variability. Weathering all this is really the difficulty of becoming an everyday player at the highest level. There are starts and stops, two steps forward, one step back, two steps back, one step forward, and then a couple more. The knowledge—along with the patience—to survive the chaotic dance takes time to develop.

The change from facing AAA pitching to the majors is a huge adjustment. For me, it was night and day. Sure, some of the AAA pitchers I faced had been in the bigs, but they hadn't quite had the quality stuff to stick around or were trying to come back from arm injuries. Then there were others—like former White Sox hurler Joe Horlen and his great curveball—who'd enjoyed good years in the majors but were now in their thirties and trying to get back without their best stuff. Sprinkled in here and there were the up-and-comers: guys like Joaquín Andújar and Jim Kern, who were on their way to having All-Star careers. But in the big leagues, there were ten pitchers (today, it's twelve to thirteen) on every staff with above-average stuff. That's a huge upgrade. Plus, in AAA you aren't going to face any Steve Carltons, Tom Seavers, Jerry Koosmans, J. R. Richardses, or Don Suttons—guys with *exceptional* stuff. No way. So the player has to adjust, if he can. And it's very seldom that someone like a Fred Lynn or a Ken Griffey Jr. or a Mike Trout comes into the league and says, "Okay, I'm a man-child, and I'll handle whatever you got from day one."

For most, it's not such smooth sailing.

"Strike three!" the umpire calls, and Conforto heads back to the dugout to figure things out. It's his second time striking out looking on the day. I don't mind strikeouts—they happen over the course of a season—but called third strikes, particularly on a fastball, are anathema to me. It tells me that the hitter is guessing. If you are an experienced veteran, okay—you know the pitcher and his tendencies, so maybe you take a chance and guess once in a while. But a youngster who hasn't been around long enough needs to stick to the basics, bear down, and go to hitting.

This reminds me of my first encounter with the legendary Ted Williams, when he grilled me on my hitting philosophy, *particularly* hitting with two strikes. It was January 1980, and I was working an endorsement gig at the largest sports trade show convention in the country at the McCormick Place Convention Center in Chicago. I'd just won the batting title and MVP in the '79 season, so there was a good crowd around my booth—folks looking for autographs—when all of the sudden I noticed a tall, confident man striding toward me. Any baseball fan worth his salt would have instantly recognized the Splendid Splinter, dressed in his typical corduroy sport jacket, turtleneck sweater, and slacks. *Gulp.* He quickly introduced himself, and before I could find the words to say "Hello, Mr. Williams," the interrogation began.

"What's your approach at the plate, Hernandez?" he asked. There was now a crowd gathered around to hear this conversation between baseball god and mere mortal, and I, the latter in that equation, was terrified I would say something stupid.

"Well," I sheepishly began, "I generally look fastball, going up the middle and adjusting to the secondary pitches. When I've got two strikes, I fight off the inside pitches and go the other way."

"Well, that's pussy hitting," Ted said, referring to my two-strike approach.

Silence. I could feel the hundred or so eyeballs upon me. *So much for not saying anything stupid . . .*

Fortunately, Ted, who I'm sure could read the room and see the panic in my eyes, said, "I'm sorry. I didn't mean to embarrass you," and quickly followed up with another question. "What's the easiest pitch location to hit?"

Stammering, I answered, "The pitch letter-high and away."

"Correct! Why?" There were no pauses between his words, like a teacher giving a sixty-second pop quiz.

"Because it's right there," I said, extending my right arm to indicate the location.

Ted then proceeded to demonstrate, as if he had a bat in his hands, taking a swing at a high pitch away, stopping the swing at "contact."

"Because it's the shortest distance for the bat to travel to the contact area," he said.

So I was 1 for 2 at the plate with Ted. *I'll take it!*[*] But I

---

[*] I had more opportunities to talk hitting with Ted, including the time when I referenced his book, *The Science of Hitting.* I told him it was the key to me overcoming swinging under a high pitch. Per the book's prescription, I got rid of the nasty habit of dropping my back shoulder on a high pitch by hanging a spare tire from my parents' oak tree in the backyard. I set the tire so that its central arc was at the letters and, as instructed, "chopped wood" all winter long. Ted loved that!

went back to the hotel that evening kicking myself, because I hadn't been able to adequately explain my two-strike approach to Williams. I never became a "Judy hitter" (the less crude way of saying what Williams had said) when down in the count two strikes. I still looked to drive the ball as drilled by my father throughout my young years. But as I stated earlier, I had the ability to fight off a tough pitch in. My "emergency swing." I can't tell you how many times I must have frustrated pitchers who felt they made a great pitch but were thwarted by the quickness and adaptability of my hands.*

But it took the better part of four years in the bigs—nearly two thousand plate appearances—for me to perfect that two-strike approach.

Again, it just takes time.

So today's talented young players, like Michael Conforto, who is becoming a star precisely because he understands that nothing comes easily in this game, will have to continue to be patient and get better with each at-bat. *Two steps forward, one step back . . .*

Well, I'm glad I'm not in the lineup today. *It's cold out there, ladies and gentlemen*—49 degrees at start time. The electric heaters are going next to our feet, and I've got on more than a few layers beneath the network's blue parka. Fortunately for Mets fans, current first baseman Lucas Duda has no problem staying warm. Two batters behind Conforto, Duda hits another home run, his second of the day and the team's fourth. *I swear this baseball is juiced.*

---

* Despite being on record as saying that "good hitters have to guess," Ted, I think, would agree with me on this point about needing to "fight off" the inside pitch if you've "anticipated"—rather than "guessed"—wrong. Our semantics and explanations may differ, but I suspect our *intent* at the plate with two strikes would be somewhat similar.

The Mets aren't the only team going deep to put runs on the board this season. In fact, the entire league is more reliant on the home run than ever before, including during the steroid era.[*] How is this possible? Are players once again doing things to their bodies that they shouldn't be doing? I don't think so. The league's drug testing has become extremely vigilant, and players today, though by and large in excellent shape, don't look as "blown up" as what we saw during the late 1990s and early 2000s.

But the league has to be thrilled with this increased dependency on the home run because the long ball helps them promote the game. We got talking about this before today's game, and Gary said the people at MLB don't seem to know how to promote the game any other way. It's just home runs and strikeouts, he said. I agree 100 percent. And for proof, you don't have to look any further than the sports-news highlights, where it seems every baseball play shown is either a home run or a fan putting a "K" sign up on a wall.

But what about a ten-pitch at-bat that taxes the pitcher and yields a base hit? Or a good sinker ball knee-high on the outside corner that the batter grounds into an inning-ending double play? Where are these elements of the game in America's daily updates? Or does America just not have enough bandwidth for such intricacies during their fast-paced, multitasking day?

---

[*] Back in 2014, one out of every three runs scored (33.4 percent) was off the home run. As Joe Sheehan of Slate pointed out, "That's a high figure historically, but not unreasonably so. In 1994, which of course seemed like a huge hitting year at the time, it was 33.5 percent. In 1961, an expansion year in which a notable home-run record was set, it was 33.7 percent" (Slate, September 1, 2017). Since 2014, however, that number has risen dramatically: 2015 saw a record set at 37.3 percent; in 2016, that record was broken, at 40.2 percent, and again in 2017, at 42.3 percent.

Of course, our fascination with the home run is nothing new. Babe Ruth, after all, was the "Sultan of Swat." And what kid doesn't want to go to a ballpark and see his heroes hit bombs? It's spectacular stuff. It was one of the first things I looked for in the morning box scores: *Who hit a home run?*

But to keep up in a progressively more self-indulgent culture, is the league stoking our fascination with the long ball too much? Because not only do they continue to sell the home run; they've also actually gone ahead and *changed* some of the field parameters to encourage more of them, like making most of the new ballparks bandboxes and all but getting rid of the gaps, or power alleys, between fields with fences arranged in straight lines and right angles, rather than bowing arcs, from the corners to center field. Citizens Bank Park, Great American Ball Park, the new Yankee Stadium, anyone? *Please…*

Why would the league do this?

For the same reason they weren't quick to curtail steroids in the second half of the 1990s. They were giving the fans a lot of a good thing: home runs to fuel new records being set at a frenzied pace. On the heels of the disastrous 1994 strike, this boom was a godsend to baseball. And I'll admit it: Sammy Sosa and Mark McGwire's home-run-chase slugfest in 1998 brought *me* back to the game. Until then, I hadn't watched a baseball game since my official retirement in 1991. Not a regular season game, an All-Star Game, a playoff, or a World Series. Zip. Nada. I had no interest. But two guys crushing Maris's single-season record? Who wouldn't want to watch that? It electrified me just like it electrified everybody else.[*]

---

[*] It just didn't quite click about the steroids, McGwire and Sosa looking like two male models auditioning for a Michelin tire commercial. How did it not register in my brain? Seven years out of the league, and I was already a dinosaur.

So Duda hits the home run, and the kids go wild in the stands. *Yeah!* But I wonder if they know that five years ago they would have had to settle for a double. Because at that time, Citi Field's larger dimensions and taller wall—the Great Wall of Flushing, as we referred to it in the booth—would have kept Duda's hit well inside the park. But after the 2012 season, the Mets brought the fences in *twice* to give the fans and the hitters a little more offensive power during the games—i.e., more home runs.[*] So it's a home run for Duda, and *Let's go, Mets!*

This sort of tinkering with the game's parameters, like bringing in the fences in order to produce a certain result, worries me.

Let's suppose you were managing a baseball game. The goal, of course, is to put more runs on the board than the other team. How will you accomplish this? Like a general in charge of an army, you need to know your team's capabilities and the environment in which you'll be playing. If only two of the players in your lineup can hit the ball out of the park with any regularity, you have to do *other* things with the *other* seven players to score runs. Like hitting the other way, drawing walks, bunting, stealing, and—dare I say—hitting-and-running. But if all of the sudden the field of play is altered and now *most* of your players can hit it out of the park, you don't necessarily need to do those other things.

Well, this is precisely what is happening in today's game—the fences are in, and management has all the "bigger, stronger" players swinging for them. Suddenly, the low-percentage shot—like with the three-pointer in basketball—has become the layup. Hence the reason why things like on-base percentage in

---

[*] I do agree that the original dimensions of Citi were as vast as the Russian steppes, on a par with the Astrodome and old Busch Stadium, where I played the majority of my career. They needed adjustment, but the second alteration was unnecessary.

today's game are at an all-time low. You don't need to do all the little things if you can do the one big thing. And to win the day, you just need to bring bigger guns than the other team.

I'm sorry if I sound like an ex-ballplayer bitching and moaning about how the game isn't played the way it was played *in my day*. You're probably saying, *Shut up, old man!* Okay, I get it. I thought the older generation was often full of BS myself. But please understand: My intention is not to put baseball down but to raise it up for the wonderful game that it is. Or at least can be. And I have tremendous respect for today's players and their abilities—they're in far better shape and train more than we ever did. But when you have a culture that increasingly seems to have a shorter attention span and that attention span is purposely being overindulged with an emphasis on only the game's "spectacular" elements, then at some point the once-robust game of baseball will cease to exist. And that would be a shame—*not* because that's the way it was played "in my day," but because baseball has so many interesting other dynamics that to reduce it to one element—the home run—is like making a western omelet with just the melted cheese.

Where's the egg? Where's the ham? Where're the peppers and onions, for crying out loud?

Does finesse have no place in today's *power* game? I'm not convinced. How would a team with a lineup full of players who executed the little things fare against these long-ball lineups? I do wonder, but I'm afraid that's increasingly becoming a theoretical question, because we simply don't see that type of team in today's game.[*] Because on-base percentage is way down, teams

---

[*] The exception was the 2015 Royals, who won the World Series despite finishing last in the AL in home runs, with 147 (0.907 per game). How? With a big ballpark, solid defense, and pitchers that kept the ball in the park and the batters off the bases. *Imagine that!* They also were second in the league

don't steal, and I can't remember the last time I saw a hit-and-run in back-to-back games. To execute these things, players have to develop the skills at a young age and in the minor leagues. But from what I can tell, these skills aren't being taught there. Instead, most of the players—and their Statcast-era,[*] uppercut swings—seem to be geared toward one end: lifting the ball over that tantalizing fence. And who's to blame them? All they're doing is responding to the league's invitation to come to a perpetual home-run derby—no performance-enhancing drugs or doctored bats required.

But the consequence is obvious: baseball is becoming one-dimensional.

I remember one game in Chicago a few years ago during which there were twenty-plus strikeouts and around seventeen walks between the two teams. *That's a lot of walks.* Jim Deshaies, the outstanding commentator for the Cubs, said, "You know, Keith, seventeen walks and [we'll say] twenty-one K's is thirty-eight at-bats where *nothing happened.* No action!" And I responded, "You know, I never thought of it that way." And we both agreed that it was a good way to put your fans to sleep. Because a game of home runs and strikeouts is boring.

---

in stolen bases, with 121 swiped bags in the season. Relative to the rest of the cement-shoed league, they did the little things to score their adequate 4.17 runs per game (third to last in the league). But consider that 121 stolen base number compared to, say, the *314* swipes by the 1985 Cardinals, who despite hitting just 87 home runs that season (0.537 per game) were an offensive juggernaut that led the league in runs scored (4.611). So while the 2015 Royals seized an advantage over the otherwise home-run-bingeing league, there was still plenty more to be had.

[*] "In 2015 the league introduced Statcast, a 'state-of-the-art tracking technology capable of measuring previously unquantifiable aspects of the game,' giving teams, scouts and players access to detailed data which is used to make the physics of hitting a lot clearer. The biggest change brought about by the Statcast data is illustrating the importance of an uppercut swing that results more often in fly balls and line drives rather than groundballs" (*Washington Post,* June 1, 2017).

So really, when you think about it, the decision to make fields smaller to "increase the drama" has had the reverse effect, and rather than bringing the fences in, teams should push them *out* and bring back the power alleys and the gaps. That would create a more dynamic game and force teams to diversify their personnel, putting more contact hitters with speed in the lineup. That's what Whitey Herzog did to the Cardinals when he took over in 1980. He took one look at the big dimensions and Astroturf of old Busch Stadium and told himself, *I need to build a team with speed, defense, and good pitching.*

What a concept!

And so by 1982, he had put together a team that hit the fewest home runs in the National League but scored the fourth most runs and went on to be World Series champs by defeating, in seven games, the powerful Milwaukee Brewers. How? By stealing bases, hitting-and-running, always taking the extra base, good pitching (particularly our bullpen), great defense, and playing sound fundamental baseball. Back then and across the league, it was almost an automatic on a double in the gap, with a runner on first, that the third base coach would send the runner home. And a close play at the plate—now *that's* exciting baseball that fans can sink their teeth into: they see where the ball is, check the runner, the ball, the relay throw, where the runner is, where the catcher is . . . *Oh my gosh, it's going to be a close play at the plate* . . . Now we're talking baseball!

And please don't get me started on the hit-and-run. I know it's sacrilegious for sabermetrics folks because, as they say, it doesn't pay off. But with the right personnel—in any sized outfield—the hit-and-run can do a number of things for a team. And, again, if suddenly you're not going to be relying on the long ball to score, then you have to manufacture runs somehow, and hit-and-runs help set up a big inning and keep pressure on the defense. I personally loved to hit-and-run, and we made a living off it in St. Louis.

"Oh, but you were on Astroturf," people will say, "and the ball gets through the infield faster."

Sure, but look at the infields today, how manicured they are. There's no long grass anymore like Wrigley Field back in the '70s and '80s. Back then, the Cubs' philosophy was basically *Okay, we have a small and windy park, so let's stock our pitching staff with sinker-ball pitchers, in the hopes of keeping the ball out of the air, and grow the grass four inches long so the infield will eat up all those ground balls, turning them into outs.* And when Whitey's speedy Cardinals would come to Chicago, they would grow the grass an inch or two longer.[*] Still, we would hit-and-run and race all over Chicago.

Even with the bandbox stadiums, I wish the Mets would do it more often. It sure has to be enticing. I mean, all the infields in the league today are fast, like putting greens—perfect for ground balls to get through. And while there are plenty of terrific athletes, many of today's middle infielders have become big, offensive guys. They lack the quickness to get to that hit-and-run ball in the hole. Despite these advantages, the Mets—like most of today's teams—don't hit-and-run. And on the rare occasion when some other team successfully executes it *against* them, I say under my breath, *Well, here you are, first and third with nobody out, and you've got a problem on your hands.*

Like with the hit-and-run, a lot of sabermetrics guys think stolen bases are to be avoided. Really? Those teams of my era

---

[*] I remember batting champ Bill Buckner, who played for the Cubs from 1977 to 1984, cursing all the way down the baseline as one of what must have been a multitude of hard-hit grounders was gobbled up by that "lion's mane" (as we used to call it) of an infield. It was hard not to bust out laughing as Buck would shout in full gallop, *"Cut the motherf—ing grass!"*

and their heavier emphasis on speed would rampage in today's game, if for no other reason than to simply rattle the pitchers. Because pitchers now come up to the big leagues not knowing how to hold runners on. Why? No one steals anymore! Look at Noah Syndergaard in 2016. When other teams actually attempted to steal, *they stole him blind,* and it affected his pitching *enormously.* He was completely rattled. But that wasn't Noah's fault—no one had really worked with him in the minors. I guarantee you that if Noah, an extremely talented player, had come up in the '60s through the '80s, he would have been better prepared to deal with this stuff. So why don't teams take this approach with other pitchers? It's not like Syndergaard is the only one with a problem holding runners in check.

It's also not just the pitchers who feel anxiety when there's speed on the base paths. Fielders, too, feel the pressure. With speed on the bases, fielders are more inclined to rush the play or throw, thus making them more apt to commit an error. But, again, you need team speed to apply that pressure, and that quality just isn't a top priority for the GMs. In the process, the game has slowed, and baseball is becoming similar to the American League in the '50s and '60s. Boring, one-base-at-a-time, home-run baseball.[*]

Yuck.

---

[*] I tried playing Strat-O-Matic baseball's late-1950s American League season a couple of years ago. I didn't last through the first month of that season.

CHAPTER 30

THE 1976 ALL-STAR break was approaching, and I was still riding pine.

Looking back, I understand where Red and Bing were coming from—it's difficult for managers and general managers to endure a young player learning to play every day in the major leagues when it means you may lose a few more games. And between 1960 and 1975, the Cardinals had finished below .500 only twice, so losing wasn't part of the tradition, especially when there were deals to be made to bring in veterans instead of playing youngsters. But as the 1976 All-Star break approached, it was obvious that the organization had kicked the can down the road a bit too long: gone were the talents of Bob Gibson, Tim McCarver, Julián Javier, Curt Flood, and Nelson Briles, to name a few.*

---

* The bottom line is that athletes age. Look at the Phillies and their great run in the mid-2000s with Chase Utley, Ryan Howard, Jimmy Rollins, Cole Hamels, Shane Victorino, etc. They all came up together and were dominant for half a decade. But the team held on to some too long, and rather than replenish from their minor league system, they traded their youth for quality veterans. This worked for a while with the likes of Roy Halladay, Roy Oswalt, and Cliff Lee as the Phils extended their post-season appearances another three years after their world championship in 2008 with yet another World Series appearance. But the inevitable came knocking, and the Phillies' last .500-plus season was in 2012.

Six games before the break, Red called me back into his office. We were now *nineteen* games back. "You'll be in the lineup every game, and it doesn't matter if you hit .190 or .400," he said. "You're in there, so don't worry about it." With all other plans exhausted, they were finally coming back to me.

I struggled a bit those first six games but went into the All-Star break with a home run off the Dodgers' Burt Hooton. Talk about the worst time for a rest! But I caught another guardian angel in Fred Koenig, now part of Red's coaching staff. A big beer-swilling guy with a Mr. Clean hairstyle, Fred was a cross between a marine drill sergeant and a barroom brawler. After the last game before the break, Fred walked up to me and offered to throw BP during the three days off. My eyes lit up. "Absolutely!" I responded.

These extra BP sessions didn't sit well with clubhouse man Butch Yatkeman. Butch had been in the Cardinals organization since 1924, when at sixteen years of age he started out as one of the clubhouse kids who performed all the menial chores. He eventually worked his way up to head clubhouse man, and through his tenure he saw the Cardinals win thirteen NL pennants and nine World Series. He was around for Rogers Hornsby, Dizzy Dean, Johnny Mize, Bob Gibson, Lou Brock, and the greatest of all Cardinals, Stan Musial.[*] But Butch was set in his ways, always bitching and moaning about something, and he worked hard to let us know that today's players weren't up to yesteryear's snuff. Typical generation-gap stuff (like me in the previous chapter) but with Butch, it was more like three generations. He was downright cranky and a pain in the ass. We would eventually learn to like each other,

---

[*] Butch would retire in 1982 after fifty-eight years of service.

but for now, Butchie didn't have much time for me, and there wasn't much love lost.

"You mean I gotta come to the ballpark and wash your clothes?" he whined after I gave him the news about the BP sessions.

"Butch," I said, "I'll take my clothes home and wash them myself."

"Well, I still gotta come to the park and open up the clubhouse."

"Butch, can't you have one of the front office people open the clubhouse for me?"

"I'm not letting anybody in my clubhouse without me present!"

Well, enough was enough. "Screw you, Butch!" I yelled, though maybe I used a different word. "It's my career on the line. So come to the *f—ing* clubhouse or have someone else *f—ing* do it. But I'm hitting tomorrow morning, and the *f—ing* clubhouse better be open!"

Lo and behold, the "f—ing" clubhouse was open the next day, and there was Butch, as pleasant as ever. I again offered to wash my clothes, but Butch, in full martyrdom, wouldn't have it. Oh well. My only regret is that I didn't offer to pay Fred Koenig a couple hundred dollars for his time and effort, or at least give him a case of Budweiser. Because that son of a gun was under no obligation to come to the yard those two blazing-hot and humid July afternoons and throw me BP. But he did, perhaps saving my Cardinals career.

Thank you, Fred! (You, too, Butchie.)

But I had good reason to ruin everyone's All-Star break—and not just because this was perhaps my last chance in a Cardinals uniform. I was making a major plate adjustment, this time against *left*-handers, who were giving me fits with the breaking ball away. It was Lou Brock, sensing that this was my moment, who'd made the suggestion.

"Why don't you move more on top of the plate [closer] against lefties," Lou said. "That's how Frank Robinson did it." Lou also told me to make this move obvious to all the opposing catchers and pitchers, by digging in *hard* so they couldn't help but see this drastic change. "You're going to go around the league for at least a month, they will see you on top of the plate, and they are going to throw you inside. Look for it and rip it! Pitchers can't relate to hitting. They don't know you're looking in there. It doesn't matter if you make an out or pull it foul, just hit it hard. Establish the inside pitch as *your* pitch. Each time you do this, they're going to say, 'Hey, that's my best fastball, and he hit the dog out of it. Maybe I *can't* get in there...' That's when you have them! Because then they're going to switch gears and throw right into your strength—the outside corner, with the barrel of your bat in full coverage."[*]

So now I was off the plate against righties, per Ken Boyer's suggestion a year earlier, and closer in against lefties, per Brock's. By "closer," I mean *real* close—like six inches off the plate. While it's not a change in mechanics, it's yet another new strike zone. So lots of BP. It also requires nerve because you're giving major league pitchers—who aren't afraid to put one in your ribs—more reason to do it. Pitchers view the plate as *their* turf, and if you stand on top of the plate, that's a declaration of war.

---

[*] Years later, I told Frank Robinson about Lou's suggestion, and he gave me a big smile. "Yes!" he exclaimed. "I learned to look in. They would always think they could jam me, but I had other ideas." I then relayed Frank's comments to former Cardinals teammate, 283-game winner, and lefty Jim Kaat, who had faced Frank many times when Frank was an Oriole and Jim a Twin. Jim's eyes lit up and he said, "Yeah, I remember seeing him on top of the dish when he first came into the league, and I said, 'I can get in there.' He *killed* me, and it took me a while to realize that was where he liked it. So I started throwing him my sinker away, and from that time on I had better success against him." A game of constant vigilance and adjustment.

Frank Robinson, Lou's example, stood on top of the plate from day one, and in his 1956 rookie season, he set a rookie record for hit-by-pitches with a whopping twenty. That led the league, and it didn't include all the brushbacks and dustings. Despite the assaults, Robinson hung tough and won Rookie of the Year that season.[*] Could *I* hang tough like that? Against ninety-five-mile-per-hour, up-and-in heat? Well, something had to give versus the lefties...

Again, *adjust or perish*.

Nerve aside, there was another, bigger challenge to working so close to the plate: I discovered that I could cover only three-fourths of the width of the strike zone at once. So when I looked *in,* I had to take the pitch on the *outer* quarter; conversely, when I looked *away,* I had to take the pitch on the *inner* quarter. Easier said than done. It required, first, *recognizing* the pitch's location out of the pitcher's hand, then deciding to pull the trigger or not, depending upon the location I was anticipating.

And *anticipating* is key here. You're not *guessing* what and where the pitcher's going to throw. Remember, I looked fastball 90 percent of the time throughout my career. You're just looking for a particular spot so you can jump on it *if* it comes. But there, too, I had to be careful, because sometimes I pulled the trigger too quickly. Particularly when looking inside. That wasn't good because it created an inside-out swing. I'd fly open with my shoulder and, recognizing that I was early, drag my hands behind, producing mostly weak fly balls or bloops to center or left field. To counter

---

[*] I remember Red Schoendienst telling the story that one time Robinson just killed the Cardinals in a series in Cincinnati, and the next week, when the Reds came to St. Louis, the Cardinals pitchers knocked him down as a sort of retribution. But it didn't matter—Frank still had a great game. And the next day, Red called a team meeting and said, "I'm calling this meeting to say leave Frank Robinson alone. Don't throw at the son of a bitch. You're just making him mad, and he's killing us."

this inclination, I remembered what my father had told me in my late-teenage years:

You have quick hands, Keith. Trust them. Don't rush. Let the ball come to you, then strike.

That's a tall order when we're talking about a pitch that seems to be on you in an instant, like an inside major league fastball. Could I make the adjustment?

We started the second half of the season on the road in San Diego. *God help us... another West Coast swing.* I came to the park expecting to see my name on the chalkboard. *Nope...* Brent Strom, a lefty, was starting that night for the Padres, so Ferguson caught and Simmons played first. The next day it was the same story: Simmons and Ferguson against another lefty, the crafty Randy Jones.* Had I been duped? Suspicious and brooding on the bench, I kept my mouth shut, and I kept coming to the park early for extra BP to stay sharp.

My brother drove me to the park on the final day of the San Diego series. Released by the Cardinals after the '75 season, Gary had recently taken a job in L.A. as a sales representative for Johnson & Johnson. We headed into the clubhouse together and saw my name up on the board. It felt like opening day. Trepidation galore. *Okay, Hernandez, this is it — time to put up or shut up.* And there was Gary: "You're going to have a great day, Keith. I can feel it." Once again, my selfless brother — my good-luck

---

* I couldn't have been too disappointed missing out on Jones. Anyone who dismissed him as a "soft tosser" missed the point: with a hard sinker and a wicked hard slider, much like Tommy John's, Randy threw his fastball hard enough to keep hitters off-balance. In 1975, he went 20–12 in 36 starts and finished second in the Cy Young balloting. This season, 1976, he came into the start with a 16–3 record, on his way to a 22–14 season in 40 starts and a Cy Young Award.

charm—was right: I went 3 for 5, with 1 run, a double, and 3 RBI in a 7–1 win over the Padres.

Then it was an hour-and-a-half flight up the California coast to San Fran with Dad waiting for me at the airport. *Don't I have enough on my shoulders? The last thing I need is to be talking baseball and hitting all night.* Thankfully, Dad was somewhat subdued and very positive. I guess Gary had called him and given him a heads-up: *Let Keith breathe. Don't force any issues.*

After a good night's sleep in my old bed, I drove to the park for the noon doubleheader and the two right-handers slated for the Giants. I went 1 for 3 against Jim Barr—the same Barr who had knocked me down in '75—with a two-out, two-run single to center that tied the game at 4–4 in the sixth. *Take that, Jim!* But Red pinch-hit Ferguson for me in the ninth against one of the game's toughest lefty relievers, Gary Lavelle—a hard-throwing power pitcher with a power slider. The second game was another 1 for 3, and again Red pinch-hit for me against Lavelle. I started the series finale the next day, going 0 for 2 with 2 walks, and it was adios to Mom and Dad, who were all praise after the game. It was a double relief: Dad's words filled my sails like no others could while at the same time I was delighted to be escaping his scrutiny.

We wrapped up the road trip after two games in L.A., where I sat, of course, against lefty Doug Rau but hit a double off right-hander Don Sutton in the second game. On the whole, it was a good stretch: 5 games started, going 6 for 18 with 3 runs, 2 doubles, 2 walks, and an impressive 5 RBI. *But what about the lefties?* Red was keeping me from them. *Why?* If I was going to be an everyday player in the bigs—which was the goal—I had to face the southpaws.

We opened the home stand with a four-game series against

the Cubs, who threw all right-handed starters. I went a whopping 6 for 11 with 2 doubles, 2 RBI, and 5 walks in the series.

One at-bat in game three was a turning point: I was facing Bill Bonham, a hard-sinker/slider-throwing right-hander. Bonham had me 1–2, and I just knew he was going to pound me inside. I knew it! So I anticipated the pitch and, sure enough, Bonham put a fastball right there—inside corner, on the black, just above the belt. *Patience. Front shoulder in…anticipate, coil, attack…* Whack! A BB up the middle for a single.

Perfect execution. No anxiety. Relaxed like a cold-blooded assassin.

But that's only half the story. The other piece is that I executed it without overcommitting. Instead, I had this assumption in the back of my mind—*I think this is what he's gonna throw*—but with two strikes, I still had to protect the plate; I couldn't commit 100 percent to the inside pitch. A lot of hitters are unable to do this, which is why the game has seen a multitude of "guess hitters" over the years. For them, guessing—or "selling out on the pitch"—is their way of responding to major league pitching. But in this at-bat against Bonham, I proved to myself that I could do it better and hedge my bets. Because as the ball shot up the middle, I understood that I'd still had enough time to adjust if the pitch had been somewhere else. That knowledge—*You have enough time, Keith*—was like being handed a trump card at a blackjack table: no matter what the pitcher dealt, I had an answer.

"From then on," as I later recounted to the *Post-Dispatch,* "I had it."

Like in Tulsa the previous two seasons, I was taking off. By the end of the month, I was 16 for 43 since my return to the starting lineup, hitting .372 with 9 runs scored, 6 extra-base hits, 9 RBI, and a slugging percentage of .558 in 13 starts. Moreover, I got on base an incredible 58 percent of the time with 9 walks and only 3 strikeouts. That meant I was getting the National League pitchers' respect—I was no longer "the easy out."[*]

On August 7, Red started me against lefty Jim Kaat. He did it again the next day against lefty Steve Carlton. *What's this? Two premier lefties and I'm starting?* That's when I realized I'd be playing every day. Righties and lefties.

In retrospect, Red handled me beautifully against the lefties. Rather than just throwing me to the lions, he sat me down those first few weeks against the likes of Randy Jones, Doug Rau, Gary Lavelle, Tommy John, Woodie Fryman, John Candelaria, and Jim Rooker. All tough lefties—all lions. Then, as I got hot with the bat, he put me in the lineup against these guys.[†]

I had a solid August, hitting .315 in 21 starts with 16 RBI and a .365 OBP, and I put the pedal to the metal for the remaining 36 games of the season, batting .331 with 26 runs scored, 17 RBI, and 20 walks (a .420 OBP and a .515 SLG). The power line drives were coming now, too, yielding 8 doubles, 2 triples, and 4 home runs.

The home runs were especially gratifying, as 3 were off left-handers, including the Mets' Jon Matlack and Jerry Koosman.[‡] Against Matlack, I led off the inning, which isn't my favorite thing to do because you have to run off the field, put your glove and cap down, get your bat and your helmet, get in the on-deck circle, and rush your warm-up ritual. *Thank God I didn't wear batting gloves.* I preferred time to get into the on-deck circle, prepare my bat with the proper amount of pine tar and resin, take a

---

[*] Or, to borrow a term from my esteemed colleague in the booth, Mr. Ron Darling, I was no longer "a lamb." (As a player, Ron would break the opposing lineup into two categories: those he wouldn't let beat him and the lambs.)

[†] I went through the second half of the season in chronological order, box score after box score, provided by that wonderful website Baseball-Reference.com, and I saw there was a method to Red's madness. Red sat me down later in August against Randy Jones and Don Gullett, but that was it.

[‡] The third home run was off lefty Buddy Schultz, a September call-up for the Cubs.

few swings with the weighted donut on the bat, and finally settle on one knee to watch the pitcher work the batter ahead of me. But Dad had always preached to me the importance of starting a rally, and my on-base percentage for leading off an inning was .409 that season. So I got up there, and Matlack threw me a nasty 3–2 slider—knees and black—and I crushed it to right-center field over the 386 sign at old Busch Stadium. Per Lou's advice, I was on top of the plate versus the lefty so the fat of my bat could cover the outside corner. Mike Phillips, a utility infielder with the Mets, later told me that Matlack came into the dugout all pissed off and shouted, "I'll knock him on his ass if he thinks he can lean over the plate like that again!" *Ahhhh, music to my ears, folks!* And after that home run, my batting average for the season stood at .290—exactly 100 points better than where it was at the All-Star break.

Four days later, I went deep off Koosman in the eighth inning at Shea. He was pitching for his twentieth win of the season, and "dealing." Protecting a 3–0 lead, he threw me an up-and-in fastball. *Bam*—a line drive into the Mets' bullpen in right. Jerry had never won twenty in his career, so he wasn't laying one in for me. *He wanted that shutout.* And I remember rounding the bases, thinking, *I've hit home runs off Matlack and Koosman! The cream of the crop!*

But the most satisfying home run that month was off Steve Dunning of the Expos.

I didn't care for Dunning. The right-hander was a former all-American from Stanford, and I'd played against him in AAA. He'd started one game in Denver and was crying at the umpire for most of the night. Bitching and moaning, and in my third at-bat I disgustedly said from the batter's box, "Quit your whining and throw the ball over the plate." He looked at me in absolute surprise and said, "What?" I motioned sweepingly with my left arm over home plate, inviting him to throw a strike, thinking for sure he'd put one in my ear. Instead, he threw me a changeup, and I grounded out to second base. *What a wuss.* Now in '76, we were going against each other again, and he threw me another lousy, straight, high change over the middle. I sent it over the scoreboard and into the swimming pool beyond. A very satisfying, monster two-iron off the tee at Parc Jarry.

Now, that's what I'm talking about! That's the Keith I know! Where the hell have you been hiding, for crying out loud?

So I *killed* it that September. Really, the whole second half was a romp: in 296 plate appearances, I hit .331 with 17 doubles, 3 triples, 7 home runs, 43 runs batted in, and 35 walks for an almost .500 slugging percentage. The only bummer was that the season was over, but I was also grateful. Luck had been on my side, because circumstances could have been very different. What if, like in 1975, the team had been in a divisional race? I don't think I would've made my way back into the lineup every day in the second half. What would've happened then?

KH BATTING PROGRESS (BY SEASON)

Year	Games (G)	At-Bats (AB)	Batting Average (BA)	On-Base Percentage (OBP)	Slugging Percentage (SLG)
1974	14	34	.294	.415	.441
1975	64	188	.250	.309	.362
1976	129	374	.289	.376	.428

While career saving for me, the second half of 1976 was the end of the road for our manager. The season had been a disaster for the organization, finishing fifth in the NL East with a 72–90 record. It was the first time a Cardinals team had lost 90 games since 1916 (63–93), and the lowest finish in the standings since the advent of the two-division system in 1969. So after a twelve-year tenure,[*] which brought two pennants and a World Series title, Red was fired at the end of the season. I felt bad, of course. I liked Red, and my struggling the first half of the year hadn't made things easier for him. Despite that, he'd kept his word, inserting me into the lineup the second half of the season. He'd been yet another angel on my shoulder, and I was sorry to see him go.

For the first time, I didn't return home to my parents for the off-season. Instead, I remained in St. Louis for what turned out to be one of the coldest winters on record. The snow never melted; it just froze until the next storm came and covered it. To stay warm, I rolled joints and spun records, blues mostly—J. J. Cale's *Troubadour* and Roy Buchanan's *A Street Called Straight* were particular new favorites—and stayed in decent shape because the Cardinals had instituted an off-season workout program. It was like *The Jack LaLanne Show* of the '50s and '60s: mostly calisthenics with a bit of running, stretching, and agility drills. Today's players would laugh at this regimen, but it was better than being a complete couch potato throughout the miserable winter.

I also hung out with a girl I'd met during the season, Sue. I'd spotted her in the stands one day while I was still riding pine in

---

[*] Tony La Russa's sixteen seasons managing the Cardinals, from 1996 to 2011, surpassed Red's for the longest tenure with the club.

the first half of the season. Her father was in the lumber business, and once a year he'd get box seats behind the Cardinals' dugout for his big German-Catholic family. Four daughters, three sons. Sue was his eldest. I couldn't help but notice her. I gave one of the clubhouse kids a note asking for her phone number. I'd never done that before. She obliged, but of course I lost it.

A few months later, I was doing a promotional event at a bank, signing autographs, when she showed up with her sister. I recognized her immediately. She was twenty-one, a year younger than me. We didn't party—Sue had a two-year-old daughter, Jessie, from a previous, short-lived marriage. We just sort of hung out at my place or over at her folks', who were terrific people, and that was fine with me because I enjoyed being back around a family.

I was becoming more recognizable around town and didn't know how to handle all that came with being a local "celebrity." It's one thing to be noticed when you're surrounded by teammates but entirely another to be out there on your own in the off-season and have someone say, "Hey, aren't you Keith Hernandez?" Back then, I'd get nervous—sometimes even start stuttering—and would duck into a grocery store or a bank with sunglasses and a hat pulled down. Anything to avoid being recognized.

Hanging out with Sue let me skip a lot of that. Then winter was over and it was time to head to Florida again.

Play ball!

Part III

CONSISTENCY

CHAPTER 31

Long Island

AFTER YESTERDAY'S WIN AGAINST Atlanta, the broadcast crew flew out to the West Coast with the team, while I drove home for a nice dinner with friends and eleven days off to work on the book. *And relax.* This afternoon, I'm getting together with my friend Paton Miller. Paton is a fabulous and well-respected local artist. He sells to me at the "friendship price"—to date, I have seven of his paintings hanging on my walls.

I love to collect art.

Books, too. I started collecting Easton Press when I was twenty years old, and I have a soft spot for first editions if I can find a good deal online. I can't say I've read the entire collection, but it's here for anyone who wants to visit. Some players surround themselves with a lot of trophies and career mementos. Gary Carter, my former teammate and co-captain on the Mets, basically had a shrine to his career in his office. I haven't kept much—though sometimes I wish I had. As it is, all I've got on display is my MVP trophy and three Emmys for broadcasting. The rest is put away in closets or collecting dust in the basement.

When I was growing up, we had my father's artwork all over the house—paintings, woodwork, mosaics. I think Dad's artistic talent was the part of him that Mom loved the most, and his creations never ceased to amaze us. I have two of his mosaics, *The Corsican Sailor* and *The Three Wise Men,* hanging in my living room. They're made from stones we collected on Pebble Beach, a two-hour father-and-sons jaunt down the Northern California coast. Dad would hand Gary and me a couple of empty Folgers coffee cans, setting us loose on the beach to collect the various shapes of green, brown, white, and black stones.

I remember he instructed us to look for three tan elongated pebbles—a nose for each of the wise men—and I stumbled upon the perfect Roman nose. It was just lying on the beach among the millions of other stones. I rushed up to Dad and said, "Dad, I got a nose for you!" He took it and, holding it flat against the palm of his hand, inspected it, smiled, and said it was perfect. But it was Gary who had the find of the day: the lip of a 7Up soda bottle that had broken off and been smoothed over by the sea—the perfect jewel for the sailor's ring.

Dad was always taking bits of this and that for his creations. Like when he made a teepee for us in the backyard. A real Plains Indian tripod teepee. He used eucalyptus tree branches, whose limbs were long and strong—like poles—and Dad cut them down to size, about fifteen feet long. For the cover, Dad used pieces of fabric he'd gotten from Ed and Jim's Union 76, the same gas station that sponsored our Little League teams. They would occasionally have tire or service sales they'd advertise with signs made from big canvas sheets. When the sale was over, Dad would ask for the signs and take them home, usually for his oil paintings. But this time he stretched the material over the eucalyptus branches, like the American Indians must have done, using twine to combine the various pieces until the fabric completely enveloped the tripod. And using the pictures from our history books, Dad painted Indian symbols in oils on the outside of the teepee. Finished, he anchored the teepee in the ground and let us sleep outdoors during the rare hot summer nights in Linda Mar Valley.

Gary and I were so excited—*we were real Indians sleeping in our teepee out on the Great American Plains.*

Dad also painted two individual portraits of Gary and me in warbonnets (though we felt we didn't look very Indian-like because he had us smiling, and Indians were always portrayed as very stoic). We were in the center of the paintings, and on each side, flanking us, was an Indian on horseback: one was a medicine man dressed in a breechcloth and a buffalo hat with two horns; the other was in a full warbonnet and dressed in deerskin leggings, his spear and shield draped along the side of his Appaloosa. Below our group, off in the distance, a US cavalry troop was making its way through the hills, and the Indians were looking down at those men and pointing. It was fantastic. I still have mine, which I cut into sections. I framed each Indian, and they hang in my master bedroom in Sag Harbor. I wish I had kept the whole painting as one, but it was just too large to hang anywhere.

Though my brother got most of Dad's artistic talent, I love to draw. At least I used to before professional baseball. When I retire from announcing, I'll pick it up again.

One thing I've discovered is that lots of artistic people like baseball. Like at Elaine's. It was just a great place to hang out—the people were so interesting. The restaurant was up on 88th and Second Avenue. When Elaine started it in the '60s, a literary crowd came in there. They were all aspiring guys—George Plimpton, Gay Talese, Norman Mailer, Kurt Vonnegut—and they were all broke. All these names. She let them eat, and they paid her when they could, so she developed this long-standing loyal following. The food was never the greatest, but nobody cared—it was all about the crowd. Established actors, screen-writers, choreographers, writers—you name it. It was their hangout, and it was phenomenal.

And I found that a lot of the "artists in residence" wanted to talk to me as much as I wanted to talk to them. So it was a good quid pro quo: baseball for art.

My good friend Bobby Zarem, the most famous publicist in New York, was responsible for introducing me around. Bobby knew everyone in the arts. I remember going with Bobby to a rescreening of *Lawrence of Arabia* at the old Ziegfeld Theatre. Peter O'Toole and David Lean, the film's director, were there, and we sat with them afterward at the party back at Elaine's. I asked Peter, "What did you think of the film?" And he goes, "You know, I've never watched the film." And I go, "No!" And he goes, "I don't watch my films. I must say, T. E. Lawrence was a very interesting character..." And I'm thinking, *You gotta be kiddin' me*.

So here I am, little Keith from Pacifica, California, sitting down at a table with David Lean and Peter O'Toole, and they're talking about making the film. Peter said, "I hated those fucking camels. It was so hard on my ass. I had to put about six inches of foam padding on it, on the top of the saddle."

And I sat with Elia Kazan one night. He occasionally came into Elaine's and one time he called me over. Huge baseball fan. He just started talking about all his films. James Dean, when they did *East of Eden*. Raymond Massey. It was incredible. I would sit there, just listening to these people go.

One of the most memorable times was meeting Plácido Domingo, after the one opera I've ever been to at the Met. Not exactly my favorite kind of music (I can't even remember which opera it was), but Bobby took me backstage after the show to meet Plácido. We walked in, and he was sitting on his chair like a king on a throne. He screamed across the room: "Keith! I am so sorry. I sang like a .230 hitter tonight. I have a cold. I promise you, next time I sing like you, a .300 hitter." So he was just a piece of work, and evidently a baseball fan.

My cell phone buzzes next to my computer.

It's Jo Craven McGinty from the *Wall Street Journal*. We'd set up the morning call, but I'd sort of forgotten about it. She's writing a Behind the Numbers column about Joe DiMaggio's fifty-six-game hitting streak. It's the seventy-fifth anniversary of the streak, and she wants to know if I think the record will ever be broken.

"Well, if anybody could have done it, it would have been Pete Rose," I say. "Tenacious as he was." But Pete stopped at forty-four, and now I don't think anyone will do it. It's not an impossibility, I explain to McGinty, but I think Joe's record is safe. Rose got as far as he did despite what was, at the time, extensive media coverage—the TV networks rearranging their nightly programming so folks at home could follow Rose's at-bats. And who knows? Maybe the attention wore even him down.

Imagine what it would be like in today's game, where if a player makes it to just twenty-eight games—halfway there—the twenty-four-hour, can't-even-buy-gas-without-a-screen-in-your-face media kicks into high gear. Pete didn't have to deal with Twitter, Instagram, and Facebook. There wasn't even *SportsCenter*! It was the dark ages, comparatively, and I'm not sure any person could stay relaxed in today's bright spotlight for the two months it would take to break the record.

McGinty and I talk for about ten more minutes. She's wondering if any changes in the game over the past seventy-five years—specifically, the increases in travel and league size, the number of pitchers faced, and the types of pitches they throw—

might also prevent the record from being broken. She's got a point on all of these, but there's also a flip side to consider with each one.

Regarding the increase in travel, what's the difference between today's six-hour flight to L.A. from New York and the 1930s six-hour train ride to Boston? And with the level of wealth and extravagance in today's game, you could make the argument that Joe DiMaggio's travel time was a more "roughing it" experience. I mean when I was coming up, the old-timers thought we were living in the lap of luxury, and compared to their day, I guess we were. Imagine what they would say about today's players with their concierge lifestyle, prescribed diets, million-dollar training rooms, huge clubhouses, and, in Atlanta's new SunTrust Park, a "quiet room" and a "sleep room" with bunk beds—*I would have loved that after staying out late on a Saturday night!*

But players didn't have three time zones to travel until 1958, when the California teams came on line. And the schedule for today's players, with seven teams out west and interleague play, is far more grueling than ever before. There's a lot of back-and-forth. In the days of two divisions, we made two trips to the West Coast a year, each trip stretching to ten days so we would acclimate to Pacific time. Now players may make four or five short coast-to-coast trips a year. Even for me, a guy who just picks his nose up in the booth, it's taxing.*

When you had two divisions, there was better continuity

---

* It's always easier to travel west and play, but coming back *is a bear*. Even if you get the much-needed off day after traveling, it takes two days to really recover. When I was playing for the Mets, I always felt sluggish that first game back after a trip out west. Former Angels third baseman Doug DeCinces told me that every time the Angels traveled east, they would open in Yankee Stadium. They would play a night game first, but the Yankees' owner, George Steinbrenner, would always schedule the second game during the day. Why? He knew the Angels would be on fumes, and the Yankees would kick their butts.

because the teams played each other more frequently and in quicker succession. And as a hitter, it was nice to see the same pitcher within a week or ten days because the previous encounter was fresh in your mind. But today, that continuity is gone: you can have the Dodgers' ace Clayton Kershaw throw a three-hit shutout in L.A. and then you don't play the Dodgers again for a month and a half. Well, that stinks. Without all this expansion and interleague play, you might see Kershaw just ten days later on a home stand.

So, yes, all these new teams and expanded bullpens mean more pitchers faced, and there's less familiarity for hitters to know what's coming at them. I buy that 100 percent. I would rather face a good starter with his best stuff going that night in four at-bats than have to face four pitchers.[*]

The increase in the *types of pitches* thrown is perhaps the strongest argument for an untouchable fifty-six. Stan Musial, who faced a diet of fastballs, curveballs, and changeups through most of his career, was on his way out of the league when pitchers started throwing the slider, and he admitted that the pitch made it harder to succeed as a batter. I've said many times on the air that if there ever was a serious upset in the balance of power between pitchers and hitters in MLB, it was when the slider was introduced. Why? Because it was the first time pitchers had a breaking ball that was close to the speed of their fastball, making it difficult for hitters to pick up. During my career, we were all

---

[*] But what's the quality of those relievers? Again, with the four-team expansion in the '90s came a long-term watering down of the talent pool, and with talks of future expansion always floating around, it's a consideration that probably isn't going away. So you could make the argument that while Joe DiMaggio (and, later, Pete Rose) faced fewer pitchers over the course of fifty-six games than a batter would face today, he was going against the cream of the crop more often. Not to beat a dead horse, but Rose and DiMaggio also weren't swinging for the fences every at-bat.

adjusting to the split-finger fastball, which was introduced and perfected by Bruce Sutter, then a closer with the Chicago Cubs and a future Hall of Famer. That particular pitch enabled otherwise average pitchers, like the Giants' Mike LaCoss, to become much more formidable foes. It made the Astros' Mike Scott a Cy Young winner. In today's game, the *pitch du jour* is the "circle change," a five-finger pitch with the thumb and index finger forming a circle around the inside half of the ball, which can be lethal because it looks so much like a fastball coming out of the pitcher's hand. So it's true that each time pitchers put a new arrow in their quiver, hitters have their hands full.

But, again, hitters adjust. When I was with the Mets, I faced a left-hander for the Cardinals named Greg Mathews for the first time, and he threw me a high changeup inner half.

Wait, what's this? A lefty throwing a left-handed batter a changeup?

That strategy just wasn't around in my day. The pitch jammed me in on the hands and I hit a weak ground ball to the second baseman. As I ran to first base, I thought, *Okay, it's a new pitch. What did I do wrong, and what do I have to do to counter it the next time I face this guy?* As a batter seeing something for the first time, that thought process instantly starts churning, and you begin to figure out how to combat it. I did the same thing with the split-finger, and Musial did the same thing with the slider.

Ted Williams, who, like Musial, left the game as the slider was coming in, was asked if he could have still hit .400 against pitchers armed with the slider, and he said, "I would've learned to hit it." And that's exactly what good hitters do. We adapt. Whether or not that means it's tougher now to hit in fifty-six consecutive games, I don't know. But I do know that hitters find their counterpunches: I mean it's not like after the introduction of the slider or the split-finger, hitters stopped hitting over .300, right?

The one disadvantage for today's hitters that the reporter failed to mention is the players being *bombarded* with too much statistical information to put together a fifty-six-game hitting streak. These hitting charts, bar graphs, and stat tables—it's all useful information, but as I mentioned before, there's that point when it reaches paralysis by analysis. I have to laugh every time there's a pitching change and I see the hitting coach bring out his big binder to show the batter what the new pitcher likes to throw and when. It's all this "He throws 30 percent breaking balls on a 2-and-0 count and 16 percent fastballs away on full counts." I feel this is overkill for these batters, who, the last time I checked, were baseball players, not engineers working for NASA with degrees from MIT.

The reason the batter's getting paid a lot of money isn't because he's got a genius IQ; it's because he has split-second reaction time that allows him to do what is almost theoretically impossible: hit a baseball slung by a man with a cannon for an arm who's just sixty feet six inches away and is motivated to not allow a hit. That's tough stuff, so "Don't think too much, stupid."

When I played, I was known as a thinking man's hitter, and it's true: I would go up there with a plan and could be fastidious in my approach. *But a player can overdo it,* and if I were a coach today, I'd throw half of that statistical stuff out and tell the players to rely more on these two sources of information: *their eyes and ears.*

It's amazing what we can pick up when we get our heads out of the data for a moment and *let our senses soak in the game* right before us. For example, the pitcher I faced the most during my career was Hall of Famer Steve Carlton. Against him, I hit .321 with 17 walks in 154 plate appearances. The key to that success was my paying attention to *how Carlton faced my teammates*. Steve always tried to "extend the strike zone"—getting the hitter to swing at his nasty slider that, at first, looked like a strike but scooted well off the plate just before it arrived. Carlton would feed that slider in the same location the entire game as if it were spit out of a computer. That's the kind of command he had, and because it looked so enticing every time, a lot of very good hitters consistently took the bait. My Cardinals teammate Garry Templeton was a prime example. I would be in the on-deck circle and watch Carlton cast his spell on Tempy, who just couldn't lay off.

Well, if Tempy, who, along with Darryl Strawberry, was one of the most talented hitters I ever played with, couldn't lay off that pitch, I sure as heck better.[*] So I had to discipline myself not to swing—*Don't take the bait!*—forcing Carlton to grab more of the strike zone with his slider. (Easier said than done. Because Steve was also a *power* pitcher, who just happened to throw 90 percent sliders. That's kind of a paradox—most breaking-ball pitchers are not power pitchers.)

When it comes to gathering information, I would also tell hitters to talk more with other players—even players on other teams. *Ask* them questions and *listen* to what they have to say.

I remember Lou Brock told me once that when Steve Rogers came up pitching for Montreal in 1973, everyone in the league

---

[*] Like me, Templeton faced Carlton more than any other pitcher over his career (.261 in 111 at-bats). Interestingly, Tempy had more success against Steve after being traded to the Padres in 1982, where he saw Steve less frequently. As a Cardinal, Tempy hit just .205, striking out 15 percent of the time, in 78 at-bats against Carlton, but as a Padre, he hit an extremely impressive .394 in 33 at-bats and reduced his strikeout rate to 12 percent. So despite becoming less familiar with Carlton, Tempy obviously figured out how to lay off his nasty slider.

was trying to figure him out.[*] The right-handed Rogers had really good stuff—a great curveball, cutter, sinker, and a straight fastball—and he knew how and when to use all of them. Lou, *who hadn't faced Rogers yet,* started looking in the papers every time Rogers pitched and noticed that Rogers was throwing three-hitters, two-hitters, four-hitters, but *not* striking many batters out. The ball was being put in play, yet Rogers was walking away with shutouts.

Being the curious player Lou was, this piqued his interest, and he went to Billy Williams, the Hall of Fame left fielder for the Cubs, who'd faced Rogers. Like Lou, Billy was a left-handed hitter, and Billy told Lou that Rogers predominantly liked to go outside—that he could paint the outside corner with his outstanding curveball and nasty hard sinker. "He will pitch inside to keep you honest, but his bread and butter is the outside corner." Well, that explained the lack of strikeouts: Rogers wasn't overpowering guys, but he threw hard enough to keep them honest, and he knew how to pitch to contact. For lefties, that meant a lot of weak "rollover" ground balls to the right side of the infield.

So a few days later, Lou and the Cardinals finally faced Rogers, and when Lou got into the box, he crowded the plate, almost sitting on top of it. Why would he do this? To take the outside corner away from Rogers and make him pitch inside. Well, most pitchers don't like to pitch inside for a living—they get paranoid they're going to either hit the batter or leave one out over the middle of the plate—and Rogers was no exception. That adjustment on the fly gave Lou, who hit .358 in 67 career at-bats against Rogers, the upper hand against one of the game's more dominant pitchers.

---

[*] Rogers was second in Rookie of the Year balloting in 1973, posting a 10–5 record with a 1.54 ERA.

Maybe a player like Brock, ever a student of the game, would have made the same deduction about Rogers with pie charts and graphs. But it's a lot of information to sift through in a very sterile, static learning environment, and despite all the headphones and video games in today's youth culture, we are all still social creatures. Our minds better process information when we're interactive—even if it's just watching our teammates from the on-deck circle, or through conversation with our hitting brethren around the batting cage.

Of course, any knowledge you bring into the batter's box—be it from experience or pie charts—isn't going to tell you nearly as much as what you'll learn once you've stepped in and seen a couple of pitches. That's why I took the first pitch in almost every first at-bat over my career.[*] I wanted to gauge in that first at-bat the quality of the pitcher's stuff on that particular day or night, in that particular inning. *How hard is he throwing? What kind of movement? How sharp is his breaking ball?* In a perfect world, the pitcher would miss on his first pitch, usually a fastball. *Okay, now I'm 1–0, and I can take another pitch in the hope that he'll throw a different pitch.* Then, if he missed with that one, I would be 2–0, a hitter's count, and would have seen his fastball *and* breaking ball.

Ready to swing the bat.

Of course, that's the best-case scenario. Because if the pitcher threw a strike on his first pitch, I had to get to hitting. Maybe I hadn't seen his breaking ball, but at 0–1 I no longer had the luxury of taking another pitch. (Still, I was willing to go 0–2 in the count if necessary. Say the pitcher then came

---

[*] The only time I swung at a first pitch in my first at-bat was if I was red-hot and had runners in scoring position. But most of the time, even when I was red-hot, I took the first pitch.

with a "bastard" pitch, catching a piece of the black that I couldn't handle. Then it's two-strike hitting, and I was a good two-strike hitter.[*])

And hitters have to accept that sometimes they just won't have much information before pulling the trigger. Countless times I came up with the game on the line, with a reliever on the mound, and maybe I was familiar with him, maybe I wasn't, but I didn't have the luxury of taking a strike to gauge him. *I just have to go up there and see the ball and hit it.* If I'd made it more complicated than that, I would have frozen up. Instead, I trusted my eye at the plate and did what my dad had taught me as a kid: fall back on primordial instincts.

Dig in, growl, and hiss, recognizing the crisis of the situation, and say, "They're going to have to kill me if they want to get me out," and fight to the last breath.

In those sorts of do-or-die moments—and I'm sure both Rose and DiMaggio ran into many of them over the course of their respective streaks—there is no place for overcomplicated analysis.

Instead, rely on those multimillion-dollar reflexes, and see the ball, hit it.

It's like what Frank Robinson told me in his office when he was managing the Expos and I was just getting started in the booth: "They have got to throw it over the plate, Keith. I don't

---

[*] Albert Pujols once asked Stan Musial the definition of two-strike hitting. Stan's answer was "a great knowledge of the strike zone." *Absolutely!* Why? If a pitcher has you 0–2, you are in trouble. The hurler has pitches to waste, and most will attempt to get you to chase something out of the strike zone. *Don't fall for the bait!* If you have a good eye at the plate and don't chase those bad pitches, you can extend the count closer to your favor.

care what they got. Trick pitch? Illegal pitch? They've got to throw it over the plate."

Moments after Frank said that, a young intern from the GM's office entered Frank's office with about a *two-inch* stack of daily stat sheets. When the kid left, Frank picked out around fifteen pages and then turned to me and said, "Keith, here's what I think about the rest of this," and he threw the remainder in the garbage.

CHAPTER 32

Long Island

I'M OFF THE PHONE with the reporter, but I'm still thinking about DiMaggio and Rose. *What is it that allows a man to hit safely in fifty-six straight games, like Joe, or forty-four games, like Pete?*

A little luck, certainly, but it's no coincidence that those two men were also two of the most consistent players of all time.[*] Rose is the all-time leader with 4,256 hits (talk about a record that may never be broken), and DiMaggio's lifetime average was .325, despite taking three years "off" during World War II to serve in the army.[†] To accomplish these tremendous feats, each man just didn't have too many enduring slumps.

Streak or no streak, such fortitude is what we should

---

[*] A bleeder through the infield, or a bloop single off the end of the bat, and the streak stays alive. But the converse is also true. The day DiMaggio's streak was snapped, he hit the ball hard in every at-bat—but right at 'em. And the night Rose's streak ended, on national television with 31,000 Braves fans on their feet, the Atlanta hurlers pitched Pete as if it were the seventh game of the World Series, and Gene Garber, who ended Rose's streak (and the game) with a strikeout, celebrated as such when the game ended.

[†] More impressively, DiMaggio's career strikeouts (369) are almost identical to his career home runs (361). That nearly exact one-to-one ratio is the lowest in history of anyone with more than 300 home runs. Add his career doubles (389) and triples (181) to the mix, and the man was two and a half times more likely to get an extra-base hit than he was to strike out.

marvel at: not only to have the ability and skill to do something difficult—like hit a baseball slung by a major league pitcher—but also to do it consistently over such a long period of time.

I can tell you firsthand that even approaching that sort of consistency is extremely difficult, and just because I'd made the necessary adjustments to major league pitching by the end of 1976, that didn't mean I would be able to succeed against it game by game, week by week, month by month, year by year. In 1977, my first season in the bigs as a full-time regular, I hit .291 with 91 RBI—a good season, but not .300. The following season, 1978, I fell apart after the All-Star break and finished the year at .255 with 64 RBI.

KH BATTING PROGRESS (BY SEASON)

Year	Games (G)	At-Bats (AB)	Batting Average (BA)	On-Base Percentage (OBP)	Slugging Percentage (SLG)
1974	14	34	.294	.415	.441
1975	64	188	.250	.309	.362
1976	129	374	.289	.376	.428
1977	161	560	.291	.379	.459
1978	159	542	.255	.351	.389

It made no sense!* I was young, healthy, and playing every day. So things should have gone smoother. Sure, sometimes pitchers would try new tactics, but nothing fooled me for long. I just wasn't able to play at a high level *consistently*.

Why? I don't have the answers. Maybe the second-half rut of 1978 was a sophomore jinx. (Dad said I was feeling for the ball. He was probably right, but I didn't want to hear that.) It was yet another shot at my confidence. Maybe players like Rose and DiMaggio didn't need help in that department, but evidently I still did. Where would I get it? Thankfully, fate stepped in and dealt me a good hand, and once again, it was Ken Boyer coming to the rescue.

And so I'm sitting at the kitchen table, about to leave to visit my friend Paton, and despite my best intentions to take the rest of the day away from the game, I'm lost in another one of its memories. Something that happened years ago, and, as time passed, would be the turning point in my career:

May 6, 1979

Airplane rides in the major leagues can be pretty fun. I'm on one now, traveling 600 miles an hour from St. Louis to Houston. The team is in good spirits. That afternoon we won the rubber match against the venerable Pirates, 4–2. With studs like reigning MVP and two-time batting champ Dave Parker, and seven-time All-Star Willie Stargell, the Pirates are the club to beat this year. After that good win and heading into a day off tomorrow, the guys are letting loose a bit. There's a lot of card games and bantering. And a lot of beer.

---

* Maybe I pressed. I'm sure I did. As a team, with only twelve clubs in the NL, we ranked last in on-base percentage and on-base plus slugging, eleventh in runs per game (3.7), tenth in runs (600), ninth in batting average (.249) and home runs (79). Offensively, we stunk it up.

But I don't feel like cutting loose. I can't. Because I'm off to a bad start—another hole in April that I've dug for myself.

Are you kidding me? I'm twenty-four years old now—I can't afford this!

Back in '76, I got benched after a lousy April. Now, three years later, it's happening again. Today, against the Pirates, I had a good day at the plate. I went 3 for 4 with an RBI.

Great. My average jumped from a putrid .216 to a still-putrid .237. But beyond the numbers, there's something else: my swing feels off.

"I still don't feel comfortable yet," I told the reporters after the game. Because I am a perfectionist and a worrier (always have been and always will be). And I am obsessed with my swing. To be overcritical of your swing is like being overcritical of the very way you breathe. And when I question it, tinker with it, dream about it, pray about it, curse it, beg it . . . that one simple thing becomes a maze and chokes me off. That's what I'd meant when I told the reporter, "I still don't feel comfortable yet." I'm suffocating, dammit!

Years later, a manager of mine will understand my torment and say that if Keith Hernandez didn't worry about his swing so much, he'd have a good chance to hit .400.

The plane levels out, and the flight attendant brings me a Michelob. I take a long sip. Half the beer is gone before I open my eyes again.

My swing is off . . . *It keeps repeating inside my head. My nemesis—I will only be satisfied with it when I'm red-hot. But that seems unlikely, because now we're heading to the Astrodome, where I'm just 8 for 52 in my career.*[*]

---

[*] I despised the Astrodome. Maybe I still had in the back of my mind those powerful San Francisco Giants teams of the mid-1960s and how many

I take a second pull from the beer. The flight attendant brings another round.

This year is of immense importance to my status as a major league player. The past two seasons I had been Jekyll and Hyde. After tearing up the second half of '76, the '77 season had been a breakout year. I had finally gotten off to a much-needed good start (no hole to dig out from) and finished the year at .291, 15 home runs, and 91 RBI.[*]

But not so fast, Mr. Hernandez. The next season, '78, I'd had a good first half but then fell apart in the second half, hitting a paltry .228 with only 21 RBI. The only good thing that had happened was winning my first Gold Glove Award for fielding excellence.

Big deal. Stargell hasn't won a Gold Glove and he's in his eighteenth season, a sure Hall of Famer. Pittsburgh's Herculean first baseman had mercifully sat out today's game, and there, spitting seeds on the Pirates' bench that afternoon, he had looked as relaxed and happy as a man at a country club. A year away from forty and he's hitting .333.

Yet I know that my glove is keeping me in the lineup.

---

times their pennant hopes were dashed in September because of their inability to win there. The Giants hitters always complained how the Dome had a bad backdrop, which created what Mays and McCovey called a problem with "depth perception." Most stadiums have a black or dark-green wall over the center-field fence so the hitter can distinguish the white ball coming out of the pitcher's hand. The Dome had no such black wall. It was just this big, wide area that drifted deeper into nothingness toward a service entrance, some fifty yards behind the center-field fence. It was like some deep, dark, mysterious cavern that could have been a perfect prop for Gandalf and Frodo of *The Lord of the Rings* to enter at their own peril. Like the ancient Mines of Moria. And if you took extra BP in Houston, always at three or four in the afternoon, those service doors were wide-open, and the daylight from the outside would come spilling in, directly behind the center-field fence. It was like hitting into a setting sun. Brutal.

[*] An 0-for-21 skid over 7 games in August cost me a .300 batting average and maybe a 100 RBI season.

Our manager, Kenny Boyer, had said as much to the press during the previous home series against the West-leading Astros. I'd gone 0 for 5 in the first game, while in the second game Roger Freed had come off the bench and launched a game-winning grand slam in the bottom of the eleventh. "Any chance you'll give Freed a couple of starts at first base?" some press members had asked.

Boyer had stuck by me, answering, "Freed realizes his role as a pinch hitter...Hernandez is so good defensively at first that I can't take him out, even when he's in a slump at bat."*

My dad had drummed into my head as a kid that if you excelled defensively, the manager would be less inclined to bench you when you were in a prolonged slump. Well, Boyer probably shudders at the thought of Roger Freed's glove "handling" our infielders, especially hard-throwing shortstop Garry Templeton. Last season, Tempy, who's a bit loose with his throws, made forty errors at short, and my "golden" glove must have prevented twenty more.† So the Cardinals—and the St. Louis writers, who'd lobbied for that Gold Glove largely because of my adventures with Tempy's freewheeling style—were well aware of how important my skills were at first base.

Still, the day after Boyer's comments, I went 0 for 2, and the press descended on my locker. I survived the inquiry, mostly by agreeing with them. "First base has got to be a productive position," I said. "If you're not helping on offense,

---

* *St. Louis Post-Dispatch*, May 2, 1979.

† Templeton threw from over the top, which made his ball rise and run either to the left or right. Plus, even when he was on top of me, coming in on a slow roller, Tempy still liked to show off his incredibly strong arm, and I didn't have much time to react. As electrifying as he was to watch make plays, I still have nightmares about some of the throws.

you're not doing your job. And batting no. 3—that guy's gotta hit."*

I tried to come across as confident, like I was weathering the storm, saying:

"The pitcher is out there doing the best job he can, and I'm sure not going to help him any if I'm upset about my hitting"
and

"It's a team effort and I have to contribute the same as always on the field"
and

"If I'm in a slump, I just wipe it out of my mind."

What a load of crap! I can't just wipe it out of my mind, because I know that in the big leagues, shortstop and catcher are the only positions where managers can afford to keep a guy in the lineup just for his defense. First basemen are hitters, and sooner or later the team will reshuffle the deck.

The second beer is gone, replaced by a third.

And, yeah, sure, maybe my glove is keeping me in the lineup. But I don't want to be just another major league player. I want to be a Mickey Mantle. I want to be a star. My dreams, ever since I was a kid, were lofty. And I grew up a Cardinals fan. The uniform means a lot. I understood "Cardinals Pride" since day one, even before they drafted me and I thought, Holy cow, there's twenty-six teams and I get drafted by the Cardinals, the team I love!

So what? Lots of people have big dreams. When it comes down to it, maybe you're just a .250 hitter . . .

I close my eyes again—anything to slow down the train running at full steam inside my head. Keep this up and

---

* *St. Louis Post-Dispatch,* May 3, 1979.

275

you'll never climb out of this. You're your own worst enemy...

When I open my eyes, I notice Ken Boyer strolling toward the rear of the plane. The same man who was my manager in Tulsa in '74 and '75 when I was "wearing it out," and who took over the Cardinals last season. Now Boyer is making his way from first class, and he doesn't stop to chat with anyone until he's next to my seat.

He leans over to me and says, "Nice hitting today," referring to my 3-for-4 at the plate.

I say, "Thank you," and want to ask, Hey, Skip, any chance we can tell the pilot to go somewhere else — any place other than Houston and the lousy Astrodome? *Instead I take another long sip, and Boyer starts talking again.*

"I've seen you hit, Keith, and I know that you are something special. I knew that back in Tulsa. And I'm telling you right now that you are my first baseman. You'll be in the lineup every day, even if it costs me my job. So stop worrying. Go out there and have fun, and do the things on the field I know you're capable of doing." Finished, Boyer pats me on the arm, smiles, and moves on.

The next game, I'm in the Astrodome, facing Ken Forsch. I go 4 for 4, scoring a run in the 4–1 victory. My swing feels like a well-oiled machine. I'm no longer suffocating. I'm breathing.

I stand up from the table. It's been almost forty years since that plane flight, when Boyer came to my rescue. They were the most important words spoken to me over my career. Without them, I think maybe I wouldn't have made it in the big leagues. Who knows?

I glance at the digital clock above the stove (out of the game this long, but my eyes are still like a hawk's). Time to meet up with my friend Paton. But before going out, I walk into the guest bedroom and head to the closet. I turn on the light, and there, tucked in the corner, is the Silver Bat Award I got for winning the batting title that year, 1979. I should put it up on the wall with the artwork, but it's so damn heavy—it's pure silver.* Still, I need to get around to buying or constructing a wall mount.

I guess I've been saying that for a while now.

---

* I believe 1979 was the last year the bat contained a large amount of silver. After that, I heard, they were silver-plated only. I could be wrong, but my Silver Bat is darn heavy.

CHAPTER 33

MY SUCCESS IN 1979 was catalyzed by two events.

One was the confidence booster from manager Kenny Boyer on the airplane—"You are my first baseman." *No matter what.* The second actually took place *a year earlier,* during a conversation with none other than the Reds' Pete Rose. Along with the Pirates' Willie Stargell, the Phillies' Dick Allen, and the Dodgers' Steve Garvey, Pete was often very encouraging to me during my early years when I struggled, despite being a rival player. He would land on first base and say things like "I like the way you swing the bat, Hernandez. You keep going the way you're going, and you'll be just fine." On this particular occasion in 1978, the Reds were in town, and I'd had a decent series so far. Pete was hanging around the batting cage, and he watched me take a couple of rounds of BP.

"Keith! You can hit!" he exclaimed as I exited the cage.

Wait, what? Pete Rose *is saying that to me? Wow!*

"Shoot, you're a .300 hitter, Keith!" he said. "And that's the goal, isn't it? To hit .300?"

"Sure," I said to Pete, who'd hit .300 or better in *thirteen* of the past fourteen seasons.

"Well, some guys make that tougher than it really is, Keith.

You just gotta remember that baseball is every day over six months. That's a heck of a long time. You can't worry about your average on a day-to-day or even on a week-to-week basis. *It will drive you nuts.* Instead, think in terms of every 100 at-bats, which is about a month's worth of work."

I nodded. A full-time player got about 600 at-bats a year, depending on how often he walked and where he was in the lineup. So, yeah, 600 divided by a 6-month season was 100 at-bats a month.

Pete continued. "Now, 30 hits per 100 at-bats is a .300 average. So what's 30 multiplied by 6?"

I replied, "180."

"Right! So in 600 at-bats, 180 hits is .300 on the season. Now, what's 25 multiplied by 6?"

"150."

Pete nodded. "What's *that* batting average?"

".250, Pete."

"Precisely. The difference between a .250 hitter and a .300 hitter is 30 hits. Think about that: 30 hits spread out over the 600 ABs in a season is what separates the average from the great. That's less than one additional hit every five games! Now, think of all those at-bats you give away in the course of a season, like those last at-bats in a blowout game in the eighth or ninth. *Never give those at-bats away!* If you have 2 hits, you want 3; if you have 3, you want 4."

This all made perfect sense to me. *Don't let any at-bats go to waste—it might be that extra hit!*

Then Pete expounded, "If you hit .320 in the first 100 at-bats, you only have to get 28 in the next round to still be hitting .300. But *never* settle for that, Keith. Keep building your chips so after the fourth 100 you're playing with house money."

Pete Rose's words of wisdom—to break down the season per

100 at-bats—may sound obvious, but a simple outlook can be tough to practice if you're struggling like I was in 1978. I was just too anxious and uncertain to put Pete's words to good use. It wasn't until 1979—after Boyer's assuring me that I'd be in the lineup every day—that I settled down enough to digest the season per Pete's prescription.

In my first 100 at-bats of 1979, I got 22 hits—8 short of the goal of 30 (remember: 30 hits per 100 at-bats equals a .300 average). So, accordingly, my goal for the next 100 at-bats was the prescribed 30 hits plus 8 more to make up for those first 100 at-bats. That was a tall order, but I was just beginning that second set when Boyer had his chat with me on the airplane, and instead of 38 hits, I got 40, including one stretch where I was 20 for 43. That was more like it! Now, to maintain my .300, I only had to get 28 hits for my *third* set of 100 at-bats. But remember, Pete had said, "Be greedy." So once again I exceeded my quota, getting 34 hits and raising my season average to a fairly awesome .321.

Quite a turnaround.* What's more, I was killing both righties *and* lefties, and driving in runs at a monstrous clip: forty-one in fifty-five games. I couldn't wait to get to the ballpark every day.

Unfortunately, the team was headed in the opposite direction. Tied with the Expos for first place on June 11, 1979, we began the first trip of the season to California: Dodger town, San Francisco, and San Diego. We won the first game in L.A., but then proceeded to lose the next seven of eight. I stayed hot at the plate, going 17 for 38, and was now hitting .331 for the season. That was good enough for the sixth-best batting

---

* Since Boyer's talk, I'd batted .392 (47 for 120) with 5 HRs, 25 RBI, a .455 OBP, and an off-the-charts 1.064 OPS. Smokin'!

average in the NL, behind Pete Rose (.358), Dave Winfield (.354), Lee Mazzilli (.343), my teammate George Hendrick (.339), and George Foster (.332). But that early in the season, who cares? All I knew was that I was incredibly hot, in the top ten in batting average, and I wanted to help my team win more ball games.

After the West Coast disaster, we limped home in fourth place and then dropped 8 of 14 against the Mets, Expos, Phillies, and Pirates. We were a promising outfit—rebuilding since yet another disastrous season in '78, when we'd finished 74–88—but we just weren't ready for prime time against the more seasoned teams. By the All-Star break, we were taking our lumps (but were only six and a half games back, in fifth place).

But I was still going steady at .325, batting .356 (89 for 250) with 43 RBI, 27 extra-base hits, and a .961 OPS since May 1. In fact, the only hitters hotter from May through the break were the Padres' Dave Winfield and the Phillies' Mike Schmidt. Winfield, whose .331 average, 22 home runs, and 72 RBI made for one of the best first halves in baseball history, and Schmidt, who was on pace to hit 55 home runs that season,[*] were clear early favorites for National League MVP and two of the highest vote getters for the 1979 MLB All-Star Game.[†]

I, on the other hand, wasn't voted to the All-Star team. *How is that possible?* Three reasons: Steve Garvey, Pete Rose, and Willie Stargell. These first basemen were superstars, former MVPs with *twenty-six* National League All-Star selections between them. And though not as strong as mine, their first

---

[*] Thirty-one home runs at the break.

[†] The first "half" of the MLB season is actually longer than the second, as the All-Star break falls a few games or so *into* the last 81 games (there are 162 games in each season). In 1979, the break came after game 86, leaving 76 games left to play.

halves had all been solid: Garvey, "Mr. Clutch," had hit exactly .316 in each of the first three months of the season; Rose had cooled off a bit after a hot start but was still batting .304 at the break;[*] and Stargell, who didn't make the All-Star cut that year, was enjoying a .306, 18 home run, 41 RBI first half in just 51 starts. So imagine baseball fans sitting down in major league ballparks across the country, filling out their All-Star ballots, and seeing those three guys as first base candidates along with their home team's first baseman. Then add my name to the mix. Outside of St. Louis, I'm sure the only consideration I got, if any, was *Who in the hell is Keith Hernandez?* Hence, I was left off the showcase's twenty-five-man roster,[†] and I resigned myself to spending the three off days at home. Was I disappointed? *Hell yes!* It wasn't going to be easy to break through that Garvey-Rose-Stargell ceiling.

Things changed, however, when I got an unexpected 10 a.m. phone call. We were back in Houston, playing the Astros for a final three-game series before the break. *Who's calling me at this hour?* I dragged the phone receiver across the hotel sheets to my ear and said a groggy hello.

It was John Claiborne, Bing Devine's replacement as the Cardinals' GM. "Congratulations, Keith!" he said. "You made the All-Star team."

Wow! Maybe Keith Hernandez was a household name! Not exactly—the manager of the National League's team, Tommy

---

[*] Rose had batted .360 in his first 100 at bats, followed by .350 in his second 100 at bats, giving him plenty of breathing room for the following month-and-a-half-long slump when he hit just .234. In the game following the break, Pete would go 0 for 4, dropping his average to .301. But he would go no lower the rest of the season. Typical Pete, who was a pure force of will and determination.

[†] Set in 1939, the twenty-five-man roster increased to thirty in 1982, thirty-two in 2003, thirty-three in 2009, and its current number, thirty-four, in 2010.

Lasorda, had chosen me to replace an injured Dave Kingman on the roster.*

Later that afternoon, after Claiborne's phone call, Rick Hummel of the *St. Louis Post-Dispatch* asked if I planned to accept the invitation and head to Seattle for the game. "I'll go and I'll enjoy it," I told Rick, who wanted to know if I felt "slighted at all by being picked on the rebound." But I meant what I'd said, and bouncing back from that lousy April, I was thrilled that Lasorda, who had chosen me over Stargell, had recognized my effort.†

There was another reason I was happy to stay away from St. Louis for the break: I'd gotten married in the spring of 1978, and by 1979 the union was showing cracks in the foundation. Sue, the girl I'd spotted in the stands back in '76, and I just weren't well suited for a "baseball" marriage, in which I was more committed to my game than to her. We were able to avoid that obvious fact when I was playing ball every day. But the prospect of being stuck in the house for three days, going stir-crazy and waiting for the second half of the season to start, just wasn't my idea of a respite. (Sue did come to the All-Star Game, and we had a great time together.)

Crisis averted, for now . . .

When I flew into Seattle for the All-Star Game, the first day's

---

* Kingman was unavailable to play after being hit by a pitched ball on his left arm earlier that week in Atlanta. His comeuppance for bulldozing me in 1976! Speaking from experience, I'm sure the ball suffered more damage coming into contact with one of Kong's limbs than the other way around. Dave was out of action for ten days as a result of the hit-by-pitch but was back in action July 21, pinch-hitting for the Cubs in the ninth inning against the offending Braves to deliver the game-tying RBI and score the winning run. He would go on to be the NL home-run king that season, with forty-eight, beating out Mike Schmidt's forty-five.

† In today's game this could never happen, as managers no longer can name players to the roster, lest they be accused of "homerism" by selecting their own players and/or avoiding players from rival clubs. Sort of dumb, in my opinion.

routine was simple: head to the park, gather for a team meeting, take a few rounds of BP, and make yourself available to the media. But when you lace up your spikes in front of your locker, look up, and there's the likes of Johnny Bench, Joe Morgan, Dave Parker, Larry Bowa, Steve Garvey, Pete Rose, and Mike Schmidt, it's not just any "normal" day.

On All-Star weekend, even the guys who aren't too crazy about one another during the regular season genuinely enjoy one another's company. Take Expos All-Star catcher Gary Carter, for example. Gary had a knack for rubbing some players the wrong way during the regular season. I think it was the way he carried himself—always strutting, shoulders back, chest puffed out, and a smile you suspected was more adoration-loving than genuine. I didn't know him well, but we'd had our moments. Gary was very athletic behind the plate—he'd committed to going to UCLA out of high school as a quarterback on a full scholarship but decided on baseball instead—and I remember one game in Montreal when he ran me down, back toward third base, and tagged me out. But rather than just lay on the tag, he steamrolled me. It was completely unnecessary—like a boxer squeezing in an extra jab well after the bell. I never forgot that one. But now here was Gary, one of baseball's premier catchers, a few lockers down from me. I had tremendous respect for his game, and it was an honor to be around him and my other fellow All-Stars.

Behind the good-natured laughter and genuine camaraderie going on in the clubhouse was also a serious intent: *to win*. National League president Chub Feeney came into our clubhouse on the workout day and exhorted us to make good on his annual gentleman's bet with his American League counterpart, Lee MacPhail. He reminded us that the National League had dominated the American League the previous seven meetings and had won fifteen of the last sixteen contests. It may have been called a "showcase," but the All-Star Game was no circus act. It was a real contest where a score was kept, and I sensed that every one of my teammates wanted to be on the winning side to prove ours was the better league.

The next day, after an All-Star luncheon, where each first-timer was presented with an oil-painted portrait of himself with his team cap on,* I went to perhaps the best cocktail party in history. The drinks were good, of course, but among the guests was a who's who of the morning-paper box scores when I was a kid—baseball's titans of yesteryear. I remember talking with the legendary Ernie Banks, "Mr. Cub," when Warren Spahn strode up. Cigarette in hand, the winningest left-hander in baseball history started bustin' Ernie's chops, saying, "I used to love to play you guys. I'd look ahead in the schedule for my next start, and if it was Chicago, I'd get all excited and send a limo for your lineup."

Well, I waited for Ernie to laugh first, which he did with great joy, and I joined in.† *Somebody pinch me! I'm in absolute heaven!*

Spahn then turned to me and said, "Boy, Keith, I would've liked to have you at first base when I pitched."

"Warren," I said, "thank you very much, but you had Joe Adcock over there."

"Yeah, Joe could hit," replied Warren, "but I've never seen anyone with your glove. Plus, you can hit, too."

Holy shit! Here was Warren Spahn telling me—a twenty-five-year-old player who'd never hit .300 for a season—that I was his preferred first baseman! This is the same man I'd watched "toe

---

* And first-timers with *new* teams, so I would receive another in 1984 with a Mets cap on.

† I looked it up, and sure enough, Mr. Spahn was 49–19 with 4 saves in his career against the Cubbies. He just may have sent that limo...

the slab" and twirl a gem at Candlestick Park back in '63, when I was nine, my father remarking the whole game what a great pitcher he was.[*] Well, if that doesn't pump a player up, I don't know what will.

Bring on the American League!

I got my chance the next day, in the game's eighth inning, when Lasorda pinch-hit me with two outs after Lee Mazzilli's home run to tie the game at 6–6. I stepped into the box to face Cleveland's stopper, Jim Kern. I'd battled Jim in AAA more than a few times in my Tulsa days, so I knew he had a blazing fastball but a slider he was uncomfortable throwing to lefties. I approached this virgin All-Star at-bat as if I had two strikes on me. I was ready to swing at the first pitch. It came, a fastball about nine to twelve inches outside at the knees.

"Strike one!" yelled home-plate umpire George Maloney.

I looked back at him. "That ball's a foot outside," I said.

"Swing the bat, sonny," Maloney retorted.

Swing the bat, sonny? I couldn't have hit that pitch with a ten-foot pole!

Of course, I didn't say anything. It was my first All-Star appearance, so it wasn't like I was going to argue with the umpire on the first pitch I saw. *I'm sure he'd be delighted to throw me out of the game if I beef.* But I was fuming—*Thanks, jackass, because now, instead of 1–0, a hitter's count, I'm down a strike*—and it got the best of me and my concentration. I went down swinging on three or four pitches.

Fortunately, we won the game (and Chub Feeney won his gentleman's bet) after Mazzilli drew a walk with the bases loaded

---

[*] Spahn would return to San Francisco that same season to throw another *complete* game, this time taking the loss after giving up the game's only run in the *sixteenth*!

off Ron Guidry in the ninth. But I never forgot that big, blind umpire, Maloney.* *Too bad the San Diego Chicken, the Padres' hilarious mascot, wasn't present in his white doctor's jacket with an eye chart.*

Oh well—on to the second half of the season.

---

* Actually, I did forget Maloney, because I thought for years the home-plate ump that night was Marty Springstead, and I told the story countless times as such. So, my apologies to Marty, who passed away in 2012. To George Maloney, who died in 2003, all is forgiven. *But, for crying out loud, how could you call that pitch a strike?*

CHAPTER 34

TWO WEEKS AFTER THE All-Star break, Winfield was leading the league in hitting at .345. But if I've said it once, I've said it a thousand times: *it's a long season,* and after a dismal August, when he batted just .175, Winfield was down to .312. I kept steadily climbing, hitting .333 in July and .384 in August—good enough for NL Player of the Month—and I sat atop the league at .345. It was while playing against Winfield and the Padres, in a series that stretched into September, that I began to really think about the batting title.

We'd arrived in San Diego on a roll, taking two of three in L.A., then two of three in San Francisco. No Cardinals team had done that—won both of those series on the same road trip—since *1969. Could we finally exorcise the ghost of West Coast past?* First we had to deal with Winfield and the *three* southpaws the Padres were running out against us. In game one, Winfield reminded us that, despite the slump, he was still one of the most dangerous hitters in baseball, when he put the Padres on the board with a three-run shot in the bottom of the first. But fourteen innings later, I had the final say with a game-winning double—a bullet to left center—in the top of the *fifteenth* off lefty Bob Owchinko.

Now, that's a game-winning RBI!

I started game two with an RBI double off Randy Jones in the top of the first, and with the game tied 2–2 in the top of the seventh, I got Jones again, this time with a three-run bomb to put us ahead for good. Another game-winning RBI. I remember feeling positively on fire after that home run—like they couldn't get me out—and Mike Phillips, our backup shortstop from Texas, sat down next to me on the bench after that at-bat and asked, "Why do you take so many first pitches? You're starting off 0 and 1 most of the time. They're grooving you first-pitch fastballs."

"Mike," I said, "I'm just too nervous! I go up there all wound up. I need a pitch to settle in."

It was true: I took the first pitch almost every at-bat that whole season. I was just too unsettled to go hacking away. Instead, I'd step in the box, take a deep breath, watch the pitch, take another deep breath, and get to hitting.

"Man," Mike said with that Texas drawl, "I wish I could do that."

But that's how well I was seeing the ball: I could be down 0–1 and still have the confidence to be patient, waiting for a pitch I could drive. And if the pitcher gave it to me, I drilled it; if, instead, he put it off the plate or in the dirt, I didn't chase. The knowledge of the strike zone that my father had drummed into me was paying off. I looked fastball on every pitch that year, even if I was facing a junk-baller. Again, I had the ability throughout my career to look fastball and adjust to any and all secondary pitches.

Part of the reason I was so hot at the plate was because our cleanup hitter, Ted Simmons, was back in the lineup. Ted had started off the first two months of the season on a tear, hitting .321 with 18 home runs (season pace of 48) and a whopping 52 RBI (season pace of 152), and his strong performance had helped open the door to my big rebound in May and June, because pitchers didn't want to come after Simmons, a proven veteran and .300 clutch hitter from both sides of the plate. Instead, the pitchers would come after me, a relatively unproven 3-hole hitter, hoping they could get the out and pitch around Simmons. In short, with Simmons striking fear into the opponents, I was seeing good pitches to hit.

But those rules of engagement went out the window when Ted went on the DL on June 25 for a month and George Hendrick bumped up to the cleanup spot. George was having a tremendous year, hitting .341 with 6 home runs and 31 RBI at the time. But it wasn't Ted Simmons–like power, and more important, George wasn't a switch-hitter.

So lefties still came after me, but righties were a bit more careful, and I was seeing fewer good pitches to hit. Proof of this was in those 26 games without Ted, when I hit only .299 but walked at a much higher rate. I was still contributing at a high level—with an on-base percentage of .417, and delivering in the clutch with 16 RBI—but Ted's absence was having an effect. Upon Ted's return on July 24, opposing pitchers resumed their caution, and that meant better pitches for me to hit the rest of the way.

Well, Simmons went deep in game three against the Padres, and we swept in San Diego. I remember feeling further energized when Ted did that, because he'd been in a slump since coming back to the lineup. *If he gets hot, the team could have a really good September*. The only problem was that the Pirates weren't losing. Even after we swept the Cubs, finishing our road trip at 9–2, we picked up only a half game on Pittsburgh, and we were seven games back with less than a month to play. That was a bit of a backbreaker for us. Anything was possible, but Willie Stargell's "We Are Family" campaign in Pittsburgh was turning into a movement, galvanizing the steel town and its base-ball team, and they showed no signs of softening.

The Chicago series had been another boost for me. I went 4 for 7 in the 2 games with 2 walks and a double off Willie Hernandez, another lefty, and I finished the road trip 11 for 22 (.500!) with 3 doubles, 1 HR, and 6 RBI. I now sat "comfortably" atop the league at .348, with everyone else a good bit behind: my pitching teammates had checked Winfield, keeping him just 2 for 12 in our San Diego series, and his average dropped below .310;[*] the Braves' Bob Horner, the 1978 NL Rookie of the Year, who had put together a great month coming out of the All-Star break, batting .387 to raise his season average to .329, was now at .316; Lou Brock, who had been up to .327 on August 15, was at .314; and Garry Templeton, our Cardinals teammate, who'd batted .342 since the break, was still 22 points behind me at .326. So despite my usual anxiety before every at-bat, I felt like the batting title was within reach.

Quite a turnaround from 1978's .255.

But just when I started to feel like *Oh my goodness, I can win this thing,* Pete Rose got hot. *Red-hot.* Never allowing himself to fall below .300 on the whole year, Pete hung around .310 for most of the second half. Then he batted a ridiculous .468 in 62 at-bats from September 1 through September 16, raising his average to .327, 18 points behind my .345, with two weeks left to go.

Could he get 18 points in fourteen days? Let's quantify that: Pete would have 59 more at-bats between September 17 and the end of the season on September 30. For him to jump the 18 points to .345, he'd need 30 hits in those 59 at-bats. That's a bat-

---

[*] St. Louis pitching got the best of Winfield that season: 9 for 44 (.205 average).

ting average of a whopping .509. But there was no guarantee that I was going to keep my stats up. What if I fell into a slump during those last fourteen days of the season? Let's say I got only 10 hits in my remaining 45 at-bats—a .222 average—then my season average would drop to .336, and I would meet Pete halfway. *Gulp.*

Well, who else would come to town for a three-game series to kick off those final two weeks but the Philadelphia Phillies and their tenacious and irrepressible first baseman, Pete Rose. *Folks, I can't make this stuff up.* Here we were, master versus apprentice, sharing the same field: me watching him, him watching me, and all the reporters and fans watching us both. Our respective teams may have been out of the divisional race and squabbling for third place, but we were just as much in the national spotlight as the Pirates and Expos, who were neck and neck atop the division. *Hey, Ma and Dad, look at me! I'm in every paper across the country!* Now I was becoming a household name *not* because I was winning the race, but because I was the man "Charlie Hustle" was chasing. And it didn't hurt that Pete himself was praising my accomplishments to the reporters huddled around his locker before and after every game. Even after Pete's 3 for 4 and my 0 for 2 in game one cut the lead to just 14 points, Pete had some pretty nice things to say to about me to the press: "If .335 is going to win the title, then I think I can do it. But Hernandez is a fine hitter. I think he should be the most valuable player. Me, I don't think I should get it. I've been having the same kind of year every year."[*]

Of course, and as the papers pointed out the next day, "beneath this facade [was] a hungry man gunning for his fourth

---

[*] *St. Louis Post-Dispatch*, September 18, 1979.

batting title."* In part, Pete's flattery was intended to get me to crumble a little—nothing burdens a man like strapping on medals before he's crossed the finish line. But by then, Pete wasn't the only one offering such praise. With the St. Louis press really getting behind me, and then the national attention of the batting race, I'd started to hear my name more and more frequently in the NL MVP conversation. As Kenny Boyer pointed out numerous times to the press during those final weeks, "How [else] do you rate a player who scores 100 runs, drives in 100 runs, hits the way he does and is the best fielding first baseman in the league?"† So my play—offensively and defensively—was making a pretty good argument for the league's highest individual accolade.

But none of that was in my control. The batting title, however, was mine to lose; and with the team's divisional chances gone,‡ it was the one thing I wanted. But first, I had to withstand Pete's relentless assault, and in that second game against the Phillies, Pete was 2 for 3 while I went 0 for 4, and the race was suddenly down to just 10 points. *10 points!* The Phillies then left town, and I broke out of my mini slump, going 2 for 5 in a double-header against the Cubs, but Pete kept the pressure on from afar, as reported by the *Post-Dispatch* the following day:

The Phillies' Pete Rose continued his torrid hitting with three safeties in the two games [going 3 for 7]. He has 35 hits in his last 66 at-bats and has hit safely in his last 17 straight games. He's boosted his average from .306 to .333,

---

* *St. Louis Post-Dispatch,* September 19, 1979.
† *St. Louis Post-Dispatch,* September 23, 1979.
‡ Ten games back on September 16, we were all but mathematically eliminated. That formality would come one week later, September 22, when we were twelve games back with eleven to play.

293

nine points behind the Cardinals' Keith Hernandez in the fight for the NL batting title.[*]

Rose was like the mummy from those horror films that all kids growing up in the '50s loved but also dreaded. As a boy, I had this recurring nightmare in which I'd be running through the creek and into the woods near our house and the mummy would be chasing me—dragging one foot and limping, one arm outstretched to grab me—and no matter how fast I'd be running, I'd turn around, and that son of a bitch would be gaining on me. Well, that was Pete, and in less than a week, my 18-point lead had been cut in half!

What was that "hypothetical" number I stated previously? Pete had to hit something ridiculous, like .509, to catch me? Well, he was bettering that by 21 points, hitting .530 over that week's span, and was now *30 for 50* since September 8. *That's batting .600 for over two weeks!*[†] And what was that ridiculous *low* number to which I had to collapse in order to meet him halfway—.222? Well, I was worse than that, hitting just .214 over the previous two series.

Of course, I'm breaking this down six ways to Sunday and nearly forty years later, using newspaper articles, a calculator, and wonderful stat sites like Baseball-Reference.com. But I probably was doing some rough number crunching in my head at the time; regardless, the reporters were in my ear before *and* after every game with stat scenarios rounded off to the nearest millionth.

You have to remember what a batting title means to a player.

Historically, there are *three* coveted batting stats: home runs, runs batted in, and batting average. *The Triple Crown.* Of the three, batting average is the most prized (at least, it was before the earlier mentioned home-run craze), especially in a close race in which every at-bat counts. It gives September the air of a Kentucky Derby, and in 1979, baseball's favorite horse, Pete Rose, was the one making the late charge, bringing the grandstand to its feet.

What was my MO now? Sure, I knew where I was: 78 at-bats into my sixth set, hitting .346 for the term. But so what? There were only ten games left in the season! There was no "next 100 at-bats" to make up lost ground. If I was going to beat Pete—who was 2 for 3 on September 20 and now just 8 points behind me—I had to get hits *now*! The only problem was we were heading up to New York to face the last-place Mets and their whole batch of September call-ups.

Advantage Hernandez? I think not!

Remember what Dick Selma told me back in 1974: to keep track of what pitchers threw me. "That way, the next time you face them, you've got an idea of what might be coming down the pike." Great advice, and it was certainly part of the reason I'd been able to do well in 1979. In the 698 plate appearances I had that season, 264, or 37.8 percent, were against pitchers I'd seen *ten* or more times; 534, or 76.5 percent, were against pitchers I'd seen five or more times. So I'd gotten a taste of pretty much everyone and had at least a little intelligence walking up to the plate. But in late September, against a team like the 1979 Mets, who had been mathematically eliminated from the divisional race for almost a month, such familiarity went out the window. Why? Because September call-ups—the young pups—take on the lion's share of the work, especially on the mound.

And the Mets, no longer with the services of Seaver and Koosman, Ltd., were tossing up new arms, right and left, hoping something would stick for the next season.* Names like Mike Scott, Jesse Orosco, Juan Berenguer, Jeff Reardon, Roy Lee Jackson, and John Pacella. *Wait…who?* Of course, a few of these guys would go on to have terrific careers, but at that point, they were all unknown. Their motions, deliveries, release points, pitch actions, strategies—it was all new information to be digested. And that lack of familiarity doesn't increase the odds for a good series at the plate.

So I would have to call on yet another piece of advice—this time from Dad and our BP rounds together since I was a kid: "Son, sometimes you're just gonna have to get up there, grit your teeth, and bear down." Well, that's exactly what I did. In game one of a doubleheader, I singled off the right-handed Pacella in the first; singled off Jackson, another right-hander, in the second; homered off Jackson in the fourth; singled off Dwight Bernard in the seventh; and hit the ball hard off Ed Glynn but right at the second baseman, Doug Flynn, for a groundout to lead off the ninth.† Boyer rested me the second game, and I was 0 for 3 in the finale, but I left New York (and their enigma pitching staff) 4 for 8, my average kicked up to .346, and we bussed down to Philly for one final series against Rose and his compadres, who'd just wrapped up three games against the Expos.

The next day, Pete was waiting for me by the batting cage. "How in the hell did you go into New York and go 4 for 5 against

---

* Seaver was traded to Cincinnati midway through the 1977 season, and Koosman was now in Minnesota, earning his second 20-win season. Craig Swan remained with the team, managing 14 wins and a 3.21 ERA despite the lack of support.

† Neither Glynn nor Bernard was a September call-up, but I was 1 for 3 lifetime against the two of them *combined* prior to these at-bats. So, again, not a lot of familiarity.

all those September call-ups?" he asked. My performance that first game had put the pressure on him against Montreal, where a couple of 1 for 2s wouldn't do him much good; only more 3 for 4s and 4 for 5s could help him climb the ladder fast enough. He'd gotten a hit in each of those three games—extending a hitting streak to twenty-one games[*]—but concluded the series just 3 for 14, and we were back to double digits between us with a week to play.

Looking back, I relish the moment: here I was, standing with one of baseball's all-time greats, who later *that day* would collect his 200th hit of the season, setting a major league record for the most 200-hit seasons—ten—a record he had previously shared with Ty Cobb. And he was bustin' *my* chops, feigning incredulousness, about the batting title. I *should* have stopped right there, relaxed, smiled, and just taken it all in for what it was. But I couldn't. There would be no relaxing until I had nailed down the batting crown.

So while I remember being thrilled any time Rose or any of the big stars would come shoot the breeze around the batting cage or during a game while standing on first base—and I could be a chatterbox—I didn't, in my core, feel like I was quite a peer yet. I guess I'd felt the same way during the All-Star Game—a bit of an outsider. *Why?* Who the hell knows, but not even with Pete basically conceding victory did I chill out. And looking back at the numbers now, with the pressure off, the race was essentially over. I'd clinched it in New York, and Pete, for all his competitive grit, knew it. With six games remaining in his season, there really wasn't enough time for him to catch me.

But each time Pete came up to the plate, I was intently hoping

---

[*] Pete's hitting streak lasted two more games.

for an out. By the second game, my lead cut back down to 11 points, I felt like my head was going to explode: I hit a fly out to center, but Pete singled. *Oh shit.* He came up again and grounded out to the pitcher. *Phew.* I hit another fly out to center field. *Uh-oh…*

Round and round we went—him 1 for 3, me 0 for 3—until the top of the eighth, when I ripped a double to left-center field off reliever Tug McGraw. I ran by Pete, who was playing first base, going "Ooooooh!" all the way to second. Evidently I was still in battle mode, and Pete just looked at our first base coach and said, "What's wrong with him? Is he crazy? He still thinks I can catch him. I can't catch him."

So, yeah, Pete knew that I had it in the kipper, and a week later, after I went 7 for 15 at the plate over the remaining 5 games, it was apparent to all—even dumbass me. The season was over, and despite batting an incredible .421 for the month of September, Pete ended at .331, 13 points behind my .344.[*]

I'd won the National League batting title, becoming the first infielder to win a batting title and a Gold Glove in the same season.

---

[*] In Rose's 628 at-bats that season, 8 more hits would have given him .344. That's just 1 more hit every 78.5 of those at-bats. But with Pete, you know he never took any of those at-bats for granted. And my pitching teammates really picked me up, holding Pete to just 2 hits in 13 at-bats in that final series. In fact, had Pete hit St. Louis pitching that season (22 for 72) as well as he hit the Cubs (33 for 74), he would have had me.

KH BATTING PROGRESS (BY SEASON)

Year	Games (G)	At-Bats (AB)	Batting Average (BA)	On-Base Percentage (OBP)	Slugging Percentage (SLG)
1974	14	34	.294	.415	.441
1975	64	188	.250	.309	.362
1976	129	374	.289	.376	.428
1977	161	560	.291	.379	.459
1978	159	542	.255	.351	.389
1979	161	610	.344	.417	.513

CHAPTER 35

YOU KNOW THOSE SCENES in the movies where a character is stranded on an island, and to keep from going insane, he begins to tally on a big rock his total days marooned? Well, that was me in the weeks that followed the 1979 season. I was bored to tears, counting the hours until spring training, five *months* away. Again, domestic life just wasn't for me, especially on the heels of a batting race with Pete Rose and playing in front of 40,000 people on their feet every time I came up to the plate.

Why did I get married? I think when Sue and I started dating, she filled a void: she was a nice girl who kept me company during the long, cold winter months in St. Louis. And I'd spend weekends and Thanksgiving and part of the holidays with her big, loving family—she had great parents and younger siblings—and I took refuge in all of that during a time when I was lonely and insecure. I also grew up with *Leave It to Beaver, The Donna Reed Show, I Love Lucy, My Three Sons*—all family-oriented television series that probably influenced my expectations of what adulthood should look like: wife, kids, dog, car, mortgage, etc. I think this was typical of my generation, and perhaps it helped push many of us into marriage before we really understood the dedication and sacrifice it requires.

My father tried to warn me. Sue and I were thinking of getting married after the '77 season, but Dad asked me to wait another year. He was leery of me taking on so much responsibility and its effect on my burgeoning career. So we waited the year, and then we got hitched. Had we waited just one more year, the marriage never would've happened.

Because I was taking off. And as my career, along with my confidence, was being rocketed into the stratosphere, I suddenly needed less and less support to hold me up. One more push, and I'd be weightless. As it turned out, that final stage ignited with yet another morning phone call:

Me: (groggily) Hello?
Caller: Keith, it's Jack Lang with the Baseball Writers' Association. You wouldn't mind sharing the National League MVP with Willie Stargell, would ya?
Me: No, sir, I would not!
Caller: Good. Congratulations.

For the first (and only) time in history, the voting for NL Most Valuable Player ended in a tie, and Keith Hernandez—out of little Pacifica, California—was one of the winners. I thanked Mr. Lang, and called my parents and Gary. *If ever there was a justified case of "black cord fever"!*

It was only after I'd hung up with my family that I started to think about the strange way Mr. Lang, the secretary-treasurer of the Baseball Writers' Association of America, had dropped the news. Actually, it was more of what he had *not* said that I found odd. He didn't say:

Keith, congratulations, this is Jack Lang from the Baseball Writers' Association. I'm calling to inform you that you have won the MVP along with Willie Stargell. It's the first time there's ever been a tie for MVP, but you and Willie Stargell are the National League co-MVPs. Congratulations.

That would have been fine. But instead he had asked *if I would mind* sharing it with Stargell.

Why was he asking *me*? I wasn't a writer—I had no say in who won the MVP. What if I had said, "Yes, sir, I do mind sharing the award"? Would that have yielded a different result? Because part of me felt that Willie Stargell, superstar that he was, didn't deserve the MVP that year. With 32 home runs and 82 runs batted in, he'd had a great season, but it wasn't a *full* season. In fact, with only 424 at-bats and 105 games started, it was two-thirds of a season. Yes, he was the glue that had kept that team together to win the World Series, whereas we had finished a distant third, but, again, he hadn't played close to every day.

I wasn't alone in this thinking: While the ever-popular Stargell led the way with ten first-place votes from the twenty-four writers who made the decision, *four* writers omitted him from their top ten, citing Stargell's frequent absence from the field. I, on the other hand, led in both second- and third-place votes and was the only candidate to make *every* writer's top ten—in fact, I cracked every writer's top five.[*]

Given Lang's choice of words—delivered in a seemingly sheepish, almost apologetic tone—I started to think that maybe I'd won the award outright and the powers that be were making it up to the twice-a-bridesmaid Stargell, who had placed second

---

[*] To be fair, I received only four first-place votes. But the reason the ballot is designed the way it is—with ten placed finishers—is to reduce the effect of any potential bias from hometown sports journalists and provide a more complete picture of the field. I should also note that while not one of the four journalists who omitted Stargell was from St. Louis, *two* were from Houston, which is head-scratching, given Stargell's success against the Astros that season (.302 in 43 ABs with 6 HRs and 13 RBI).

in '71 and gotten absolutely screwed in '73, when he'd led the league in home runs, runs batted in, doubles, slugging, and on-base plus slugging.* And maybe now they couldn't deny Willie a third time—not with all that "We Are Family" stuff. Whereas I was just the new kid on the block who'd never hit .300 in a season—a kid the Writers' Association thought would be content just to be included.

And if that was true—if the writers had produced such a convenient outcome—I couldn't help but wonder if my last name had made it easier for them. "Are you a wetback, Hernandez?" I never forgot what that heckling fan way back in AA ball had asked me, or that even some of my teammates failed to appreciate my European-Spanish heritage: "C'mon, man, you're a Mexican." And though I'd never felt mistreated or racially targeted by the press, a teammate, a coach, or an organization, I'd heard comments from some of the Latino players suggesting Latinos were just as discriminated against as blacks, but without the national attention to combat it.† *Is that what this was with the MVP?* Would Lang have asked me if I'd "mind sharing" the award if my father, rather than my mother, had been Scots-Irish with the last name Jordan (my mother's maiden name)? *Did that name on the back of my jersey make a difference?*

Justified or not, all this entered my mind after that phone call.

Even so, my suspicions were minuscule compared to my delight that I'd won the award, and sharing it with Willie only further proved just how far I'd come after April's terrible start: here I was, sharing the spotlight with the great Willie Stargell,

---

* The 1973 MVP results: Pete Rose (274 points); Stargell (250).
† I believe that in the '60s, '70s, and '80s, the Latin player was perhaps the most overshadowed, underappreciated player. Fortunately, with the great number of Latino players in today's game, times have changed.

fellow Bay Area boy and the same cool and confident man spitting seeds on the bench that day in St. Louis while my average
sat at .216, just hours before Boyer's fateful talk with me on the
airplane. It never diminished the award, and I considered it an
honor to share it with him.

I'd first met Stargell back in '74 at an awards dinner. It was
a really big event, up in Napa somewhere, and Willie was there
along with Pete Rose. Superstars. I was thrown in at the last
moment simply because I was a Bay Area kid, and I remember
the moderator, Lon Simmons, the broadcaster for the Giants and
49ers, saying, "I'm really sorry, Mr. Hernandez. Please forgive
me. I don't have a lot of information on you." So I really had no
business being there. (Willie, of course, was just a big ol' teddy
bear who treated me like gold, as if I was a major leaguer.)

Six winters later, we were sharing the podium once again.
Only this time it was in New York City, at the awards dinner
hosted by the Baseball Writers' Association of America, *the
biggest of all dinners,* where they handed out the Rookie of
the Year Award, the Cy Young Award, and the MVP Award.
DiMaggio came to these things, the commissioner and league
presidents, too, and here I was, center stage with Willie, in front
of the cameras and reporters in that huge ballroom with all those
people.

Rubbing elbows with big shots.

Everywhere I turned, there was baseball royalty, past and
current, and all of them were very conversational and wanted
to talk baseball *with me.* Even Joltin' Joe, whose aloofness was
well known, struck up a conversation. I was sitting next to
him, and maybe it was an uncomfortable moment—I don't
know—but he turned to me and asked what pitch gave me the
most trouble. I was shocked that he'd asked me a question, so
I just blurted out the first thing that came to mind: "The break-

ing ball." And he said, "No, no. I can't believe that. I loved the breaking ball." Then he said, "*I didn't like the hard sinker, down and in from a right-hander.*" I said, "Well...I guess I don't like that pitch either."[*] So Joe was probably thinking, *Look at this stupid guy,* but that was fine: I was an MVP, the 136th ever selected in the history of Major League Baseball, talkin' shop with Joe DiMaggio.[†]

After New York, I spent much of the next month going around the country to different awards dinners. The various chapters of baseball writers from all over hold these things. It's like a circuit, and I loved every minute of it.

I'd go alone because Jessie was in school, and Sue, who was now pregnant, stayed at home. So while they were living in one reality, I was being swept up in another, where I was the center of attention on a grand scale. For a person with a history of poor self-esteem, the experience was intoxicating.

Here I was, coming off this amazing chase with Pete Rose and winning the batting title, only to have it all stop. Then they called me with the MVP thing and it kicked everything into high gear again. I was not playing ball, but it was fun to be on the road in the off-season. I did the dinners, and there were all these

---

[*] Joe was a right-handed batter, so whereas he had problems with the right-handed pitcher's sinker, my fits came from the southpaws. Lefty versus lefty. Righty versus righty.

[†] Years later, around 1989, I would have a similar fumble with the actor Sean Connery. I was in London, at a dinner for, like, fifteen people, and Marty Bregman, the movie producer, was there, as was Connery and his wife, Micheline Roquebrune. And Connery, who was a super-gregarious guy, but intimidating—everything he is on the screen he is in person—suddenly looked at me from across the table and, with a big smile and that confident Scottish cadence, asked, "Who are the toughest pitchers you faced and *why*?" Everyone turned to me, and I blanked and said, "I don't know." And he said, "I can't believe that you don't know." I continued to fumble for words, but nothing of substance came out—like Ralphie with Santa Claus in *A Christmas Story*, I was in such reverence of the big man that I sounded like an idiot.

other players, the best of the best. And they were not only from baseball but from other sports as well. Like the Dapper Dan, the writers' event in Pittsburgh, included all the Steelers players: Terry Bradshaw, Joe Greene, Franco Harris. Then, a few days later, there was one up in Erie, Pennsylvania, and I got to talk with Joe Paterno, the legendary coach from Penn State. Even at the St. Louis dinner, I hung out with the best of all those sports teams—guys from the St. Louis Blues and the football Cardinals, like Jim Hart, Dan Dierdorf. All of the sudden, I wasn't just another baseball Cardinals player.

I also began to realize then that it wasn't that difficult to talk to girls I didn't know. They were there. Lots of beautiful women, and some of them had their eyes on me. And, yes, I cheated on Sue, who was home and pregnant. And I'm not proud of it, but it's true. It was like I'd suddenly broken out of a shell that had been containing me my whole life, and I wanted to exercise that new freedom and the elation that came from it. Well, I'm far from perfect, and it was hard not to want something I'd never had before—even if being married meant I was supposed to pass certain parts of that something up.

They always had huge cocktail parties, and reporters would come up to me, and then other athletes, and then the women. I'd shake hands and mingle and have a few drinks. I'd go from cocktails into dinner, and all the people who had been flown in were staying there at the hotel so the party kept going. There'd be drinks and girls.

Maybe even some cocaine. I say "maybe" only because I'm not positive that I did do it on any of those trips, but 1980 was the first time I tried the drug. (In the 1980s, coke was the drug of choice, so it was around.) Though I wasn't completely stupid. I knew it was a hard drug—much more serious than marijuana. But I remember that I felt on top of the world during that MVP cross-country circuit, and if someone offered me some coke, I probably said, "Sure." Because people were fawning over me, and I was riding the wave. I was now twenty-six years old, and for the first time in my life, I felt really good about myself.

Those were heady days for me: like that Frank Zappa and the Mothers of Invention album *Over-Nite Sensation,* I went from obscurity to stardom, and I just got swept up in it.

But it wasn't all peaches and cream. I do remember that when I went to the Dapper Dan, I got a frosty reception from the audience, which made sense because it was all Pirates country, and they didn't like Stargell sharing the MVP with a "singles hitter." I remember reading that in the Pittsburgh paper—this "slap guy" next to big powerful Willie. And when I went to Kansas City, I overheard Royals favorite George Brett make a snide remark. When I was being honored as the MVP, they played a highlight reel of my season. Brett was sitting behind me, about fifteen, twenty, feet away, and at one point the video showed me hit an up-and-in fastball that I had to inside-out, and I hit a freaking bullet down the left-field line. A great piece of two-strike hitting. Brett started giggling: "Inside-out Judy hitter." And that pissed me off. *I'd like to see you* pull *that ball, George.* But I didn't say anything to him. *What am I going to do, get in a fight with George Brett in Kansas City?*

I don't know why he felt compelled to do that. We were both the toast of Missouri: him in Kansas City, me in St. Louis. And I wasn't competing with George Brett. *He's in the other goddamn league!* I was just happy to meet him and talk baseball with a fellow hitter—not make some nasty remark about his game.

But I got the feeling from some of the big hitters in baseball that they didn't respect *my* game. Particularly those in the American League who just saw my stat lines, and because I hadn't hit a lot of home runs, they assumed I was just some inside-out hitter, when in fact I hit more line drives—gap to gap—than perhaps anyone else in the game. I just didn't try to lift the ball—I was trained to hit the top half of the ball, *not* the bottom half (and good thing, playing in Busch Stadium, the second-biggest park in the league). I'm not sure if my insecurity was reasonable or I was just being paranoid, but I sensed what I sensed.[*]

And I'd always think, *Well, all you guys are great players, but I'm pretty goddamn good, too.*

---

[*] Seventy of my 210 hits in 1979 were extra-base hits, exactly one-third, as reflected by my 105 RBI despite only hitting 11 home runs. That's not slap-hitting, folks, and that some people thought I was a Judy hitter still irritates me today. I most definitely was not.

CHAPTER 36

METS GAME THIS EVENING. I'll be in the booth.

But I'm already on my way into the city for a card show. That's where fans pay to have current and former ballplayers sign a bunch of their memorabilia, like baseball cards, bats, balls, and stuff. It'll be a few hours of autographs and taking pictures. Easy money.

The first time I heard about the memorabilia business, I thought it was a crock: *like someone's gonna stand in line and pay for that* . . . This was in the mid-1980s. I was playing for the Mets and hanging out with a buddy of mine, Brandon Steiner. I remember him telling me, over dinner, his idea to get a bunch of professional athletes under contract and start his own memorabilia company.

I told him, "You're crazy."

Well, Brandon, who was just out of college at the time, built Steiner Sports into a multimillion-dollar business, wound up selling it for, like, $80 million, and still runs the company today.

So what do I know?

I still do a few shows a year for Steiner. I may not have played ball in a while, but we old-timers can still pack 'em in. The events are very structured: there's someone to my left to put the fan's merchandise in front of me while I sign and pose for a quick photo with the fan; there's also someone to my right to move it all along when I'm finished. *Next!* It's not exactly intimate, but like kids waiting at the mall to see Santa, the fans don't seem to mind the assembly-line approach.

I wasn't such jolly company when I first started to make appearances. It was back in the '80s and I was still playing ball, and I was too on edge, as per usual. *I just played a double-header yesterday and now I gotta sign people's stuff for four hours?* Well, I guess my lack of enthusiasm showed because one of the assistants, a Brooklynite named Don Lipeles, got tired of my nonsense and let me have it: "You know, Keith, these people waited in line and paid a lot of money to get your autograph. And you're treating them like garbage. Quit being an asshole."

You have to love that New York honesty, and, moreover, Don was right—*It's not like anyone is forcing me to do this.* So I got my act together. Granted, there's always some Yankees fan who's a schmuck, and it's sometimes very stressful to move the line because there might be four hundred people in the queue. But it doesn't take much to say "Hello" and ask folks how they're doing. And people are lovely—they're excited to be face-to-face with ballplayers they've watched for a while, and I've enjoyed interacting with them over the years.

Those early days in the memorabilia business were like the Wild West: you were paid in cash, no oversight. I did a show in Brooklyn once where I signed for around four hours, and I left with a shopping bag full of dough. Maybe twenty-five grand—more money than I had made in either of my first two seasons in the bigs. (I negotiated my 1975 contract on my own with assistant GM Jim Toomey. It was the off-season, and I was on the kitchen phone in my parents' house. Dad said I should ask for $22K, which sounded reasonable to me, but Toomey started chuckling on the other end when I put the number to him, and without a leg to stand on, I wilted and signed a one-year deal for $18K. A year later, I again negotiated my contract, and I got $24K out of Toomey. *A 33 percent raise!* I hated doing those contracts, and later in 1976, I hired an agent.[*])

Anyway, I probably could have made more than the twenty-five grand, but those fourteen letters that make up my name take a toll on the assembly-line production, plus I like to make sure that each fan gets a perfect signature. (The greatest name ever for autographs was Ed Ott—just five letters.)

Still, it was a lot of cash. I remember signing one day with Pete Rose, and Pete, who got paid a lot more per signature or inscription, went out the door with a briefcase full of bills. He and his buddies—*Pete always had a couple of buddies*—had a limo waiting to take them to Belmont:

> **Me:** Pete, where you going?
> **Pete:** The track.
> **Me:** Okay.

But those trade shows were publicized events, and it didn't take long for the Feds and the IRS to get wind of them. Some guys, like Pete, went down because they failed to declare the income on their tax returns. (*Not even the standard 80 percent, fellas?*) So now it's all very much aboveboard: written contracts, W-2s and 1099s. And you're paid by check—no more shopping bags full of cash, which is probably a good thing because, sooner or later, someone was going to get robbed.[†]

---

[*] Late in the second half of the 1976 season, when I was wearing it out, I followed Lou Brock's advice and started using his agent, Jack Childers, out of Chicago. Phew!

[†] Because I was walking out with all that money, they had a limo waiting with two security guys in it—one of them packing a pistol—to take me home.

Those early card shows were somewhat indicative of a star ballplayer's life from the late '70s to the early to mid-'80s: suddenly, there was a lot of money coming in, and nobody knew exactly what to do with it. Remember, guys like me who went pro in the early '70s did so when there was still a reserve clause. Even if we'd had success on the field, we didn't expect to make scads of dough. After retirement, we thought we'd have to do what all former ballplayers did: *go out and find a job.*

Baseball, for a *long* time, had a way of chewing up and spitting out everyone—even its stars—after their careers were over. For example, Whitey Ford, the future Hall of Famer for the Yankees and their winningest pitcher in franchise history, was given just two weeks' severance pay after he had to walk away from the game midseason in 1967 because of an elbow injury. He was thirty-eight years old, his one-in-a-million skill set suddenly expired, with no pension and little savings. He is still the winningest pitcher in that illustrious franchise's history. Makes you wonder what sort of treatment the non–Hall of Famers got...

But who needs to get a job when you're making $25K in one afternoon signing autographs?

What happened? How did we get here? The short answer is that beginning with free agency, organized labor—on the backs of the previous generations of ballplayers*—continued to win us

---

* Most notably, Curtis Flood, Dave McNally, and Andy Messersmith. After being traded to the Philadelphia Phillies in 1969, Flood filed a suit against MLB alleging that the reserve clause violated antitrust laws as well as the Thirteenth Amendment, which barred slavery and involuntary servitude. The case went to the Supreme Court in 1972. The Court ruled against Flood in a 5 to 3 decision, ultimately destroying the thirty-three-year-old's All-Star career. Three years later, another attempt was made to challenge the reserve clause when pitchers Dave McNally and Andy Messersmith refused to re-sign with their clubs and filed a grievance. The case went before an independent arbitrator, Peter Seitz, who decided in favor of the players on December 23, 1976. After a failed appeals process by MLB (owners), the reserve clause was finished. But so too was McNally, who retired at the

a larger piece of the pie. And it was at a time when the pie itself was getting bigger, and bigger, and bigger. TV coverage, which had been growing steadily since the '60s, started to take off after the famous 1975 World Series, when Carlton Fisk hit his home run to cap Game Six, and by 1980, TV contracts with local and national broadcasts accounted for 30 percent of the game's $500 million in revenue.

That was a far cry from when I was a kid, when all you had was one Saturday *Game of the Week.*

Beyond the direct revenue from TV, the increased exposure had a trickle-down effect: more televised games meant more commercials and more player endorsement opportunities, resulting in even more exposure and, ultimately, additional revenue streams, like card and memorabilia shows with people lining up out the door to get autographs from baseball players—the famous men on TV.

So my generation of stars was fortunate in that we were just hitting our stride when all these things started happening. In 1976, the first year of free agency, the highest-paid player in the league was Hank Aaron, at $240K. The following year, that number more than doubled for baseball's new highest-paid player, Mike Schmidt, at $560K. Three years later, 1980, it was up above a million dollars—Nolan Ryan this time—with players like Dave Winfield reportedly asking for $2 million.[*]

---

end of 1975 after playing for the same salary he had earned the previous season. Messersmith, who also played on his previous year's contract terms, finished 19–14 with a 2.29 ERA in 40 starts and 321⅔ *innings pitched.* So the Dodgers had pitched him to death, only to unceremoniously trade him to the very bad last-place Atlanta Braves after the season. A previous runner-up for the Cy Young, he was never quite the same after that abusive season.

[*] Ryan signed a three-year deal for a guaranteed $3.5 million over the course. The next season, Winfield was signed for $1.4 million per year, almost six times what Aaron had made only six years previously.

For me, the timing was fortuitous: not only was 1979 the year I catapulted into the upper echelon of players, but it was also the final year of my contract, and in the 1980 off-season, I signed a $3.8 million contract for five years. Wow! My 1979 annual salary of $75K had just grown *ten times*.

The Cardinals didn't really have a choice—the market was what it was, as reported in the *St. Louis Post-Dispatch* by syndicated columnist Murray Chass of the *New York Times* just one month before my signing:

> The information, obtained from management officials and agents, shows that club owners, who often have lamented the spiraling salaries, committed themselves to spending nearly twice as much money on the first 22 players who signed in this market than on the first 22 who signed in last off-season's market.[*]

Gussie Busch, who was as old-school as any owner out there, could bitch all he wanted about how players were making too much money, but the Cardinals' GM, John Claiborne, clearly understood the new cost of doing business: it was a seller's market, and you had to pay the players if you wanted to be competitive.

The only thing left to determine was my value, and after a batting title and an MVP at the tender age of twenty-five, with my prime years still in front of me, the Cardinals couldn't argue my elite status (especially when they were the ones who'd been saying that I was "the next Stan Musial"). Sure, they could have kicked the can down the road and negotiated a one-year deal,

---

[*] *St. Louis Post-Dispatch*, January 8, 1980.

but that would have just raised the price: the benefit of a long-term deal is you secure a player for the future at today's rate, and by all indications, those rates are going to keep going up (the risk is that your "star" is just a flash in the pan and you wind up over-paying him in subsequent years).

Perhaps the biggest incentive for keeping me happy and playing ball in St. Louis for the next five years was that the Cardinals, who hadn't won the NL East since the two-divisional system was introduced in 1969, wanted to get back atop the league. And with Templeton, Hernandez, Simmons, and Hendrick in the top half of the lineup, they certainly had the pieces to build a successful franchise.*

So the timing was perfect: I suddenly had the security of a lucrative, long-term contract with guaranteed big money.

But, by the same token, it also raised the expectations of *Cardinals fans*. Every morning, those fans woke up and glanced at the paper, where they saw two trends: baseball players were getting richer by the day and the rest of the world was going in the toilet. Rising unemployment. Stagnant wages. Rising cost of living. Gas crisis. Hostages in Iran. Russians in Afghanistan. It was a pretty bleak time in the United States and the world beyond, and while we players felt justified in our pursuit of happiness—after all, a highly skilled and select labor force plying their trade in a meritocracy with an ever-growing demand is what capitalism is all about—it was impossible to ignore the hardships around us. Especially in a blue-collar town like St. Louis, where economic recessions always seem to strike the hardest. (The same week I signed my contract, General Motors

---

* Both Simmons and Hendrick were already tied to long-term deals. One month after the Cards made the investment in me, they signed Templeton to a long-term deal.

announced it was shutting down a manufacturing plant inside the city, resulting in the loss of thousands of jobs and $10 million in tax revenue for St. Louis.)[*]

So which Keith Hernandez was going to show up for the St. Louis fans: a premier player who "earned his bread" or an overpaid sub-.300-hitting "bum"? I wasn't sure—I might have just won an MVP and a batting title, and then gallivanted around the country thinking I was the cat's pajamas, but self-doubt about my abilities still lingered.

Again, what is greatness? To do something not only well but *consistently* well. Could I do that? Could I repeat my performance in the years following my MVP?

---

[*] As reported by the *Post-Dispatch*, February 1, 1979. Other *P-D* headlines that month of my signing read: NEW ACTIVITY BY SOVIETS IN AFGHANISTAN; FORD SAYS IT LACKED PARTS TO FIX PINTO; NEIGHBOR CALLS GACY "NICE, GOOD MAN"; NO RELEASE BEFORE APRIL, KHOMEINI SAYS; CARTER CONSIDERS PLAN FOR 4-DAY WORKWEEK; MORTGAGE RATES HIGH, LIKELY TO REMAIN SO; WHO ARE THE REAL VILLAINS IN INFLATION?; STEEL INDUSTRY DOES NEED HELP; BUSCH COMPLETES ACQUISITION OF SCHLITZ BREWERY; FORGOTTEN VIETNAM VET?; US POWER LOSS AFFECTS ELECTION; CHILDREN CAN COUPON, TOO; CHRYSLER ASKS STATE WORKERS FOR A LOAN; BALLPARK FIGURES HARD TO CALCULATE; '79 COST IN BASICS CALLED LARGEST IN DECADE; FATHER OF 5 OFFERS TO SELL BODY PART.

CHAPTER 37

MY MEMORY STINKS. HERE'S the story I had planned to tell you:

I went into the 1980 season on pins and needles, wondering if 1979 was just a fluke, but I stepped into the batter's box on opening day against the Phillies' Dick Ruthven and ripped a one-out double down the line to short-hop the fence. My first at-bat of the season. And then and there—the ball careening off the wall—all the uneasiness that I'd had going into the season simply evaporated: With that one good swing, I knew not only that I belonged in the major leagues but that I was worthy to be considered among its elite players. The roller-coaster ride—one good year followed by one bad year—was over.

There's just one problem with this account: that at-bat against Ruthven didn't happen.

What?

At least not on opening day, 1980. Because I'm looking on Baseball-Reference.com, that all-knowing eye in the sky, and we didn't even match up against the Phillies on opening day. Rather, we opened up against Pittsburgh. So wrong team, *and,* to add insult to injury, I didn't even get a hit that first game: I went 0 for 3.

Damn you, Baseball Reference! I've been telling folks that story for years![*]

But my uneasiness going into the season was very real. It was all about April and getting off to a good start. Through 1975, 1976, 1977, 1978, 1979, and 1980, April was always front and center in my life, like a shadow hanging over me and the season ahead.

When I was very young, I sometimes had horrific nightmares. I'd wake up in the middle of the night, scared to death, determined to flee my bedroom. But I'd still be half asleep, dreaming, and if I moved too fast, my bedroom walls would suddenly grow in size and close in on me, or if I moved my hand or a foot too fast, it would appear to suddenly start ballooning in size until it was smothering me. I was imagining it all, of course, but I was terrified, like I was living in my very own Wonderland.[†]

Well, that was April for me: a lurking nightmare. And the press during that 1980 spring training didn't help: *Sports Illustrated* put me on the cover of their Special Baseball Issue with the caption "Who's Keith Hernandez and What Is He Doing Hitting .344?" Rick Hummel put out a column in the *Post-Dispatch,* basically asking, "Will the real Keith Hernandez please stand up?"

But any doubts about my 1980 season at the plate were just like the phantoms of my childhood: unfounded. Because my ap-

---

[*] I'm not sure what pisses me off more: the fact that I went hitless or that I'm getting too old to remember such things.

[†] The trick, I discovered, was that if I moved very slowly nothing would balloon and the walls would stay put. So I'd get out of bed—at a snail's pace—and cautiously make my way into the hall, calling out to my parents. Mom and Dad would come out of their bedroom, and I'd scream, "Slow down!" because if they moved too quickly, they, too, would grow in size. So Mom and Dad would inch their way over to me and sit me by the heater, then Mom would head into the kitchen, warm me up a glass of milk, and eventually I'd calm down and come back to my senses.

proach at the plate was built on a solid foundation. There were simply no holes in my swing, and I could adjust to whatever pitchers had in store for me. So unless teams were going to walk me every time I got up, I would get pitches to hit. It was now very rare that a pitcher could make me look bad. Like a master craftsman who puts ten thousand focused hours into his trade, I was an expert in my craft. And it wasn't just mechanics; I'd built an *approach*—between all those at-bats and advice sessions from veterans—and it had all come together. The year 1979 hadn't been a fluke. The year 1979 was proof that I'd arrived.

Sticking with Baseball Reference, I see that after the 0-for-3 opener, I went 2 for 4, including a triple off John Candelaria, for my first hit of the season. Really, when I look at my numbers, it just was a solid month for that entire April, hardened by my 5 for 5 on April 27 against the Phillies.[*] So it wasn't an opening day but an opening *month* success story—after a career in the majors, I should have recognized that 1 at-bat wouldn't make the difference. "Think in terms of every 100 at-bats..."

That 1980 April was when I first understood that I was a quality player. With my being the reigning MVP and a batting champ, pitchers were pitching me extra carefully. I still had Simmons hitting right behind me, but opponents knew they had their hands full, and I was more than handling it. One month into the season—my *sixth* month in a row of hitting .300 or better—I was right where I had left off in 1979.[†]

And that's a legitimate confidence booster.

---

[*] The first two of those hits were off the right-handed starter Ruthven. But they were each singles—no doubles. I'll keep looking...

[†] I finished April at .329 in 73 at-bats. Nine days later, I completed my first set of 100 at-bats, and my average was up to .321 with 9 extra-base hits and 20 RBI. *Raking!*

Especially when I think about the toll those opening weeks in previous seasons had taken on me. It was like I had to put my back up against the wall and feel that I was under attack in order to perform. I couldn't just relax—be a Lou Brock—and take it as it came. But after that April, I had my .300. *Okay, I'm on my way. I can hit, and this is where I belong.*

As for my peers, they seemed to agree. That first month of the 1980 season, Dave Parker, two-time NL batting champion for the Pirates and one of the most talented players I've ever seen, came strolling up to Ted Simmons and me after witnessing a round of BP in Pittsburgh, and exclaimed, "You two are the *hittingest* white boys I've ever seen!" Simmons laughed, and I loved it:

I'm Keith Hernandez, Hittingest White Boy.

I've talked a lot about Pete Rose because his example can't be overstated. Not only for me but for every other player of that era—from the majors down to Little League—because Charlie Hustle, like Derek Jeter in a later generation, *visibly* pushed himself on every play, in every game, in every season. "*Never* give those at-bats away!"

Simply put: Pete fought like hell.

This approach may seem standard for all major league players. It isn't. (Otherwise, Pete Rose wouldn't be Pete Rose, and Derek Jeter wouldn't be Derek Jeter.)

I remember José Cardenal, a veteran playing on the Phillies, landing on first base one game during the previous season, and asking me, "What are you doing hitting .330, Keith?"

I said, "What do you mean?"

"People will expect you to hit .330 every year. That's a lot of pressure. If you hit .305 next year, they'll say you had a bad year.

Whereas you could hit .280 with one hand tied behind your back."

I chuckled, said something like "Yeah," and the game got back under way, but I was surprised that Cardenal had said this. In his prime, Cardenal had been solid for the Cubs, batting .296 over six seasons, and in 1979 he was a very good bench player on a talented, younger Phillies team. *The man could hit.* Yet here he was, suggesting I *not* give it my all. (José played the game free and easy, so maybe he thought I was just too high-strung for what was ahead.)

That year I was in the middle of the batting race, so it sorta went in one ear and out the other, but I remember thinking, *I can't do that. My father always taught me to be the best I can be. If I can hit .330, I'm gonna hit .330; if I can hit .350, I'm gonna hit .350.*

What Cardenal said may seem as unacceptable to you as it did to me, but when you think about it, it's also understandable. Like any other occupation in which you're expected to perform at a high level day in and day out, baseball gets to be a grind. And once you reach a place where you feel like *Okay, I've made it,* it's tempting to put the car into neutral and just coast down the hill. Especially when you're talking about *managing expectations*—the press, the fans, the organization, and, most important, yourself. I mean, here I was in 1980, having just won the MVP, and it seemed like the question on everyone's mind, including mine, was "Can Keith Hernandez repeat his MVP performance?" It's a completely legitimate question, but wearing nonetheless. And as a player, it soon gets interpreted as just another way of saying "Hey, Keith, what have you done for me lately?" Because the better you perform, the more will be expected of you.

From that perspective, José Cardenal's suggestion to temper those expectations by *not* grinding out every single at-bat begins to make a lot more sense. He wasn't advocating brilliance, certainly, but he also wasn't advocating mediocrity. Instead, he was advocating *sustainability* for the long road ahead.

What separated Rose from almost everyone else was his ability to say "Screw that" and approach every one of his 14,053 career at-bats like it was Game Seven of the World Series. But Pete was the exception, not the rule. *Could I even come close to that level of persistence and tenacity?* That was the challenge that lay ahead of me, not only in May, as I set off to make it my seventh month in a row of hitting .300, but for the rest of my career.

I still intended to be the best I could be.

Two weeks into that May, we were in San Francisco for a three-game series. It was the first time I'd been home since the MVP, and when I came into the house, Dad had the old film projector and screen set up in the living room. Just like when Gary and I were kids. He sat me down and said, "I want to show you something," then he turned off the lights and started the projector.

It was one of the old Little League films Mom used to shoot, and I saw myself up on the screen, eleven years old, at the plate. Dad said, "Look at this stance, look at this swing. That's when I knew you were special."

I was stunned. Seeing Dad behind the projector, so proud of what he was showing on the screen, I realized why he'd been so hard on me.

When I was thirteen, playing my first year in a Pony League, I hit a double and was rounding first when I felt something "pop" in my right quad muscle. After I scored that inning, Dad could see me limping and came out of the dugout, asking what was wrong. Later that night, when we got home and I was limping more and more because my leg had stiffened up, Dad just lit into me: "You shouldn't be pulling muscles! Those never go away,

Keith! They come back and nag you!" He was just screaming at me, exclaiming, once again, that I must be lazy because "*active thirteen-year-olds don't pull muscles.*" And I thought: *What are you talking about? I hit a double and I'm running to second base and I'm halfway there and something pulled. I don't know why! I'm playing ball. I'm playing sports. I'm riding around on my bike. I'm walking everywhere. I'm an active kid and I'm lazy?*

Thirteen years later, sitting in that living room with him, I finally understood: I might have won the batting title and MVP in 1979, but Dad had seen the potential years before. And anything that might derail my progress, like a lousy pulled muscle, had been a threat to his vision and had made him angry. I was his second chance to make the bigs...

The footage was his proof: "That's when I knew you were special."

EPILOGUE

I'M SITTING AT MY brother's kitchen table in San Francisco, drinking coffee to shake off the morning cobwebs. I arrived last night after broadcasting a three-game series in L.A., and we were up late reminiscing and looking over Dad's scrapbooks. There are four scrapbooks, covering his whole baseball career, starting with his time at Mission High School. Gary found them up in the rafters at my parents' house after Dad's death from cancer in 1992, eighteen months after I retired. Last night was the first time I'd seen them since before I left home for the minors in '72.

I sip my coffee and look at the collection still spread across the table. Dad probably put the clippings together himself, at least early on. Later, when he was playing in the minors and in Hawaii for the war, he probably sent the clippings home to his sister, Pep, who chronicled them.

I focus on a picture from 1945. A group of young men in uniform—Stan Musial among them—squatting over a barbecue pit on Waikiki Beach. It is just after sunset; the men have dug a big pit in the sand, where the fire blazes as dinner roasts. The black-and-white photo was shot from the ocean, capturing Hawaii's most famous beach. The landscape in the background is so pristine—not one development or building, just palm trees.

The scrapbooks make it obvious how much Dad loved base-

324

ball. I remember sensing that even as a kid when Dad would go through the pages with us. Along with photos, there are some hand drawings. Sketches my dad did of his favorite players, most notably Charlie Gehringer, a Hall of Fame second baseman. The drawings are impeccable. Graceful yet direct strokes. He was a very talented man, my dad. If not for his love affair with baseball, I wonder what else he might have become.

But that seems impossible: *Dad without baseball.* I think about how these players, like Gehringer, must have lived inside my dad's head as a kid. When he was growing up in San Francisco in the '20s and '30s, there was no MLB team to follow locally. Just box scores and World Series radio broadcasts.[*] No TV.

Perhaps we should be envious of a time when a kid was free to go about his day with mighty baseball heroes and their fantastic 3-for-4 adventures playing inside his head, unfettered by "the tube." I mean where would Greek mythology be if people way back when had had a TV camera and TV set to tell their stories instead of the oral tradition? *Would these stories have been as mystical and magical? As impressive?* Baseball is like that—there's something about the battle between hitter and pitcher that captivates a person's imagination. *Achilles vs. Hercules.*

It certainly was enough to stoke Dad, who, despite falling short of his dream to play in the major leagues, never lost his passion for the game.

And when baseball eventually went to the tube, Dad loved it. Every weekend when we were kids, we'd watch the Saturday *Game of the Week,* and Dad would always be commenting on the game, the swings, even though the coverage in the early days was terrible—they shot from above the press box behind home plate.

---

[*] Regular season games for teams weren't nationally broadcast until 1950.

I remember Dad always getting upset because we were look-ing down the back side of home plate, and it was impossible to tell where the pitch was. But when broadcasts later adopted the center-field camera, Dad was ecstatic, because we could now see the pitch and its location along with the action in the field: double plays, rundowns, outfielders making catches, hitting or missing cutoff men. It was all there in plain sight, and Dad would always comment on the mistakes or on the proper plays. It was like watching a game with a special instructor—unfettered color commentating at its best.

You couldn't get that from a box score.

I close the scrapbook with the drawings of Charlie Gehringer and move on. I come across a clipping from the Oklahoma City paper printed in 1947. The article explains that my father was given his outright release after a dustup with his minor league manager.

I remember the story well; my father narrated it for Gary and me on numerous occasions.

He had begun that season in the very tough Texas League (AA), playing for the Oklahoma City Indians, a Cleveland affili-ate. On that team was future Hall of Famer Al Rosen. My father was the starting first baseman.

But Dad was in a slump and got benched by the manager. There were three managers for the Oak City squad that season. That particular manager was a big drinker, and his backup first baseman was a drinking buddy. Acting on his quick temper, his loathing of authority, and his aggressive nature when he felt wronged, my father stormed into the manager's office. I remem-ber Dad saying he punched him out. Gary remembers it differ-ently. He remembers Dad saying there was a heated exchange.

Either way, my father was released from the team, and the St. Louis Cardinals organization picked him up and sent him to their Houston AA club in the same Texas League. He had a terrific year, hitting over .300, with a team high of 18 homers, and led the team to the Texas League championship. He was named the club's MVP.

The irony isn't lost on me. In 1983, just seven months after we'd won the World Series, I was traded by the Cardinals to the New York Mets, while that same organization, thirty-six years earlier, gave my father a fresh start.

They picked him up. They let me go?

Being a Cardinal was everything I'd dreamed of as a kid. Everything I'd worked so hard for. (It wound up being for the best. I'm a New Yorker—not born and raised, but naturalized.)

And now, seeing my dad's scrapbooks and all the places he played and how so much of what's in these books represents his life, I wish that I had done a better job of holding on to things.

So now I've written a book. And I realize that, in a way, I've finally started to create a scrapbook of my own. Like my father before me, I've cut and pasted the memories together and tucked them into one place. I focused on the early years, and while those may not be the most celebrated, they were the "hard" ones. The most instructive.

When I first started this process, I thought, *There's so much there, and I'm not sure how to arrange it all.* But like a crossword puzzle, I just went one way, then another, and another, until it was put together. That's how I remember things. I always have. I can go up and down, left and right. It isn't a rigid progression. It's fluid.

Like a good baseball swing.

ACKNOWLEDGMENTS

Thank you, baseball. I've always said that when I leave the game I'll walk away for good, but this project has reminded me just how much baseball has shaped me. There's no leaving that.

The *St. Louis Post-Dispatch* and its writers, especially Rick Hummel, and Baseball-Reference.com. Thank you for providing such detailed windows into that baseball past.

Family, friends, former teammates, and colleagues. Thank you for indulging me with your stories and recollections these past two years. Especially my brother, Gary, who, as always, was willing to lend a hand, be it confirmation of a certain recollection or just chatting on the phone about this and that. Our stories are so intertwined that it is impossible not to benefit from even the most casual of our correspondence.

Kai Thompson Hernandez, for your remarkable literary eye, honesty, and intelligence. Thank you.

Ian Kleinert, for bringing this book to Little, Brown and steering it home. Philip Marino, John Parsley, and all those associated with the publisher over the course. Thank you for giving me the opportunity to share this story. Your patience has been remarkable.

Finally, to Mike Poncy, whose vision and dedication made this work possible. Mike promised me a year, and I took two. I'm extremely grateful to him and his family, and I look forward to our continued friendship. To Mike's support team and to the University of Virginia Library: public access to their periodical collection and digital archives, particularly from the *St. Louis Post-Dispatch,* ensured the team's investigative success.

INDEX

Note: The abbreviation *KH* refers to Keith Hernandez.

ABOUT THE AUTHOR

Keith Hernandez is a former Major League Baseball first baseman who played the majority of his career with the St. Louis Cardinals and the New York Mets. A batting champion and five-time All-Star, Hernandez was corecipient of the 1979 NL MVP and won two World Series titles, one each with the Cardinals and Mets. He earned more Gold Glove Awards—eleven—than any first baseman in baseball history. Since 2000, Hernandez has served as an analyst on Mets telecasts for the SNY, WPIX, and MSG networks, and he is a member of the FOX Sports MLB postseason studio team. He divides his time between New York and Florida.